Contempt

Contempt

A Memoir of the Clinton Investigation

KEN STARR

SENTINEL

Sentinel
An imprint of Penguin Random House LLC
375 Hudson Street
New York, New York 10014

Most Sentinel books are available at a discount when purchased in quantity for sales
promotions or corporate use. Special editions, which include personalized covers, excerpts,
and corporate imprints, can be created when purchased in large quantities. For more
information, please call (212) 572-2232 or email specialmarkets@penguinrandomhouse
.com. Your local bookstore can also assist with discounted bulk purchases using the Penguin
Random House corporate Business-to-Business program. For assistance in locating a
participating retailer, email B2B@penguinrandomhouse.com.

ISBN 9780525536130 (hardcover)
ISBN 9780525536154 (ebook)

Printed in the United States of America
10 9 8 7 6 5 4 3 2 1

Dedication

An old saying holds that there are no atheists in foxholes. When you're in a foxhole, fervent faith abounds and a powerful sense of camaraderie blossoms. Mindful of the message on the banner we hung in the office during the Whitewater trial that "we are honored by our friends and distinguished by our enemies," I lift up this dedication, first, to my fellow foxhole friends, the intrepid men and women who served courageously in the Office of the Independent Counsel, both in Little Rock and in Washington, D.C. This memoir is not mine alone; it is instead our shared story. I am deeply honored to have been at the battlefront with each and every one of them. They are listed in the acknowledgments. I wish I could say more.

Second, to the good and gracious residents of Little Rock, who were unfailingly courteous and hospitable to this mission-focused stranger during my long sojourn in the beautiful Natural State, I am deeply thankful. Many Arkansans doubtless felt I overstayed my welcome, but they never showed it. For years, Little Rock was my home away from home.

Yet at day's end, there's no place like home. To my wife, Alice, and our three children, who lived through those tempestuous times and were called upon to make their own very substantial sacrifices of service, I give abiding thanks. It is my hope that this memoir will help explain to our growing brood of Starrs, Doolittles, and Roemers (Randall and Melina, Carolyn and Cameron, Cynthia and Justin, and our precious seven grandchildren) those five long years of seeking the truth and trying my best to serve the cause of justice. For Alice, Randall, Carolyn, and Cynthia: you were there alongside me, even when we were miles apart.

CONTENTS

INTRODUCTION

F OR YEARS, PEOPLE HAVE COME UP TO ME AND ASKED, "Why don't you write a book about your experience during the Clinton investigation? People don't know your side of the story." They were right to guess that I had quite a lot I could tell. But they were wrong to imagine I was eager to tell it.

Think back to the rough outlines of the story: Twenty years ago, after a four-year investigation resulting in fourteen criminal convictions in Arkansas and leading to the resignation of the sitting governor of the state, the Whitewater investigation took a bizarre twist. It was revealed that in 1995 President Bill Clinton had begun an extended Oval Office affair with a twenty-two-year-old White House intern, Monica Lewinsky, then tried to cover it up.

In the fallout from the president's misdeeds, the nation went through wrenching political turmoil. Much of the drama was tragically unnecessary, a self-inflicted wound by a talented but deeply flawed president who believed he was above the law. In the long and painful saga, he showed contempt not only for the law, but for the American people, whom he willfully misled for his political self-preservation. He also demonstrated a shockingly callous contempt for the women he had used for his pleasure.

Yet ultimately, the president was lucky. An indulgent and prosperous nation readily forgave Bill Clinton and instead blamed the prosecutor.

That would be me.

I became the most criticized man in America and found my hard-won reputation for integrity and fairness under assault. I had a thick skin, but that kind of attack can't be borne forever without pain. And hurt feelings aside, my family suffered immeasurably, all thanks to the Clintons and their vicious surrogates. According to them, the nation went through the trauma of impeachment not because of Bill Clinton's offenses, but because of an overly zealous prosecutor.

In the face of these attacks, I was resolutely silent. I knew I had to grin and bear it. Prosecutors are severely limited in what they can say. The truth would have to come out eventually, but I could not—under my professional obligations—play the Clintons' game.

And in the following years I maintained that silence. I hadn't sought out the job as independent counsel and frankly hadn't wanted it. I wasn't burning with desire to live through the unpleasant saga all over again by writing about it. I wanted to move on with my life, to focus on my work in the academic world, where I served as dean of Pepperdine law school before becoming president (and later, simultaneously, chancellor) of Baylor University in my native Texas.

Then, in 2016, I found myself unexpectedly freed of all these considerations. On June 1, 2016, I was stripped of the Baylor presidency in the wake of serious allegations of sexual violence at an institution that stood for the best values and virtues in human life: treating all persons consistent with the teachings of Christ Jesus and, in particular, the Golden Rule.

Although I had not been personally implicated in any direct way in the university's scandal, I was nevertheless in charge of the institution. Captains go down with the ship. As a matter of conscience, I soon resigned from my role as Baylor's chancellor. I likewise amicably terminated my formal relationship with the Baylor Law School, where I had concurrently held an endowed chair in constitutional law. All this was filled to overflowing with personal anguish, but I found myself suddenly freed from the all-consuming daily responsibilities of the academy.

Then, in the fall, the 2016 presidential election brought an unexpected and crushing conclusion to the political career of Hillary Rodham Clinton. A seeming shoo-in to follow Barack Obama into the Oval Office, Hillary had suffered bitter defeat at the hands of the disruptive newcomer to American politics, Donald Trump. The Clinton era was over.

Not only was I freed from personal and professional constraints, but the moral compass of the country had shifted since 1998. Furthermore, as questions of presidential obstruction and impeachment have come up in the Trump administration, many are rethinking the Clinton saga and looking for what can be learned from those tumultuous times.

I concluded that, at long last, the time was right to talk about the Clintons' contempt.

By the end of this book, my personal account of the legacy of Bill and Hillary Clinton—a legacy of contempt—I believe most reasonable, open-minded people will agree with me. Or at least they should agree with my basic proposition: that President Clinton and the First

Lady knowingly embarked on a continuing course of action that was contemptuous of our revered system of justice.

I make this bold statement for one key reason: The basic facts are undisputed. The continuing debate is really about the conclusions that "We the People" choose to draw from the crystal-clear record.

In both a practical and a legal sense, the final judgment has been rendered. It was handed down by Chief Judge Susan Webber Wright, a Little Rock–based federal judge of impeccable credentials and unquestioned integrity. She stands alone in American history. By her judgment, Bill Clinton is the only president in the long national experience who has been held in contempt of court. He chose not to appeal that damning conclusion. That final judgment stands as a reminder to all of us that we live not as subjects, but as citizens under the Constitution and laws of the United States. We live in the sweet land of liberty, but liberty under law.

Prologue

In June 1992, I was in Arkansas as Governor Clinton was on the verge of wrapping up the Democratic nomination for president.

Then U.S. solicitor general, I had long been scheduled to speak at the annual meeting of the Arkansas Bar Association, to be held in Hot Springs that year. I had arrived in Little Rock on a regular commercial flight, but I was pleasantly surprised to be greeted with official Arkansas hospitality, complete with a state trooper chauffeuring me about. As I settled into the front seat of the trooper's marked car, my uniformed host immediately remarked, "That's just like Bill. That's where he sits."

The trooper, whose name I have protected to this day, had been a member of Governor Clinton's security detail, and had served a tour of duty at the Governor's Mansion. "Bill," the governor and soon-to-be president, always rode in the front seat.

With no prompting from his out-of-town passenger, the trooper gave me an earful. Out came salacious story after salacious story about the governor's notorious extracurricular escapades. The trooper's highly specific details suggested that the tales were not made up.

This was not the first time I'd heard rumors of Clinton's sexual adventures. As Clinton battled for the Democratic nomination for the presidency, his purported affairs had spilled out into the tabloids. Reporters had fanned out across Arkansas and were looking for juicy tidbits about the youthful chief executive. On January 23, 1992, a nightclub singer named Gennifer Flowers had peddled her story of a twelve-year affair with Clinton to a tabloid. He denied it.

Then Flowers produced tapes of her conversations with Bill. The tapes did not seem to lie.

The erupting controversy seemed sufficiently serious for his political future that on January 26, both Bill and Hillary appeared on CBS's *60 Minutes*. Bill, biting his lip, got close to an admission. "I have acknowledged causing pain in my marriage. I have said things to you tonight and to the American people from the beginning that no American politician ever has." His "nonadmission" admission demonstrated early on that "the Man from Hope" masterfully employed the English language to his great advantage.

While I found Clinton's behavior unadmirable, I'd not had much occasion to spend time dwelling on his misdeeds. Now I was a captive audience. My new friend prattled away. He repeated the salty language spewed out by Arkansas's First Lady when, on one occasion, she discovered a clandestine episode under way in the guest cottage of the Governor's Mansion. A former beauty pageant queen, the trooper told me, had been Bill Clinton's amorous guest.

The trooper clearly did not care for the governor's spouse. Yet he had genuine affection for "Bill." He had even told Clinton that he had not voted for him. Clinton inquired why.

"Bill, you know you don't support law enforcement," the officer said. "I have to lay down linoleum at night and on weekends as a second job just to make ends meet."

Bill responded, "You know I'm doing the best I can for law enforcement, but I had to take care of the teachers!"

"Exactly, you take care of the teachers, but you don't look after cops."

Charmed by his story, I gently probed whether the trooper had faced any recriminations because of his anti-Clinton vote.

"Bill wouldn't do that," he insisted. There it was: the genuine empathy—and relational power—of Bill Clinton. Though a Rhodes scholar and Yale Law graduate, William Jefferson Clinton was truly a man of the people.

Little did I know that in less than two years, after the governor became president, I would be tasked to investigate this magnetic, articulate politician, rightly dubbed by his biographer David Maraniss "First in His Class."

CHAPTER ONE

Growing Up Starr

Bill Clinton and I were born one month apart in the summer of 1946, not so far from each other geographically. He was born in Hope, Arkansas, and I in Vernon, Texas. We both graduated from high school in 1964 and eventually became lawyers.

Despite surface similarities—baby boomers, lawyers, from the South—Bill Clinton and I had little in common. Unlike Clinton, who was raised in a dysfunctional household with an alcoholic father, I had the blessing of growing up with both parents in a faith-filled home. My childhood was pleasant, even idyllic, despite what some might view as an austere upbringing.

It was anything but.

My father, William Douglas Starr, was a bookish minister with a practical streak. He loved to garden and often barbered on the side to supplement his income. My mother, Vannie Trimble Starr, was a stay-at-home mom. Kind but firm disciplinarians, my parents didn't turn a blind eye to my childhood temper tantrums, but they didn't react harshly either.

Soon after my birth, my parents moved to East Texas to be near family, then to San Antonio when I was in third grade. Dad was a minister in the Churches of Christ, an evangelical community emphasizing the autonomy of local congregational governance. In those days, Church of Christ members typically avoided dancing and drinking alcohol. To this day, most congregations do not use musical instruments in worship, so I grew up with a cappella singing as a major part of church services. My mother had a lovely soprano voice. Naturally musical, I loved singing at church, hearing the congregation's voices blend in four-part harmony.

As I grew older, I went to song-leader school and from time to time as a teenager I would lead worship. My mother insisted on piano lessons, and I delighted in hearing a soaring organ play Bach. To this day, I frequently say everything reminds me of a song.

I had no "road to Damascus" experience on my Christian journey. I was baptized at age twelve by my father. Reading the Bible imparted a love of language and literature. Though I later took issue with certain Church of Christ traditions, particularly its disapproval of instrumental music, I was never rebellious. I preached my first sermon soon after my baptism—for ten minutes on a Sunday night, when youngsters were allowed in the pulpit. Priceless training for a future lawyer.

My parents placed an extraordinarily high value on education. My father had attended Freed-Hardeman College in Tennessee on a preacher's scholarship. I was born just as my sister, Billie Jeayne, headed off to college at the tender age of sixteen. She later became a teacher. My brother, Jerry, six years older than I, taught economics at the college level.

As the baby of the family, I was certainly indulged, but my parents expected me to get straight As. I tried not to disappoint them. In 1961, they paid the tuition for me to attend Sam Houston High School, a public school outside our San Antonio school district. They picked up the modest tab because they viewed the academic program as stronger than the one at the rural public school I was supposed to attend.

I was a serious student, and loved to read. My favorite teacher and mentor, Roberta Mahan, pushed me to seek leadership roles, encouraging me to run for junior class president. Winning that first election was a breakthrough, teaching me the value of risking failure and giving me a taste for politics.

By now I was sociable, well liked, and popular, a big fish in a relatively small pond. An energetic debater, I also captained our school team for *On the Spot,* a local version of *College Bowl.* Fascinated with current events, government, and politics, I became a devoted reader of *Time, Newsweek,* and *U.S. News & World Report,* and began dreaming about a career in government and politics—as a Democrat. Though my parents were staunch Republicans, I was a big admirer of John F. Kennedy.

When I eventually became senior class president, I was designated to deliver my class commencement address. This was a big deal. I worked hard on that speech with Mrs. Mahan, and it was well received. My pride, however, took a bit of a hit that day.

After my speech, I was sitting onstage next to the superintendent of the San Antonio Independent School District when they announced the scholarship winners.

"Ken Starr, scholarship to Harding College."

Impressed, the superintendent leaned over and said, "Harvard College! That's spectacular!"

"No," I whispered, a bit embarrassed, "Harding College."

Harding, a Church of Christ–affiliated institution, is about sixty miles northeast of Little Rock. It's well respected, but it's definitely not Harvard. The superintendent seemed a bit crestfallen, sharing the disappointment Mrs. Mahan had already expressed. She viewed Harding as a backwater and encouraged me to study in Washington, D.C. Check out the foreign service, she said, maybe become a diplomat.

But Harding was a natural choice for my family. My brother taught economics there, and with a generous scholarship, it was readily affordable.

My tenure at Harding started with promise. I majored in political science, with the goal of becoming both editor in chief of the college paper and student body president. To that end, I ran for class representative as a freshman and won. I also worked hard as a junior reporter for the *Bison* and penned an editorial column called "Starrdust." Then, at the end of my freshman year, I got my first lesson in realpolitik.

After crafting an editorial criticizing the administration for spending too much on capital projects at the expense of building up the faculty, I was socializing in the student union when I felt a tap on my shoulder. The college president, Clifton Ganus Jr., a mountain of a man, said, "Young man, come with me."

He sat me down in his office—my only time in the president's suite—and read me the riot act. In the president's view, my sharp-edged editorial had hurt the college, and he proceeded to reprove me as if I were a child who had disrespected his parents.

"This is high school all over again," I thought. Instead of being humbled, I came to the realization that I needed to transfer. Mrs. Mahan had been right.

Even though I had been elected representative of the sophomore class, I had already been feeling restive at Harding. I had started questioning Church of Christ traditions that seemed to rest on unduly narrow interpretations of Scripture. If pianos and organs were not permitted in worship, why allow the song leader to brazenly use a pitch pipe? What about the use of hymnals? No Scriptural authority for that. If wine was mentioned throughout the Bible, why did we insist on total abstinence as a matter of doctrine?

With questions about both Harding's theology and intellectual rigor, I went home to San Antonio for the summer and began to plot my next step. My interest in politics still strong, the District of Columbia—and Capitol Hill—began drawing me like a magnet. I ended up at George Washington University in D.C. It wasn't Princeton, where I initially hoped to transfer, but highly regarded and generous with financial aid. My parents were supportive; their attitude was that I needed to go where I felt called, to use my gifts where they led.

Not long after my arrival in Washington in September 1966, I was hired as a staff assistant to Representative Robert Price, a Republican from Pampa, a small city in the Texas Panhandle. My job was to handle constituent correspondence from the 18th Congressional District of Texas. The job sounded important, but all I did was sit at a little desk just outside the congressman's office and respond to constituents' letters, which were mostly about agricultural and ranching policies, as well as veterans' issues. Not the most exciting task, but I worked hard at crafting these missives. Maybe too hard. One of the office staff good-naturedly dubbed me "Baron de Starr" for my florid writing style.

My other job was to be at the congressman's beck and call. On Thursday afternoons, when Congress was in session, I'd drive him to

Dulles airport for his flight back to Texas. Price was a hardworking rancher and a "sage-brush rebellion" Republican in a region dominated by Democrats, as most of Texas was at the time.

I treasured those trips. Regaling me with his philosophy of life, the congressman articulated a commonsense wisdom and sense of duty that has served me well to this day. Price believed that he owed his constituents his best judgment, not always the popular decision. That sometimes put him at odds with his staunchest supporters.

After being upset by a reaction from his political base, he surprised me one day by saying, "You've got to do what you think is right. If they don't like it, then they can go f*** themselves." A devout Baptist and Sunday-school teacher, Price seldom used vulgarity. But he felt strongly about this, and he got his point across: you have to vote your conscience.

In the late fall of 1966, just as I was digging into the culture of Capitol Hill and my studies at GWU, I received one of those letters that young men of my generation feared: a notice to report for a Selective Service physical.

The Vietnam War was heating up. At the time, I was mildly sympathetic to the war; the conflict had not yet become the quagmire that prompted campus unrest across the nation. My one exposure to Arkansas politics during this period was hearing Senator J. William Fulbright make a very powerful antiwar speech. But he held anti–civil rights views, which I found repugnant, as part of his Faustian bargain to retain his Senate seat from Arkansas.

Although avoiding the draft was a great preoccupation of my generation, I honestly wasn't unduly worried. Though definitely not eager to be drafted, I would have served had the call come.

But first I wanted to get my undergraduate degree. I had made the assumption that full-time students automatically received a deferment. Apparently not so. I found myself on a bus filled with nervous young men headed south on I-95 to a medical facility in Richmond, all of us facing the reality that we might soon be serving in uniform.

After being poked and prodded all that morning, I appeared to be passing the physical exam with flying colors. Then, as I left, a doctor grabbed my right arm and, pointing to a patch of skin, asked, "What's that?"

I didn't know specifically, but for years I had seen dermatologists for various skin conditions.

"That's psoriasis," he said. "The military's experience is that psoriasis is a chronic condition. Young man, would you believe it? You are 4-F."

It was good detective work on the doctor's part, because I hadn't mentioned my condition. I wasn't covered with skin lesions, so I was hardly suffering. I honestly thought the diagnosis was providential. My studies at GWU and my job on Capitol Hill would continue.

As other classmates went off to war, I lived off campus, went to school in the morning, worked forty hours a week for Congressman Price, and got paid for twenty. I wore a suit to school every day and didn't get involved in either the school paper or campus politics. I was determined to get good grades and I did. It helped that I could study at night in the gorgeous Main Reading Room at the Library of Congress.

I became close to several faculty members in the GWU political science department and developed an interest in going to law school, thinking maybe I'd teach political science at the college level. My mentors steered me to a new Ph.D. program at Brown University, in Providence, Rhode Island, where I could earn a doctorate in three years.

But I first had to make a detour to Harvard for a 1968 summer program to fulfill a language requirement for my degree at GWU, and

11

that detour was also providential. It was there that I met Alice Jean Mendell. I sat behind her in Intermediate Spanish and "pulled her pigtails."

From New York, Alice was a student at Skidmore College and also working on fulfilling a language requirement. I was drawn to her—more than she was to me—but eventually she warmed up and agreed to be my girlfriend. I had dated throughout high school and college, but Alice was my first serious relationship. When the summer ended, we began a tale-of-two-cities commuter relationship—between Saratoga Springs and Providence.

Unfortunately, the poli sci department at Brown wasn't as appealing as the one at GWU had been. I loved Brown, but there was a strong push within the department to make the discipline a "science" by emphasizing computers and statistics. I got along great with the faculty, but the department chair displayed a worrisome sign on his door: "If you can't quantify it, it's not worth talking about."

I was interested in ideas, and the process of government, not statistical analysis. I viewed the Ph.D. as an entrée to college teaching, not to conducting polls or slicing and dicing election data. My thesis adviser suggested I finish the doctorate at a program in England, where political philosophy, not numbers, remained the focus.

But I didn't have any money for studying abroad. Since the course I liked best at Brown was constitutional law, I decided to go to law school instead of finishing the Ph.D., hoping to teach law eventually. In the meantime, I needed work.

Happily, my department chair guided me to a post as a contract program officer with the U.S. State Department in the Bureau of Educational and Cultural Affairs. At the height of the Cold War, America and the Soviet Union were competing for the hearts and minds of the Third World, and this program brought young people from those parts of the world to take an in-depth look at America. The State Department wanted people to have personal experiences of Western democracy, and it was my job to escort my charges all over the country, where we were often hosted in people's homes.

As a result of my work, I got to know big-city mayors and people working with World Affairs Councils. I saw America through new eyes. And I also had space to plan the future. I lived off the State Department per diem, saved my salary, and began applying to law schools.

Duke University gave me the most scholarship money. That and its growing reputation made the decision to enroll there easy. Alice and I got married in August 1970 and one week later I started law school.

My experience at Duke couldn't have been more different from my time at Brown. I loved the entire experience and came to joke that I was a refugee from academia. My class was small enough to be close knit, and I paid little attention to politics, just studying hard. I did well enough that after graduation in 1973, I received a yearlong clerkship in Miami with Judge David Dyer, of the U.S. Fifth Circuit Court of Appeals.

Headquartered in New Orleans, the Fifth Circuit at that time covered a vast region, from Key West to El Paso. The judges heard appeals arising from a bewilderingly wide range of cases, from criminal convictions to class-action lawsuits against huge corporations. Clerks analyzed cases, made recommendations on rulings, and assisted judges in writing opinions.

Clerking for Judge Dyer was not just an honor but a delight. A lawyer who had been successful as a corporate litigator in Miami, Dyer had a rigorous legal mind and a winsome personality. I once asked the judge's executive assistant, who had worked with him in private practice, the secret of his success as a lawyer. She simply responded: "Juries really liked him." Be likable: a good lesson for anyone who practices law on his or her feet. I took note.

There in Miami I fell madly in love with the entire judicial process, loving it even more than law school. Lawyers representing clients are required to be more interested in victory than the truth. For judges, there's no such thing as a victory or a loss. Lawyers represent clients and causes. Judges seek to follow the law. That is a very affirming way to spend the workweek.

My bold ambition was to clerk for a justice of the Supreme Court, a prestigious post that would make a move into teaching law school possible. That required the enthusiastic recommendation of someone with clout, like Judge Dyer. My goal was still a long shot since I hadn't gone to Harvard, Yale, or another elite school, which had virtual strangleholds on prestigious clerkships.

To get an edge I began accompanying Alice at night to the University of Miami. While she took classes toward an advanced degree in higher education administration, I immersed myself in researching a then-hot topic in American constitutional law—whether a federal court could constitutionally order a state or locality to conduct a new election based upon voting rights violations. Thanks to my evening studies, I wrote an article that was quickly published in the *New York University Law Review.*

As my year with Judge Dyer drew to a close, I was set to begin the practice of law in California with a major firm, Gibson Dunn & Crutcher in Los Angeles. But before Alice and I packed our bags and headed for the West Coast, I figured I should at least try for a Supreme

Court clerkship. I mentioned my ambition to Judge Dyer. He smiled and responded: "I'll call Lewis."

"Lewis" was Supreme Court justice Lewis Powell, who promptly invited me to visit him in his summer chambers in Richmond, Virginia.

Justice Powell had a reputation for choosing clerks from among the "first in class" ranks. That wasn't me. More relevantly, he was also renowned for working prodigiously hard. He noticed the law review article listed on my résumé and inquired when I had had time to write it. I explained my nocturnal visits to the University of Miami Law Library. He seemed impressed.

Still, unsurprisingly, he didn't select me. Disappointed, but grateful we still had a plan, Alice and I moved to Los Angeles. She got a job at the University of Southern California in college administration; I practiced law with Gibson Dunn. Almost immediately I began arguing motions in court, something few baby lawyers in large firms get to do.

Life in California was good to Alice and me. We explored the state and for the first time had a little money in our pockets. We got involved in the First Congregational Church of Los Angeles, attracted by the church's beautiful liturgy and music. Though I had never moved away from my Christian roots, in my faith journey I had left the Church of Christ and was clearly now a seeker. My own beliefs were evolving but remained focused on the centrality of Scripture and the overarching importance of grace.

In 1973, like everyone else, I closely followed the scandal dubbed "Watergate." What was aptly described as a third-rate burglary would lead to a constitutional crisis and the impeachment of a president.

Though by now, having been heavily influenced by Representative Price, I was a registered Republican, my partisan commitments didn't keep me from seeing that the evidence against a GOP president was overwhelming. The blunder by Nixon's "plumbers" had metastasized into a massive cover-up. The president had violated the rule of law by participating in an obstruction of justice.

This obstruction was a violation of one of the beliefs I hold dearest: The law has integrity. The facts have integrity. You are not to twist, torture, or manipulate the law or the facts, as Nixon had done. Republican loyalties aside, I was relieved when the nation's thirty-eighth president resigned on August 8, 1974, and averted an inevitable trial in the Senate.

Meanwhile, Alice and I started looking for a house on the west side of Los Angeles. We were ready to put down a deposit on a small cottage in Pacific Palisades when in January 1975 I received life-changing news.

Though Justice Powell had not chosen me to clerk for him, he had picked up the phone and recommended me to Chief Justice Warren Burger. Before I had traveled to California, I had interviewed with the relatively new justice, William Rehnquist, and with Burger's screening committee. I had heard nothing for months, but now I heard what I had dreamed of for years: I had been offered a Supreme Court clerkship by Chief Justice Burger.

The day I received the offer was one of the happiest days of my life. My colleagues at the law firm were also pleased. They sent me off with their blessing, telling me to come back in a year, and I fully intended to.

Alice and I put aside the down payment and moved to Washington. Then Alice found an attractive position at Georgetown University requiring a two-year commitment, so we purchased a small town house on Capitol Hill nestled just behind the Supreme Court.

I don't know what I expected when I arrived at the majestic Supreme Court Building. Maybe the Fifth Circuit on steroids. But I was unprepared for the tension of daily life inside the Court, which was deeply divided along ideological lines. Chief Justice Burger led the conservatives; Justices William Brennan and Thurgood Marshall headed up the liberal faction. Justice Powell—and at times Justice Potter Stewart—were the all-important swing votes.

The Chief Justice had a great respect for history and tradition. He venerated the democratic process and was strongly inclined to uphold legislative choices. A son of Minnesota, Burger passionately believed in the dynamism of our federal system. As a traditionalist, he was reluctant to open new frontiers by interpreting the Constitution in a way to achieve policy goals, no matter how noble.

But there was a widely held perception that the Court, under Burger's leadership, was dismantling the liberal jurisprudence of Chief Justice Earl Warren. After all, Burger had been nominated by President Nixon, largely because he had been reliably conservative on law-and-order issues. As a judge on the D.C. Circuit Court of Appeals, which had been unrelentingly liberal on criminal justice controversies, Burger had authored numerous lower-court opinions dissenting from his court's pathbreaking decisions.

I was honored to be working for Burger, a kind, grandfatherly man, but uncomfortable with the intra-Court divisiveness. The Chief was sometimes criticized for hogging the great cases and assigning the "dogs" to other judges. Still, I was honored when Burger asked me to stay on an additional year. He was going from three to four clerks and wanted some continuity. That proved to be a glorious year.

As senior law clerk, during the October 1976 court season I wrote a bench memo for Chief Justice Burger on a complex securities law case that was widely considered a "big-time dog." I laid out the facts and presented how I believed it should come out.

"If you have any interest, I'd like to work with you on the opinion," I said. The Chief agreed and assigned the "dog" to his own chambers. After the draft opinion was circulated among the justices, Justice Stewart, one of the Chief's strongest critics, wrote "Fine piece of work. Please join me." High praise indeed. "Join me" meant to add his name to the majority opinion. Even though the case has faded into insignificance, that was one of the proudest moments in my two-year stint at the Court.

As the second year of my clerkship drew to a close, Alice and I were not eager to return to California. The lure of D.C. and Capitol Hill had gotten to me. Besides, Alice was pregnant with our first child, and moving seemed like a big challenge. Fortunately, Gibson Dunn had opened a Washington office. I became a Washington lawyer.

Meanwhile, Bill Clinton had become the nation's youngest governor. In early 1979, I crossed paths with him in a crowded elevator at the Hyatt Regency hotel at the foot of Capitol Hill. He was attending a Washington, D.C., conference, and I was staying at the hotel while sitting for the D.C. bar exam. I got on the elevator dressed in jogging clothes. Clinton, on the other hand, was sporting a sharp-looking suit. The elevator was crowded, so I did not get to say hello. But his charisma was obvious. He was charming, commanding, and friendly. As the nation's youngest governor, he was on top of the world.

I had been aware of his meteoric rise in national political circles. But I had zero involvement in politics during my time at the Supreme Court. That was soon to change. In the meantime, I was still laying the foundations of what I hoped would be a long legal career.

Back in the private sector, I was working on a sensitive criminal case arising out of the Kennedy Space Center. Our client, a contractor on the space program, had been accused of defrauding the government. It looked like the case might go to a grand jury for possible criminal charges. I was in charge of the day-to-day investigation. Part of my duty was to prepare for Armageddon if, heaven forbid, the company was indicted.

Who would be our lead defense counsel? It couldn't be a D.C. lawyer or, worse, a faraway California law firm. The situation called for home-state talent. Gibson Dunn retained Harris Dittmar, a Jacksonville litigator who had successfully defended former United States senator Edward Gurney in a corruption case. A staunch defender of President Nixon, Gurney had been indicted for perjury. To everyone's surprise, "Ditt" won an acquittal.

"What's the secret of your success?" I asked Ditt as we were driving to Orlando from Cocoa Beach.

"I let the judge and jury know that they can trust every word that comes out of my mouth," Ditt said. "I will not be proven wrong." That meant relentless preparation, plumbing the depths of the case.

Likability. Preparation. Honesty. Advice from seasoned attorneys like Judge Dyer and Ditt became my watchwords.

We averted Armageddon in Florida, and I resumed my day-to-day practice back in Washington. I drew more closely into the orbit of William French Smith, a Gibson Dunn senior partner. In the wake of Ronald Reagan's landslide victory in 1980, Bill Smith gave me various D.C.-based assignments as the presidential transition got under way.

On Christmas Eve in 1980, Smith called me at my parents' home in San Antonio as we were about to sit down for lunch. As chair of Reagan's transition advisory committee, Smith was identifying people for the Cabinet. He wanted to know if I would be interested in joining the administration as chief of staff and counselor to the new Attorney General—none other than William French Smith.

A native New Englander, Smith was characteristically sparing in his comments. A skilled listener, Bill was simply matter-of-fact. Come aboard and help me out. I accepted on the spot.

Suddenly I was back in public service, this time in the Department of Justice, the massive Greek Revival–style building on Constitution Avenue. I felt immediately at home.

Early on, I became close to FBI Director William Webster, a former federal appellate judge. "Ken, you are the conscience of the Attorney General," Webster said. "You've got to give him your best judgment. In the government, you have to turn square corners. No jaywalking."

My three years as chief of staff for the Attorney General during Reagan's first term were busy and a thorough initiation into the rancorous political process. But my professional ambition was now to become a federal judge.

In early 1983, I received the news that I was being considered for an opening on the Fourth Circuit Court of Appeals in Richmond, Virginia. The Justice Department began negotiations with Virginia senator John Warner. He had identified several candidates for the slot, all experienced federal judges from around the Commonwealth.

I was only thirty-six, quite young to be a federal judge. The DOJ reached an agreement on my nomination with Senator Warner, but he reneged at the last minute.

"I cannot support Ken Starr," Warner said at a press conference. "He hasn't graduated from the school of hard knocks."

Since Warner had married into vast wealth, his perspective seemed odd to me. Eventually, the post went to my Justice Department colleague, J. Harvie Wilkinson. A bit older than I, he hailed from a prominent Virginia family, which gave me a clue as to why he had been chosen. Warner had an eagle eye on his next election.

Knowing how disheartened I was, a friend at our church who had served in President Kennedy's legislative shop put his arm around me one day.

"Ken, you can't take this personally," he said. "These are just different people wearing the same old clown costumes."

The bitter disappointment turned out to be a blessing in disguise. My name was put forward for a seat on the D.C. Circuit, a prominent court that deals with important public law and constitutional issues. It's sometimes called the second highest court in America. My mentor, Chief Justice Burger, had been elevated to the Supreme Court from the D.C. Circuit.

Congress held my confirmation hearings in the summer of 1983.

"You are very young," observed Senator Arlen Specter, a Republican from Pennsylvania. "I realize I'll have to work very hard," I responded. No one raised any issues about my private practice or my actions at the Attorney General's office, and I was confirmed with little ado.

"Ladies and gentlemen, welcome to the monastery," said the chief judge welcoming newcomers to "baby judges school" at the Federal Judicial Center in D.C. Monastery or not, I loved it. Not long before I arrived, Reagan appointed Robert Bork and Antonin Scalia, both of whom I greatly admired, to the D.C. Circuit. And once I took the bench in October, it was humbling to work in the company of renowned judges such as J. Skelly Wright, Spottswood Robinson III, David Bazelon, Carl McGowan, Ruth Bader Ginsburg, Patricia Wald, Abner Mikva, and Harry Edwards.

I was never so happy in my professional life as being a judge, and it came at a good time in my personal life. Since the court's work was quite structured, I knew a year in advance what my schedule would be. I didn't have to travel, and I had time to focus on my family and on giving back.

Alice and I had by now been blessed with three children. Alice worked in marketing and public relations for a real estate development company and volunteered with civic organizations. We joined the McLean Bible Church, a burgeoning megachurch pastored by Lon Solomon, a Messianic Jew from Virginia who converted to Christianity as a college student. Though the trajectory of our lives had been quite different, Solomon and I became close friends. Alice and I participated in inner-city and special-needs ministries.

I taught Sunday school, coached my kids' sports teams, and was deeply involved in family life. I also entered conversations with Georgetown University about teaching a course at the law school.

But after the election of George H. W. Bush in November 1988, I learned I was the new president's choice for solicitor general, the attorney who represents the administration in disputes before federal courts, particularly the Supreme Court. While I was honored by his choice, I was in my element on the appellate court and had no desire to leave. I was on track to become the chief judge of the D.C. Circuit. In my heart, I harbored the not-so-secret ambition of someday serving on the highest court in the land.

I spurned two approaches from senior government officials. Then I got a request to meet with Attorney General Dick Thornburgh in his office.

"The administration needs you," Thornburgh importuned. "We believe you are the right person for the job."

Although it was a nice compliment, I walked back to the courthouse with a heavy heart. Duty was calling. But if I left the bench, the likelihood of returning to a judgeship was remote. I consulted with my friend Judge Webster.

"Ken, you are being piped aboard," he said warmly. I was to salute smartly and move forward. I called Attorney General Thornburgh to accept, hung up the phone, went into my private bathroom, shut the door, and cried like a baby. I said yes because of the tug of duty. I was asked to leave a job that I loved to return to a department that I adored.

In the meantime, my father had been diagnosed with cancer. I flew to San Antonio to see him just after the announcement of my nomination as solicitor general in February 1989. He was disappointed with my decision to leave the court. A judgeship was a noble calling—not to mention a lifetime appointment. For my father, being a federal judge represented the epitome of public service and success. He died the next week of a heart attack. It was devastating, not just because of the loss, but because in a strange way I felt I had let him down.

"It must have been hard for you to give up the judgeship," said Justice John Paul Stevens, after I was ushered into his chambers for the traditional courtesy call following my uneventful confirmation as solicitor general in May 1989. He understood how much I loved the court.

Despite my disappointment, I threw myself into my new work. I set up my staff, hiring John Roberts, who had worked at the AG's office when I was chief of staff, as deputy solicitor general. (Roberts would go on to the Supreme Court in 2005.) After reading in the legal press that lawyers with the office sometimes didn't seem prepared, I launched a moot court program, where attorneys presenting cases on behalf of the government tried out their arguments before "mock" judges.

As solicitor general, you are always busy, almost always managing a crisis. The work was exhilarating but exhausting. Over those four years, every one of my twenty-five arguments was challenging. I never advanced an argument I thought was unreasonable, but I also embraced a traditional practice of the solicitor general. Our role was to serve the demands of the rule of law, and if the federal government had secured a judgment that was indefensible, we would admit it. The solicitor general would go to the Supreme Court and say, in effect, "We confess error. We made a mistake." This was fundamental to our integrity. We wouldn't manipulate the facts or the law in order to win.

Throughout this period, I maintained a daily practice of personal Bible study and prayer. I regularly attended a men's Bible study group hosted by David Bradley, now majority owner of Atlantic Media, which publishes the *Atlantic*. I always had a favorite Scripture in mind when I went into an argument or attended a key meeting. One of my favorites was Philippians 4:13: *I can do all things through Christ who strengthens me.* Or Micah 6:8. *And what does the Lord require of you? To act justly and to love mercy and to walk humbly with your God.*

Faith proved to be a pillar of strength in my daily life. I found my stride, and despite the grueling schedule, enjoyed supervising a team of brilliant lawyers. Then in November 1992, Bush lost the election to Bill Clinton. The Republicans were out, the Democrats in, which meant that I was out of a job. The loss was personally difficult, because I had become close to President Bush and Vice President Dan Quayle. And to my surprise, I really loved being solicitor general, despite my initial anguish at leaving the D.C. Circuit.

On Inauguration Day, January 20, 1993, I packed up my office at the DOJ. Looking out of my office window, up Constitution Avenue to Capitol Hill, I saw thousands of people milling about, waiting for Clinton to be sworn in. I flashed back to that fleeting elevator encounter with Clinton in 1979. The idea that a youthful governor from a small southern state could unseat an incumbent president had shocked everyone but those followers who had seen his brilliant political talents early on.

Little did I know that a few months later, on March 23, 1993,

Clinton's newly confirmed Attorney General, Janet Reno, would abruptly fire all ninety-three United States Attorneys. When the opposing party takes over, U.S. Attorneys customarily submit letters of resignation, which are noted, but some are typically set aside until the president has nominees in place, so that the work of the office is not disrupted. But that was not the Clinton way.

And little did I know that this bold stroke would provide a revealing early example of the Clintons' disdain for the traditional processes of the federal government.

I turned out the lights. My time at Main Justice was over.

CHAPTER TWO

The Call

FOR THE FIRST YEAR AND A HALF OF THE CLINTON ADMIN-istration, I practiced law with the D.C. office of Kirkland & Ellis and taught a seminar on constitutional law at NYU. I enjoyed both immensely. Then, in July 1994, I got a telephone call from Judge David Sentelle.

"Ken, the Special Division is now looking into appointing an independent counsel for the Whitewater matter," he said. "Would you be willing to be considered?"

The Whitewater controversy had been in the news, but I had paid little attention to it up to that point. I had now been out of active politics for twelve years, and I wasn't planning to get back in. What thinking I did devote to Bill Clinton had been focused on his administration's decidedly mixed record on legal and judicial appointments.

Sure, I knew that during Clinton's campaign for the presidency in 1992, tales had emerged of criminal wrongdoing from the swamp of

Arkansas political wheeling and dealing. Federal regulatory authorities—in particular the Resolution Trust Corporation (RTC)—believed they had evidence that a Little Rock bank, Madison Guaranty Savings & Loan, had perpetrated fraud. The bank had been shuttered in 1989, costing taxpayers $60 million from the Federal Savings and Loan Insurance Corporation (FSLIC).

In March 1992, the *New York Times* published a front-page article about the questionable Madison Guaranty deals, including one that was particularly of interest during election season: a land-development project called Whitewater, located in the scenic Ozark Mountains of north-central Arkansas. The four owners of the property: Jim and Susan McDougal, owners of the bank, and Bill and Hillary Clinton.

No presidential candidate likes to have a bombshell story suggest that he is connected to fraud or failure, even if he isn't criminally responsible. The Clintons tried to brush the allegations off. As Hillary's close friend Susan Thomases rightly pointed out, "No one could understand the article," which involved a lot of complicated financial terms. Whitewater was just a failed land deal, a financial embarrassment, but nothing criminal, the Clinton team suggested, and Bill Clinton went on to win the election.

Yet despite the dodging and the election victory, pressure mounted, and in October 1993 the RTC submitted no fewer than nine criminal referrals to the U.S. Attorney's Office in Little Rock. But who should investigate? The Clinton-appointed U.S. Attorney, under pressure, sent the referrals to the Criminal Division of Main Justice.

The assignment to career professionals still raised a question of conflict of interest. After all, the Criminal Division reported to Attorney General Janet Reno, who reported to President Clinton.

That perceived conflict was the basic reason for the "special prosecutor law," a Watergate-era reform. The Ethics in Government Act of 1978 had created the so-called Special Division of my former court, the D.C. Circuit, for handling high-visibility criminal investigations of Executive Branch officials, including the president.

The Special Division consisted of a panel of three federal appellate judges who would appoint prosecutors. These independent counsels investigated matters that the Attorney General and Main Justice could not appropriately handle on their own due to a perceived political conflict of interest, and they brought criminal prosecutions if warranted. Different prosecutors would be appointed for different criminal matters.

The idea was simple: If the president or officials close to him were to be investigated for possible criminal wrongdoing, then the matter should be handled by someone independent of the administration.

The special prosecutor law, though, had been allowed to lapse in December 1992, right after Clinton's election in November.

Now, Reno, even if she wanted to, had no authority to go to the suddenly dethroned panel of judges and ask for the appointment of a "statutory" independent counsel to investigate Whitewater, or any other matter. Congress debated reinstating the law, but until it did, the judges could not appoint an investigator.

However, Reno could use executive power to appoint a "special counsel" to probe the same allegations. And in January 1994, one year after his inauguration, President Clinton directed her to do just that.

Bernie Nussbaum, the savvy New York lawyer serving as White House counsel, was vehemently opposed to the entire special prosecutor apparatus. With his customary panache, Bernie warned the president: "This is a dangerous institution. . . . You appoint this, it will be like a knife in your heart."

The White House spin was that there was no need to wait for a statutory special prosecutor, since there was no wrongdoing, but that nonetheless it would be good to wrap up the controversy once and for all.

On January 20, Reno named an outstanding lawyer, Robert B. Fiske, a former United States Attorney for the Southern District of New York, to take on the role. In her order, Reno gave Fiske the authority to investigate any violation of federal criminal law "relating in any way to James B. McDougal, President William Jefferson Clinton, or Mrs. Hillary Rodham Clinton's relationship with Madison Guaranty Savings & Loan Association, Whitewater Development Corporation, or Capital Management Services." The order extended to matters arising out of the above, "including perjury, obstruction of justice, destruction of evidence, and intimidation of witnesses."

Over the next few months, Fiske established temporary quarters in Little Rock. He assembled a terrific team of lawyers and investigators who built on the work done by the DOJ over the previous year. He began issuing subpoenas for witnesses to appear before a Little Rock federal grand jury.

Meanwhile, after many months of wrangling, Congress reauthorized the independent counsel statute on June 30, 1994. The Special Division of the D.C. Circuit emerged from its hiatus, once again open for business.

Judge Sentelle was the presiding officer. The other two judges were John Butzner of the Fourth Circuit in Richmond (a Democratic appointee), and Joseph Sneed of the Ninth Circuit in San Francisco (an appointee of Richard Nixon and father of recent presidential candidate Carly Fiorina).

The obvious course for the Special Division judges would have been to reappoint Fiske. That was the Clinton administration's position.

In her official request to the Special Division, Reno specifically recommended that Fiske now become the *statutory* independent counsel.

But the judges were of a different view. Again, it could be said that there was an appearance of conflict of interest with Fiske since he had been appointed by Reno. She in turn had been appointed by Clinton, the principal subject of the Whitewater investigation. This all made logical sense, but it also made the process appear suspicious. To preserve the integrity and independence of the process, the Special Division judges were looking for a Republican.

And this was why Judge Sentelle was on the phone with me.

I knew Judge Sentelle well. We had served together on the D.C. Circuit. Even after I left the bench, I continued to attend the informal monthly judges' prayer breakfast sessions held in the Superior Court dining room, usually presided over by Sentelle.

I wasn't at all sure I was going to give him the answer he wanted, though. Frankly, I harbored deep misgivings about the independent counsel law. I regarded the well-intentioned measure—a Watergate reform pushed by President Jimmy Carter in 1978—as unconstitutional. It intruded into the powers of the Executive Branch and thus violated a basic principle in our structure of government: separation of powers. The measure was also unwise as a matter of sound policy and good government, giving too much power to an unaccountable, unelected official.

The Justice Department had taken the position in 1982 that the law shouldn't be reauthorized. In fact, I was quoted as privately calling the idea "stupid, stupid, stupid."

But Congress had repeatedly reauthorized the law. In 1988, the Supreme Court had upheld the measure against constitutional challenge by a 7–1 majority. (Newly appointed Justice Anthony Kennedy recused himself from participation.) Justice Scalia was the solitary dissenter. In my view, Scalia had it exactly right. Yet now it had been reauthorized once again, and though as a private citizen and former judge I had my own views, the law was the law.

My opinion of the independent counsel law aside, I sensed that investigating Clinton, our youthful new president, was not likely to be a career-enhancing move.

Despite my lack of enthusiasm, I told Sentelle I would consider the appointment. I had never said no to a call to serve the country and wasn't going to start doing so now. But I surmised that I had drawn the short straw.

Not long after, a follow-up call came into my law office from Sentelle's assistant. The three judges wanted to see me in person. In mid-July, I presented myself to Sentelle's chambers at the federal courthouse on Constitution Avenue at the foot of Capitol Hill. Everything was familiar to me—the hallways of the fifth floor, the quiet of appellate chambers, and the friendly faces of the court personnel. I greeted many old friends.

Sentelle's long-serving assistant ushered me into the inner sanctum to meet with Sentelle and his colleague, Judge Butzner. On the phone from San Francisco was Judge Sneed, who had briefly been my dean at the Duke law school twenty years earlier.

Their question was straightforward: Was I the right choice to be the Whitewater independent counsel? They were posing their own question to me. It seemed a bit odd. I hadn't applied for the job, so why should I be called on to answer the Special Division's basic question?

Butzner was unfailingly polite, but seemed a bit wary. I sensed his inclination may have been to stay the course with Fiske. But Butzner, a quintessential Virginia gentleman, was brimming with questions. Nothing hostile, just probing.

By phone, Sneed seemed to be actively promoting my "candidacy." As the conversation unfolded, it became even clearer that Sneed was suggesting that I should be the panel's choice. After all, I had been a judge, and there was a quasi-judicial dimension to this unusual post that Congress had created. It bears noting that under the reauthorized law, the "independent counsel" was no longer to be called a "special prosecutor."

The difference from the original job title back in 1978 signaled a significant change in the role itself. The independent counsel was to reach judgments, but not necessarily to bring charges. In fact, the statute expressly directed the independent counsel merely to advise the House of Representatives if there were possible grounds for impeachment. It left the question of the president's fate to Congress.

The iconic Watergate special prosecutor, Archibald Cox, seemed to hover over our conversation. Cox, an active Democrat who had given a policy speech criticizing the Nixon administration, had been selected by Attorney General Elliot Richardson to investigate the Watergate break-in during the 1972 presidential campaign. Like me, he was appointed because of his membership in the opposition party, and, like me, had once served as an earlier president's solicitor general. I hoped our similarities would end there, since his dogged investigation had eventually led to his firing in the infamous Saturday Night Massacre.

Nixon had ordered Attorney General Elliot Richardson and Deputy Attorney General Bill Ruckelshaus to ax the resolute Cox. During their Senate confirmation hearings, the two men had assured the Senate Judiciary Committee—and the full Senate—that they would preserve and protect the special prosecutor's independence from political pressure. Neither could, in good conscience, obey Nixon's order to get rid of Cox. Instead, they resigned. So, Solicitor General Robert Bork, serving as acting Attorney General, fired Cox.

The resulting political firestorm and eventual disclosure of incriminating Oval Office tape recordings led to Nixon's resignation in August 1974 and finally, during the Carter administration, to the "remedy," the creation of the special prosecutor law.

Throughout my conversation with the three judges I was entirely comfortable. I wasn't auditioning. I certainly wasn't angling for the appointment. But as we bade farewell, I left Judge Sentelle's chambers with the distinct sense that I was likely to end up as the Special Division's choice. If so, I wouldn't decline. If I wasn't, all the better.

Within days, Sentelle called me at my law office and posed the ultimate question. Would I be willing to serve? Having consulted with Alice, I said yes. No hesitation on my part, but no enthusiasm either. Sentelle didn't indicate that a decision had been made; he just said he would get back to me before long. The call was short and to the point.

In the early afternoon of Friday, August 5, Sentelle called again. He reached me in a hotel room in New Orleans, where the annual meeting of the American Bar Association was under way. I had several speaking commitments during the yearly conclave.

"Ken, I'm about to sign the order appointing you as independent counsel," Sentelle said. "Are you still willing to take it?"

"Yes," I said.

A slight pause on the other end. "Very well. I just signed it. It'll be filed with the clerk straightaway."

I hung up the phone and immediately called Alice to alert her. She hung up, not letting on how upset she was at this appointment. She understood I had to respond to a summons to duty.

I went for a jog along the east bank of the Mississippi River. I needed to exercise and clear my head. The path was familiar. During my clerkship with Judge Dyer, his executive assistant, another law clerk, and I had flown to New Orleans each month for oral arguments in the magnificent federal courthouse on Camp Street, across from Lafayette Square. I loved the Big Easy, and had often run along the river.

Now I huffed and puffed along on the muggy riverbank under much different circumstances and mulled over my new role. In my naive thinking, I simply had a new assignment. The job ahead was all about facts and law.

There had been no mandate from the three-judge panel that I would quit my law practice. That was not anticipated by the statute; the independent counsel role was simply a special assignment. In any event, that would have been impossible, not to mention financially challenging. I still had several important appellate cases in the pipeline and those needed my attention.

I planned to return promptly to Washington after winding up my business in New Orleans, take the oath of office, and head down to Little Rock to begin my new task.

As I jogged, I had no idea a national media frenzy had just erupted. Fiske was out, Starr was in. The entire Washington press corps set out to find the new investigator. When I got back to my small hotel in the French Quarter, I found dozens of phone messages from reporters. I didn't return a single call.

I called no news conferences, nor did I hire a press spokesman. It never occurred to me. I held no press conferences as a judge. It's just not done. As solicitor general, I held only occasional press conferences in connection with policy issues, but not Supreme Court cases. In my new role, I intended to follow that familiar pattern. I had no idea that my stony silence, deeply rooted in legal tradition, would prove costly.

On Sunday afternoon, I was scheduled to make remarks at a meeting of the Federalist Society, a conservative group founded a decade earlier to promote the values of the rule of law, constitutionalism, and judicial restraint. The Society was hosting a reception for lawyers, judges, and law students. It was a public event. The meeting was besieged by a gaggle of reporters and cameramen. The Federalist Society folks loved the media attention, but I declined to comment about my new responsibility.

The media pressed ahead, posing basic questions. Who was this new guy? I found the "who's this" inquiry odd. I was well known in national legal circles, having served as a judge on a high-profile court, and as solicitor general arguing closely watched and frequently controversial cases.

Earlier in 1994, I had been selected by the bipartisan Senate Ethics Committee to conduct a sensitive review of the private diaries of Senator Robert Packwood of Oregon. The senator had been charged with various improprieties against women. My work on behalf of the committee was widely commended by senators of both parties, with even the embarrassed Senator Packwood remarking that he thought I had been "fair and certainly thorough." Those compliments well described my twin goals: to be scrupulously fair and painstakingly thorough.

I had been mentioned by President Bush as a possible nominee to the Supreme Court, but had been criticized in some right-wing quarters as not conservative enough.

"Starr's a nice guy, but he's a squish" went a common critique. David Souter of New Hampshire got the nod. I came in second, as Attorney General Thornburgh consoled me at the time.

On the day after my appointment as independent counsel, the *New York Times* described my reputation as a "soft-spoken, even-tempered professional whose work is marked by thoroughness," who would rise above his inexperience as a prosecutor "to cast a balanced eye on a difficult inquiry . . . likely to be comfortable in the inevitable glare of publicity with a personal style that is polite to the point of near blandness."

The writer quoted top legal intellects in Washington, D.C.

"There's really a small cast of people who have accumulated the kind of credentials he has," said Lincoln Caplan, who had written a book called *The Tenth Justice,* focusing on the Office of the Solicitor General. "Such people prove their reliability to the culture by transcending rank partisanship. He managed to be consistently conservative without being sharp-edged."

Even the American Civil Liberties Union had generous words: "If I was going to be a subject of an investigation, I would rather have him [Starr] investigate me than almost anyone I can think of," said Arthur Spitzer, the legal director of the ACLU's Washington office. "I don't have the feeling that he is a fervid prosecutor in the sense that he thinks that anyone accused of something must be guilty."

The *Washington Post* quoted Bush's White House counsel, Boyden Gray, who said Starr is "very level-headed and evenhanded and he is impartial in his approach to problems and his demeanor and his instincts. He's not an aggressively partisan or an aggressively ideological lawyer."

I basked in the glow of those kind words for about a day. Then the attacks started, first from the White House, charging that as a Republican I was manifestly unfit for the job.

"I think there is a real appearance of unfairness," Bob Bennett, Clinton's personal lawyer, told the *Washington Post*. "If Starr found anything wrong, I don't think anybody could have any confidence in that."

Bennett cited my publicly expressed opinion that President Clinton enjoyed no "constitutional immunity" from a civil rights lawsuit filed by Paula Corbin Jones, an Arkansas state employee, for actions taken while Clinton was governor. Bennett was representing Clinton in that case.

A week later, Bennett told a wire service that my appointment "didn't pass his smell test." He told *USA Today* that I should decline the job.

I found this shocking. I knew Bob Bennett well. He understood fully that I was a mainstream conservative with a strong respect for the rule of law.

In the months before being appointed independent counsel, I was teaching constitutional law at NYU. The issue of presidential immunity was the talk of the town among Washington lawyers, especially people interested in the Constitution's separation of powers. The president was asserting a prerogative that had no moorings in the long history of the American Republic. I viewed this as an extravagant legal claim that was doomed to fail.

In late May, I had participated in a panel discussion with several other lawyers, including White House Counsel Lloyd Cutler, on PBS's *MacNeil/Lehrer NewsHour.*

Cutler, a lion in the D.C. jungle, had taken over on an interim basis after Nussbaum resigned in March 1994. Bernie had been a New York fish out of Washington, D.C., water. Critics, as reported in the *New York Times,* said his "loyalty to the Clintons had become a liability as he appeared to step in repeatedly to shield the president and First Lady from embarrassment."

Clinton contended that any actions in the *Jones* lawsuit should be postponed until the end of the president's term. Harvard Law School professor Laurence Tribe shared his view.

I disagreed, saying, "It's a very serious step to take to say that the president of the United States is simply too busy to respond to lawsuits the way others have to, even if we're willing to bend over backward to protect his schedule."

Like many others seeking my opinion on the issue, one of Jones's lawyers, Gilbert Davis, called me. I had no involvement or interest in the *Jones v. Clinton* litigation. But I did offer my opinion that sitting presidents are not immune from lawsuits for actions that occurred prior to their taking office. Davis was not alone. I was also called by Bob Fiske, inquiring about the possibility of my authoring a brief contesting the proposition that the president is immune from civil litigation. The reason: Fiske wanted to leave open the possibility of bringing a civil action against Clinton in connection with the Arkansas investigation.

My position did not please the White House. The Clintons' lawyers and surrogates ginned up a conspiracy theory, alleging that the Special Division judges had sought out the most partisan of Republicans to go after the president.

The *Washington Post* reported that before my appointment, Judge Sentelle had lunched—as he occasionally did—in the Senate dining room with the two Republican senators from his home state of North Carolina, Jesse Helms and Lauch Faircloth, both outspoken Clinton critics and both concerned that Fiske had a conflict of interest. The implication was that Sentelle had allowed them to sway his judgment, pushing him to find someone committed to taking Clinton down.

When asked about the lunch, Sentelle said the threesome did not discuss matters concerning the independent counsel, but talked about western wear, old friends, and "prostate problems." That had the ring of truth to any man over the age of fifty.

But an anonymous source added spice to the conspiracy theory by claiming he had seen Faircloth and Sentelle board the tram underneath the Capitol engaged in an "animated" discussion. Though he had no idea what they were discussing, the source had gone to the *Post* because he felt their discussion was likely inappropriate. This was silly. Nonetheless, Democratic opposition ramped up. On August 13, the *Washington Post* ran a story with the headline: DEMOCRATIC CRITICISM OF STARR'S APPOINTMENT MOUNTS.

Sentelle's lunch meeting was "alarming," according to Rep. John Bryant, a Democrat from Texas and chairman of the House Judiciary subcommittee that wrote the independent counsel law. Senator Carl M. Levin, Michigan Democrat and chairman of the panel that had oversight of the independent counsel system, opined that "Starr's appointment was a threat to the IC system."

On August 10, James Carville, Clinton's campaign manager and one of his closest political advisers, called for my resignation.

"I think he [Starr] should never have been appointed," Carville said, pointing out that I had once briefly considered running for a Senate seat in Virginia. "Partisan politics is driving this whole thing." Carville, with his bald head, reptilian gaze, and gift for colorful phrases, found me an irresistible target. With the help of Carville, Lanny Davis, a Democrat political consultant, and Sidney ("Sid Vicious") Blumenthal, Clinton's assistant and senior adviser, I was transmogrified into a right-wing hit man.

On August 18, the *New York Times,* which had praised me two weeks before, published an editorial titled "Mr. Starr's Duty to Resign." It cited Judge Sentelle's "flamboyantly bad judgment" in having lunch with Faircloth and Helms. Now that the cloud of "personal favoritism" hung over my assignment, as a "matter of public service and personal honor, [Starr] should resign the appointment."

Practically overnight, this moderate "squish" became a pariah, a

Republican pit bull anointed by Senator Jesse Helms to maul the promising career of America's first baby-boomer president. This imagined conspiracy to scuttle Fiske and install Starr was entirely made up by the Clinton White House. Much of the media ran with the narrative.

I didn't give a moment's thought to resigning. But I was open to at least one entirely fair criticism. Though I had worked on criminal cases, had been a judge, and had argued before the Supreme Court, I had never prosecuted an important white-collar crime investigation.

How could a neophyte step into the shoes of Robert Fiske, one of America's premier prosecutors, who had served with great distinction as U.S. Attorney in one of the country's most high-profile federal districts, which included Wall Street?

These were entirely reasonable questions. At its core, Whitewater was about bank fraud and related monetary chicanery. Fiske's expertise was the prosecution of white-collar and financial crimes. Mine was not.

However, there was precedent for bringing in someone like me. Archibald Cox had been a Harvard labor law professor with no prosecutorial experience. He, however, was lucky to have the despised Nixon as his target. Two of the major subjects of my investigation, in sharp contrast, were President Bill Clinton, the lovable rogue, and his wife, Hillary Clinton, the copresident. Both were lawyers surrounded by smart lawyers.

The media storm was unpleasant, but I was sure I could weather it, since it would likely be short-lived. Ever the optimist, I anticipated taking six months to wrap things up. From the outside, the Whitewater case looked like nothing more than a failed land deal in Arkansas.

Not so.

CHAPTER THREE

Stepping into Big Shoes

ON THE MORNING OF AUGUST 9, 1994, I WENT TO JUDGE Sentelle's chambers with my briefcase and a carry-on bag. I raised my right hand, placed my left hand on a Bible, and took a solemn oath to support and defend the Constitution of the United States against all enemies, foreign and domestic. The witnesses were few. No family members, no journalists. Just the judge's staff and the clerk of the Special Division.

I signed the oath, which made the appointment official, and bade farewell. No photos memorialized the quiet ceremony. The three-judge court spelled out the duties in its order of appointment. Judge Sentelle and his two colleagues did not undertake a rewrite or reset of the investigation. Their order was, in effect, "Carry on." Fiske was performing well. Keep going.

Leaving the courthouse out the front entrance, I hailed a cab on Constitution Avenue and headed to the airport. That simple step represented my first action as the new independent counsel. No government drivers, no limos. I was simply off to take on an out-of-town project and get it done professionally.

With no direct flights to Little Rock, I had to change planes in Memphis. Checking in with my law office from an airport pay phone, I learned that two urgent calls had come in during the first leg of my trip.

One was from Attorney General Janet Reno, the other from the counsel to the president, Lloyd Cutler.

Reno was a constitutional officer, nominated by the president and confirmed by the Senate. As a matter of protocol, I called the Attorney General first.

I had never met her, but I could picture Reno seated in her back office on the fifth floor of Main Justice. I was put straight through and found myself immediately listening to a distinctive voice made familiar to the nation during her own confirmation hearings in March 1993.

"This is Janet Reno," she said. "I want to assure you of the full cooperation of the Department of Justice as you go about your work." Period. Nothing specific, no bill of particulars. All business. I thanked her and was off the line within seconds. I understood her brevity. She could not have been the slightest bit pleased that her able appointee Fiske had been sacked.

With that tersely stated pledge of DOJ support under my belt, I next called the White House. Once again, in no time at all, I was put through and found myself on the line with Cutler. He was more talkative than the all-business Reno.

"I wish you well in this new responsibility," Cutler said. No reference to Fiske, no intimation that I was off base in accepting the assignment. It was lawyer-to-lawyer professional talk. He set forth a happy vision of White House assistance.

"Ken, I view myself as the counsel to the presidency. David Kendall is the counsel to the president." He drew a neat distinction, rich in potential meaning. Cutler conceived of his role as institutional, not personal. His task was to protect the presidency and the enduring interests of the Executive Branch of government generally. For personal interests, including any potential criminal liability, the president had to look to his own private lawyer.

I stated my genuine thanks to Cutler, who I viewed as a great man, and hustled to the nearby Northwest Airlines gate.

The flight to Little Rock took forty-five minutes. The puddle-jumper flight was entirely uneventful. No press, no curiosity seekers, and right on time. Grabbing my bags, I headed to the cab stand outside the Little Rock airport.

Fiske had offered to have an FBI agent pick me up. Accepting that suggestion would have been a smart move. I'd made a dumb one instead. I had turned Fiske down, saying that I didn't want to be a burden. FBI agents should be carrying out their duties, not operating a taxi service.

I jumped in a cab and was soon zipping past the minor-league Arkansas Travelers baseball stadium. As we drove, I found my resolute calm a bit shaken, increasingly aware of a gnawing feeling that I was entering an unknown new world. I thought of Bob Fiske, too, abruptly removed by the stroke of a judicial pen. He probably would not look kindly on being benched by the Special Division, but I wasn't worried about how he would treat me, since I knew that Bob was the consummate professional.

Everything looked modern and well kept as we approached Two Financial Centre, a two-story office building just off the highway on Little Rock's beautiful west side. But as we pulled into the parking lot, I saw my tactical mistake in not being in the company of an FBI agent. The media frenzy had moved from New Orleans to Little Rock. Somehow, the word got out that the changing of the guard was to occur that afternoon.

I hadn't breathed a word. Nor, I was confident, had Judge Sentelle or his staff. But there they were: the soon-to-be-familiar media mob with their cameras and satellite trucks. I made my way as politely as I could through the scrum. All the reporters needed was a brief comment, but I was tone deaf. I could at least have said "I'm glad to be in Little Rock and very much looking forward to meeting with Mr. Fiske." But I didn't.

I smiled, politely brushed off questions, and stayed mum as the cameras flashed and rapid-fire questions were yelled in my direction. Mercifully, one of Fiske's staff members met me at the front door and whisked me out of the Arkansas heat and immediately into a comfortably air-conditioned office with the venetian blinds closed.

The offices themselves were nothing fancy. Nondescript government furniture. Virtually no décor or artwork adorning the walls. Family photos on desks represented the only human touches. The implicit message was: "This is all temporary. We'll be through and then leave ASAP."

Trim and athletic with silver hair, sixty-three-year-old Fiske shook my hand. Fiske, whom I knew well, was a Republican first appointed as U.S. Attorney in 1976 by President Gerald Ford, and kept on by President Carter. He had earned his prosecutorial reputation by trying a high-profile labor racketeering case with the help of a young FBI agent,

Louis Freeh. That young agent had later been appointed by Bush 41 to serve as a judge on the U.S. District Court for the Southern District of New York. When Clinton appointed Freeh director of the FBI, Freeh fully cooperated with Fiske by providing top-flight FBI agents and analysts.

Fiske was gracious, with not a scintilla of bitterness or exasperation evident in his greeting. I thought perhaps he was relieved. He could go home to Connecticut and resume his lucrative law practice.

Though all business on the surface, in a later memoir Fiske wrote that he was "angry, frustrated, and above all disappointed." He was close to bringing serious charges against several potential targets. But he was getting hammered by critics in Congress who thought he was moving too slow. That was a bum rap.

I could understand those feelings, but there was no sign of them on his face then. Fiske wasted no time ruminating about the disruptive effects on the investigation wrought by Judge Sentelle and his colleagues with the unexpected changing of the guard. The briefing was one-on-one for a while, then expanded to include his staff of about ten lawyers.

The Fiske team was probing, among other things, a fraud-filled Madison Guaranty transaction—what the investigators dubbed the "825 loan"—that appeared to have benefited the Clintons financially. The name given the transaction derived from the loan amount: $825,000.

A chart displaying the proceeds of the 825 loan was mind-numbingly complex, a financial Rube Goldberg, with arrows pointing in various directions. But the beneficiaries were clear enough, including six figures who would become the hub of the investigation: former municipal judge David Hale, the current governor Jim Guy Tucker, Jim and Susan McDougal, and the Clintons.

A key portion of the 825 transaction went toward a $300,000 loan to Susan McDougal, doing business as Master Marketing, supposedly to finance marketing efforts, such as a saucy TV ad featuring Susan in shorts astride a stallion, promoting one of the McDougals' real estate developments. Bank with Madison Guaranty, Susan's ad suggested, and be part of Little Rock's cool crowd.

It seemed that the money had not in fact gone for that ad, though, and that Master Marketing was a phantom company. From that loan, funds had apparently flowed not to Susan's fictitious marketing enterprise, but to remodel a house, pay personal bills, and repay various loans, including those involving Whitewater Development Corporation, owned partially by the Clintons.

The evidence was circumstantial but persuasive. It appeared that beneficiaries of the fraudulent Master Marketing loan included the president and the First Lady. The Clintons had denied involvement, though, saying they were simply "passive investors" in Whitewater. They had put up literally no money, but got 50 percent equity ownership. How could that be? I didn't know, but I could imagine that some fancy economic moves were at play and that there was a chance they were telling the truth.

Fiske indicated this was the core issue of the "Whitewater investigation": Did the Clintons knowingly benefit from funds illegally flowing from a failed, federally insured savings and loan? Fiske continued, ticking off various possible crimes committed by others close to the Clintons that had been exposed during the eight months he had been in Arkansas.

This list was long, and by the time he was done, my mind was reeling. The scope of his investigation was much larger than I had realized, and involved top political leaders in Arkansas and in Washington, D.C. It was a hydra that touched on financial fraud, government corruption, and the political future of the president and First Lady.

Fiske was moving toward seeking indictments against various defendants. These included:

- Jim and Susan McDougal, the Clintons' business partners in the Whitewater Development, for fraud relating to the looting of Madison Guaranty.
- Webster Hubbell, for billing fraud and embezzlement of over $300,000 from the Rose Law Firm, where he had worked with Hillary Clinton. He had gone to Washington as Associate Attorney General but resigned in April 1994.
- Arkansas governor Jim Guy Tucker, who had taken over as the state's chief executive when his predecessor won the presidency, for tax fraud, among other charges.

Fiske's key witness was David Hale, the municipal judge turned lender. His company, Capital Management Services (CMS), a federally subsidized lender, worked with Jim McDougal to create the fraudulent 825 loan. Hale claimed that during a meeting at the sales office of Castle Grande, a McDougal real estate project, Bill Clinton pressured him to use a portion of those funds to make the $300,000 loan to Susan McDougal, which would benefit both Clinton and Jim McDougal.

"My name can't show up on this," Bill Clinton allegedly told Hale.

If Hale's inflammatory charge was accurate, the current president of the United States would be implicated in a potential felony under federal law.

The Clintons had denied all Hale's allegations, painting him as a bitter man who lied to save his own skin. "You know, it's all a bunch of bull," Clinton told a reporter for the *New York Times* in March 1994.

Fiske had great faith in Hale's testimony, though. He had thoroughly vetted Hale's statements about shady financial dealings in the state capital, and in instance after instance, Hale's information proved accurate. Now, Hale, after pleading guilty along with two codefendants to conspiracy and fraud, had agreed to become a witness against the Clintons, the McDougals, and the others in exchange for consideration on his sentence. In the meantime, he had enough dirt on important people in Arkansas that he was living under protective custody in Louisiana.

Because Hale had confessed to his own crimes, further documentation was needed for his information to stand up in a court of law. To find that information, Fiske's team (and their predecessors) had issued approximately four hundred subpoenas for witnesses to testify before a Little Rock grand jury. His investigation in Arkansas was far-reaching and well under way.

As the sun was setting on that mind-numbing first day, the press melted away outside Two Financial Centre. But my meeting with Fiske and his staff continued into the night. On and on, the "to be investigated" list unfolded, and I was stunned by its breadth. Taking over from Bob Fiske was a tall order.

Fiske's sweeping investigative focus—financial chicanery, political fund-raising hijinks, and dubious real estate transactions—was nowhere near my professional sweet spot. I knew federal law and practice issues, but not how to put a commercial real estate deal together, or develop a multistage corporate transaction to launder assets through a fraudulent bankruptcy. I would have to learn.

As the evening wore on, I stopped taking notes and just tried to absorb it all. I understood two things well: Fiske and his team believed David Hale, who pointed an accusing finger directly at Bill Clinton, and following the leads Hale had provided would take many months, if not years.

At one point in his briefing, Bob Fiske looked straight at me and said, "Ken, move your family to Little Rock. You're going to be here for a long time."

CHAPTER FOUR

Changing of the Guard

T HOUGH I GREW TO LOVE LITTLE ROCK, MOVING MY FAM-
ily to Arkansas was a complete nonstarter.

For our three school-age children, McLean was home. All three
Starr kids (Randall, then a sophomore in high school, and his two
younger sisters, Carolyn and Cynthia) were lifelong Virginians, enrolled
at the rigorous but nurturing Potomac School in McLean. From our
house, I could jog to that almost-century-old school through the forests
and across creeks or "runs," which abound in the Old Dominion.

Alice was thriving in her own rewarding career with one of the
largest commercial real estate developers in Northern Virginia. She
was also a well-known leader in the community, serving as president
of the McLean Chamber of Commerce. Unincorporated, McLean has
no separate governance apart from sprawling Fairfax County. Due
to the breadth of her community and volunteer activity, however, I
dubbed Alice our town's unofficial "mayor."

Home, school, church, dear friends, jogging trails—all were in

McLean. We loved it there. Disrupting the children's lives and Alice's career because of my "temporary" assignment of unknown length in far-away Arkansas was not in the cards.

And so the Starr family remained in Northern Virginia. I would commute. In doing so, I took a page from Fiske's approach. Despite his advice to me, his spouse, Janet, had remained at their home in suburban Connecticut. Fiske rented an apartment in Little Rock and commuted from LaGuardia.

Beginning that August, I flew out of Washington National on Sunday nights and lived in a one-bedroom apartment during the week. It was like being a bachelor again. Reluctantly, I gave up teaching children's Sunday school and coaching Little League, but in any event, the kids were outgrowing my modest skills.

I brought the family to Little Rock over the Labor Day weekend and showed them around, kidding that we were all moving to Arkansas. But as much as I tried to maintain a routine, it was difficult to be away from home during the week. I remember talking to one of my children during a bad patch at school. I hung up and thought, "This is really bad that I'm here."

Yet despite the difficulties, the trip to Arkansas soon became routine. I flew commercial airlines (coach class) either via Memphis or Cincinnati, then to Little Rock. No government planes or helicopters. And no security. I drove myself in a modest General Services Administration–issued bright red Chevrolet.

My first goal in Little Rock, besides understanding the general shape of the investigation, was to step into Fiske's shoes professionally with respect to his personnel. He had assembled a terrific group of lawyers and investigators, and I hoped to lead them well.

The Fiske team included attorneys taking a sabbatical of sorts from their respective law firms, a few prosecutors detailed from the DOJ, and career federal agents on special assignment to a high-profile financial-crimes investigation, one that implicated both President Clinton and the First Lady.

When it came to the attorneys, Fiske had created a microcosm of his prestigious law firm, Davis Polk, in New York. Several of his senior attorneys, though still young, came with him from that firm. Others joined the effort from leading law firms on the East Coast, from Boston to Atlanta.

Unlike the attorneys, the FBI and IRS special agents were "on detail" to Whitewater from their respective organizations. For these financial-crimes investigators, Whitewater was just another assignment, rather than—as with all the lawyers—a heady interruption in their professional lives.

The FBI field office was located on the second floor of Two Financial Centre, but most of the local special agents, who lived semipermanently in the community, were largely sealed off from the ever-expanding Whitewater inquiry. That was good. Those special agents and staff members could honestly answer questions by their curious neighbors with a simple response: "Don't ask me. I don't know what's happening downstairs. I'm not part of the Whitewater investigation." As the Fiske organization grew, with reinforcements arriving from around the country, it was better and safer not to be in the know.

For eight months, they worked long hours and stuck to themselves socially. Most lived in one or two apartment complexes on Little Rock's scenic west side. They wanted to get the job done and get back to their respective homes and careers.

As I learned more about their wide-ranging work, I decided the best way to tackle the job was to pursue the twin goals of stability and continuity. This was a passing of the baton, not a reset or do-over. To carry on effectively, I wanted to keep the Fiske team intact and push their cases forward full throttle. No line of the Fiske inquiry would be jettisoned. No one would be let go. Fiske gave me no hint of having a problematic lawyer or investigator. They were all doing their jobs well.

But doing so proved to be impossible. With my arrival, almost all the lawyers recruited by Fiske decided to pack up and leave. Fiercely loyal to their boss, they had signed up to work for him, not the new guy. They felt betrayed by the Special Division's order abruptly ending his tenure.

In addition, the Fiske folks weren't entirely immune from the drumbeat of anti-Starr criticism from the Clinton White House and their friends in the media: the universally admired Fiske had been replaced by Senator Jesse Helms's supposedly anointed right-wing lawyer.

Day after day, I tried my best, urging and cajoling the few remaining Fiske team members to stay.

"You're carrying on a very important role," I implored. "That function continues, and the best way for it to be done effectively, and in the process to honor Bob, is for you to remain on the job." They were unpersuaded by my blandishments. For years, both in and out of government, my job had been to persuade, but my skills now failed me.

Over a retention-focused dinner at the Black-Eyed Pea restaurant near the Little Rock office, one young lawyer patiently listened to my plea.

"You're trying real hard, but you need to respect our decision," he said. "You need to let go. We're leaving."

I was heartsick, but grudgingly abandoned the effort, feeling I had given it my best shot. I never asked Fiske to step in to help. Perhaps I should have. But my sense was that he would have politely said no. (Only years later did I learn from Fiske that he had in fact strongly encouraged his team to stay, for the sake of the country. But away they went.)

I needed to restaff. Finding the right people was all-important. It was not just the complexity of the facts. The individuals being investigated were well known and popular in Arkansas. My prosecutors would be perceived as outsiders who had invaded Little Rock on orders of a faraway federal court.

Fears abounded in Fiske's office of a potential deep-seated bias against out-of-staters wielding federal power. To add fuel to the fire, the reconfigured Office of the Independent Counsel (OIC) was daily decried as a politically inspired witch hunt.

My first priority was to bring a senior trial attorney on board in Little Rock. I would not be the lawyer trying the cases. Not only was I the ultimate outsider, my forte was the appellate arena, or more broadly, "issues and appeals," as we called our specialty practice at the law firm.

Fiske had already approached a renowned career federal prosecutor, Hickman Ewing Jr., then in private practice across the Mississippi River in his native Memphis. As U.S. Attorney for the Western District of Tennessee, first appointed by Ronald Reagan, Hickman had come to fame for relentlessly rooting out corrupt sheriffs, politicians, and crooked law enforcement officers.

Unlike many U.S. Attorneys, Hickman tried key cases himself. He gained national notoriety for his role in successfully prosecuting the brother of Tennessee governor Ray Blanton, whose office had doled out pardons in exchange for cash and favors.

Furthermore, Hickman's powers of recall were prodigious. Former U.S. Attorney Joe Brown of Nashville assured me that trying a case alongside Hickman was "like sitting next to a human computer."

And he wasn't all brain. A Vietnam veteran, Hickman had seen combat in Southeast Asia on a Swift Boat with the U.S. Navy. A gifted raconteur, Hickman was spellbinding in the courtroom. His cross-examination skills were the stuff of legend. He connected brilliantly with juries.

Perhaps most important for the needs of the investigation, Ewing, as they say, spoke "southern." He had a Tennessee accent like a chicken-fried steak, dipped in batter, fried up, and covered in gravy.

Down to earth, easygoing, Hickman had rock-ribbed integrity, a character trait that came shining through in the crucible of hard-fought litigation. The son of a renowned high school football coach in Memphis—and a varsity baseball player himself at Vanderbilt—Hickman was a superstar, a perfect addition to the team.

We met over comfort food in Brinkley, Arkansas, halfway between Little Rock and Memphis. At the Sweet Pea's Buffet, which doled out generous portions of fried fish, collard greens, corn bread, cobbler, and enormous glasses of sweet tea, Hickman and I immediately connected.

In the South, at many restaurants you can go back for seconds in a buffet line. We did. As I chowed down, I was reminded of an old saw by a University of Arkansas law professor: "Over its glorious history, the South has suffered overmuch from two things: fried food, and oratory."

Hickman and I talked on into the evening about his experience in public integrity cases. I came away sensing that he would say yes; he would be coming on board to try the last big cases of his career. He became the heart and soul of the Little Rock operation.

Immensely talented though he was, Hickman could not do the job alone. I was thankful that two of Fiske's best attorneys agreed to stay on. They seemed to regard living in Arkansas as an adventure.

Bill Duffey, deputy independent counsel, had relocated his young family from Atlanta, where he had practiced law at the right hand of former Attorney General Griffin Bell, one of my favorite people on the planet.

Duffey wanted his children to complete a full school year in Arkansas, and the entire family seemed quite happy with their temporary arrangements. Bill and his son had taken up music lessons, and with the son playing fiddle, the Duffeys launched a family bluegrass band. His wife, Betsy, plied her trade as a professional writer. The Duffeys would chortle about living near Toad Suck and Pickles Gap, a world away from their familiar Georgia haunts of Buckhead and Sea Island. For the OIC, Duffey would master the complexities of the Whitewater investment.

Gabrielle Wolohojian, who came to Fiske's investigation from a leading Boston law firm, was a New Englander through and through. An Oxford Ph.D. as well as an accomplished young lawyer, Gabrielle found much of Arkansas life and culture charmingly exotic, like something out of an old Snuffy Smith cartoon. To get involved with the community, she began playing violin with the Arkansas Symphony Orchestra.

Cultural considerations aside, Gabrielle had not become as personally tied to Fiske as her comrades. Above all, Gabrielle loved the work and believed in the mission. She had amassed substantial evidence in the cases against Governor Tucker, a business associate, and their corporate lawyer, who had devised a fraudulent bankruptcy scheme allowing Tucker to avoid paying millions in federal taxes.

Our ranks were further augmented by two outstanding members of the Fiske team who had been "in waiting."

Amy St. Eve, a young woman with midwestern earnestness and

Cornell training, was a rising star at Davis Polk before being recruited by Fiske. She had only a few years of experience, but was smart and eager to learn. Tim Mayopoulos, a senior associate at Davis Polk, brought his formidable talents to bear in a case involving two bankers; documents showed that they, along with attorney Bruce Lindsey, had laundered cash for Bill Clinton's 1990 gubernatorial campaign.

Also joining the team was Steve Learned, a renowned career prosecutor from the Fraud Section of the Criminal Division at Main Justice, who quickly mastered the various RTC criminal referrals. Bob Bittman, a rising young state prosecutor in Maryland, became a pillar of the entire investigation.

After being recruited by Fiske, Brad Lerman, a crackerjack prosecutor, had moved from Chicago to Little Rock with his wife, Rita, and their four children. The Lermans settled in the fashionable neighborhood of the Heights and were warmly welcomed by their curious but accepting neighbors. He focused primarily on the intricacies of the 825 loan, which his quick and analytical mind promptly mastered.

As my new staff took shape, I set out a vision for recruiting the rest of the prosecutors: I wanted to create a microcosm of the Justice Department with top-notch, experienced litigators. In Little Rock and in Washington, I brought together prosecutors drawn not only from Main Justice but from U.S. Attorney's Offices around the country. With the welcome cooperation of the DOJ, federal prosecutors began signing up.

Prosecutors don't do the job alone. Given the financial focus of the Whitewater investigation, our prosecutors needed experienced FBI and IRS agents and analysts who understood complex real estate transactions and elaborate bank financing schemes. Most of those who worked with Fiske decided to stay.

Their leader was a native Arkansan, Steve Irons. Like most FBI agents, after basic Special Agent training at Quantico, Irons had been assigned to various FBI field offices around the country. A CPA with over ten years' experience in the Bureau, Irons was superbly qualified for the assignment.

"My state deserves better government than it's had," Irons told me not long after we began working together. He wasn't talking about public policy. He was all about integrity. Arkansas had not had honest government, under either Republican or Democratic rule.

Irons and I became quite close. We frequently took thirty-minute drives together, circling across the beautiful Arkansas River back to home base at Two Financial Centre.

I loved the scenery. However, these driving adventures served as a relaxed and secure setting for backgrounder briefings away from prying ears or possible tape-recording devices. Irons would talk and reflect; I would ask questions and listen.

Although his service in the FBI had taken him far away from home, Irons had maintained close Arkansas ties. But he purposefully kept a distance from the locals. He would not be compromised. He remained as lead Special Agent until the end of my service.

At Irons's right hand was a superb forensic accountant, Special Agent Mike Patkus, the go-to guy for unraveling deep financial mysteries. I thought of him as "Smoking Gun" Patkus, because he had a knack for ferreting out important documents. Along with experienced FBI and IRS financial analysts, he had built a convincing criminal case against the McDougals and Governor Tucker.

David Reign, another superb Special Agent, served as handler for David Hale, who was living incognito in Shreveport. (Fiske wanted him to be out of state, but readily accessible.) Irons, Patkus, Reign, and their colleagues believed in the truthfulness of Judge David Hale.

Time and again, Hale pointed the team to a particularly shady deal. Time and again, the documents backed him up. He was never proven wrong.

Hale became the epicenter of the Arkansas investigation. Through his testimony, the mysteries of Whitewater and other financial crimes were illuminated. If Judge Hale was right, Bill Clinton was a potential felon, assisted by Hillary.

After spending time in Little Rock getting the office restaffed, I turned my attention back to Washington, D.C., to a troubling area of Fiske's investigation that I feared needed a reexamination.

I was right.

CHAPTER FIVE

The Vince Foster
Death Investigation

O N JUNE 30, 1994, THE SAME DAY BILL CLINTON SIGNED the independent counsel law reauthorization, Fiske issued two short reports. The first, from the Little Rock office, concluded that the evidence was inadequate to show improper political interference with the RTC investigation by the Clintons.

The second report, from the Washington office that Fiske had opened, was brief. In summary, according to Robert Fiske's later auto-biography, it said: "Vincent Foster committed suicide in Ft. Marcy Park on July 20, 1993. Although the contributing factors to his depressed state can never be precisely determined, there is no evidence that any issues relating to Whitewater, Madison Guaranty or CMS played any part in his suicide."

Often referred to as courtly, regarded as one of the most talented lawyers in Arkansas, Foster had been at the vanguard of the incoming Clinton administration. A smooth professional who carried himself with great dignity, Vince Foster was perfectly situated to be a franchise player. Smart and experienced in Arkansas legal matters, he went way back with the Clintons.

In the 1980s, the three Rose Law Firm partners—Webster Hubbell, Hillary Clinton, and Foster—not only had worked together as attorneys, but were all close friends. Hubbell and Foster were staunch Hillary champions in a part of the country where she was viewed with disdain or suspicion by more traditional southern women.

Hillary Rodham had grown up in Chicago as the daughter of a hardworking Republican business owner and went off to her freshman year at Wellesley in 1965 as a "Goldwater Girl."

But in the tumultuous '60s, she shed her midwestern upbringing and became an antiwar Democrat. Many students in the Ivy League did the same thing, a common reaction to their revulsion as images from the Vietnam War dominated the media.

Hillary was profoundly influenced by the radical Saul Alinsky, whose "rules for radicals" included tips for budding community activists such as: "Keep the pressure on, never let up," "Ridicule is man's most potent weapon," "Go after people and not institutions," and "Pick the target, freeze it, personalize it, and polarize it."

She'd written her ninety-two-page senior honors dissertation on Alinsky, whom she quoted as saying that gaining and holding on to power "is the very essence of life, the dynamo of life." While researching her paper, she met three times with Alinsky, who offered her a job when she graduated. She declined. "After a year of trying to make sense of his inconsistency," she later wrote, "I need three years of legal rigor." Alinsky's loss was Yale Law School's gain.

But Hillary had absorbed many of his ideas. At her commencement ceremony, Hillary listened carefully to the keynote speaker, Senator

Edward Brooke, an African American Republican from Massachusetts. She then got up in front of her fellow seniors and denounced him. Her rude grandstanding at a revered rite of passage garnered attention. For this "soft" form of contempt, Hillary was written up in *Life* magazine as a voice for her rising generation.

Once they achieved national prominence, the Clintons often deployed Alinsky's strategies. But it hadn't always served them well. Our files were filled with examples of wrongdoing by both Clintons that could have been avoided if they'd followed the Golden Rule instead of Alinsky's rules for radicals.

During their years in Arkansas, Hillary worked at her husband's side during campaigns and launched her own legal career at the Rose Law Firm in the late 1970s. She had found in Hubbell and Foster true companions who helped her navigate Arkansas politics and culture.

Now, Hillary was paying them back. Both men had come to Washington at her behest to play pivotal roles in the new administration, Hubbell as the third-highest official at the DOJ and Foster in the White House Counsel's office, as the deputy to the counsel to the president, first the rough-and-tumble Nussbaum, then Lloyd Cutler.

Once in Washington, Foster became the new administration's point man for key issues, including vetting Cabinet nominees. In its first six months, the young administration suffered its fair share of political setbacks, including the failed nomination of Zoë Baird as Attorney General. Baird was terrific, and would have been the nation's first woman to serve in that post. But "Nannygate" scuttled her nomination when it was revealed she'd hired an undocumented nanny to care for her children, as well as an illegal immigrant as a chauffeur, then failed to pay their Social Security taxes. The nominations of Kimba Wood as Attorney General and Lani Guinier as an Assistant Attorney General also failed.

Foster got blamed.

Then there was the matter of the nine hundred errant FBI files that ended up in the office of a colorful Clinton operative named Craig Livingstone. A former bouncer who had dressed up like a chicken or Pinocchio to disrupt Bush campaign events, Livingstone had been rewarded with a position of singular authority and sensitivity: reviewing background checks of political appointees.

The White House assured the press that the misuse of the files was a simple bureaucratic snafu. But many of the files related to Republicans who had served in past administrations. It looked more like dirty tricks than an accidental dump of documents in the wrong place.

Fiske also subpoenaed numerous documents, including Hillary Clinton's billing records from the Rose Law Firm. Strangely, those records had disappeared. Mrs. Clinton insisted she had no knowledge of their whereabouts. This was highly suspicious. Billing records under subpoena don't get up and walk out of law firms. Some investigators suspected that Foster or Hubbell had stolen them for the First Lady.

The response from the Washington press in the first six months of the Clinton administration was disparaging. "Who's Vincent Foster?" asked the *Wall Street Journal* editorial page. At each administration misstep, Foster was being attacked, painted as a slimy political operative with no integrity. I could well imagine his pain.

Vince Foster was struggling to put out fires and getting blasted by the *Wall Street Journal*. On May 8, 1993, two months before his death, Foster gave a commencement address to the law school graduates at the University of Arkansas, his alma mater. He seemed reflective and, in hindsight, troubled.

"The reputation you develop for intellectual and ethical integrity will be your greatest asset or your worst enemy," Foster said. "You will be judged by your judgment. . . . There is no victory, no advantage, no fee, no favor, which is worth even a blemish on your reputation for intellect and integrity. . . . Dents to [your] reputation in the legal profession are irreparable."

Days later, yet another furor erupted over the Clintons' purge of the entire White House Travel Office, which arranged travel for the press corps that followed the president.

The seven career employees, who had served Republican and Democrat administrations going back to the Reagan years, were summarily fired. Director Billy Dale, who had worked in the office since 1961, was charged with several crimes and had to hire a lawyer. One of Hillary's cronies from the campaign, a Hollywood producer named Harry Thomason who had his own air charter business, took over.

Catherine Cornelius, Bill Clinton's second cousin, had been spying for Thomason inside the Travel Office, removing documents and reporting rumors and innuendo that the Travel Office people were skimming money and living far beyond their means.

Based on these rumors, and on Thomason's assurances that Dale and his employees were dirty, the First Lady pressured members of her staff to get rid of the career folks and get their own people in. "We need those slots," she told a member of her staff.

Her attitude was: Off with their heads!

The Travel Office staff served at the pleasure of the president. It was certainly within the prerogative of the new administration to fire or reassign those employees. But the abrupt housecleaning and the manner in which it was carried out smacked of an ugly form of political patronage. Members of the press condemned the White House for the lack of due process and besmirching the employees' reputations.

Hillary told Foster to clean up the mess.

On the plus side of the new administration's political ledger, the Supreme Court nomination of Ruth Bader Ginsburg had been well received, and was destined to sail easily through the Senate even though she'd been an ACLU women's reproductive rights lawyer before she went on the D.C. Circuit. Foster had been a pivotal member of the team that vetted and shepherded Ginsburg through the confirmation process. That was a huge victory for the fledgling administration.

But White House life is filled with exhilarating ups and depressing downs, sometimes on the same day. The mistakes landed on Foster's desk, and he was tasked with sorting them out—and at all costs, protecting his bosses.

His close friend Hillary didn't seem grateful. She excoriated Foster within earshot of others, then gave him the cold shoulder for weeks.

Shortly after lunch on July 20, Foster grabbed his coat; bade farewell to his executive assistant in the White House Counsel's office, Linda Tripp; gave her some mints from the White House Mess; and left.

Tripp was the last known person in the White House complex to see Vince alive.

Heading west across the Potomac into Virginia, Foster drove north on the George Washington Parkway toward Maryland, and pulled into a small park named after the fort that, during the Civil War, had protected the southern banks of the Potomac.

Foster parked his car, locked it, walked into Fort Marcy Park, and sat down on a berm that had been a Civil War fortification. He pulled out a pistol that had been in his family for two generations, put the gun in his mouth, and fired. No witnesses. No suicide note left behind. No farewell call to his spouse, or to anyone else. His body was discovered a little after 6:00 P.M.

The news of Foster's death shocked and perplexed everyone. He had no known enemies. Everyone liked and admired Vince.

Making his suicide even more inexplicable, Vince's wife and children were moving from Little Rock to D.C. that summer. His family would be reunited and at least three and a half years of prestige-filled service in a coveted West Wing office remained ahead of him.

The provocative question inevitably emerged: Did a depressed Foster really take his own life? Or was he murdered?

An investigation by the U.S. Park Police confirmed that he committed suicide, but questions remained. What happened to the bullet? Why had the White House prevented the Park Police from searching his office in the aftermath? The official finding didn't quash the rumors. Conspiracy theories began to spread, alleging that Foster had been murdered by the Clintons' operatives, to protect them from his testimony or to prevent him producing records damning for the Clintons. These rumors took hold of the public imagination.

Seeking to put the matter to rest, Fiske opened an investigation. His investigators confirmed that Foster had committed suicide in the place where his body had been found. They found no evidence of foul play. Reflecting Fiske's Yankee personality, his team's report was short, succinct and to the point. The case was clear, so there was no need for elaboration. Unfortunately, Fiske's report was dismissed in various quarters as unconvincing at best and a whitewash at worst, raising more questions than it answered. Adverse reactions to the terse death report were strong, and they didn't subside over the ensuing days.

Vince Foster's death haunted me. In many ways, I was a lot like him: serious about the law, conscientious, and loyal to a fault. Foster had been needled by the media, which I knew all too well could be brutal, especially for someone not used to the public eye.

A note he had written had eventually been found torn to pieces in the bottom of his briefcase: "I made mistakes from ignorance, inexperience and overwork. I did not knowingly violate any law or standard of conduct. . . . I was not meant for the job or the spotlight of public life in Washington. Here ruining people is considered sport."

I understood that a sensitive man, plagued by the media and depression, might take his own life. I also understood that the brief investigative report would not satisfy the public.

Years earlier I had worked with lawyer David Belin, who had been senior counsel to the Warren Commission, chaired by Chief Justice Earl Warren to investigate the assassination of JFK. Warren was a man in a hurry and believed the nation needed to know what had happened as soon as possible.

Belin concurred in the commission's findings, but lamented that in the final report they had not discussed and debunked various conspiracy theories. Released on September 24, 1964, the report failed to knock down the wilder stories that sprang up. Consequently, they grew exponentially. Belin was so upset by this fallout that he wrote his own book: *November 22, 1963: You Are the Jury.*

Learning from Belin's experience, I decided the investigation into Foster's death would begin anew. I was stepping into Fiske's shoes, but I would not simply retrace his path. I would start over and take a second look.

He had personally directed the Washington office's operations out of Little Rock. We would augment the ranks for a more in-depth investigation.

The question of leadership for the OIC's Washington office loomed large. There was no senior lawyer like Hickman Ewing at the Washington office. To my relief, I was able to recruit Mark Tuohey, a friend and prominent leader of the D.C. bar. He was entering a stage of professional transition, ready to move from his Pittsburgh-based law firm to a more national platform. He came on board as senior deputy.

Tuohey set a significantly different tone in the D.C. office. A great raconteur who could charm birds out of trees, Tuohey was a people person with street smarts. And he knew everybody who was anybody in Washington.

A highly accomplished lawyer in private practice, Tuohey had limited but intense experience at a policy level at the DOJ. Though he wasn't a career prosecutor, he was well known to local federal judges, especially in the District. A devout Irish Catholic, he was an active Democrat who had supported Clinton's election. The White House could not attack him as a partisan out to get them.

Looking ahead, I thought that prosecutorial experience was less likely to be important in the Washington office. We were more likely to run into complex issues of law and policy, and to have significant interaction with Capitol Hill. I began developing a D.C.-based "brain trust" of young lawyers I knew well. The intellectual firepower assembled in our Washington office was strong, rounded out by a singular hire: the "Legendary Sam" Dash (aka LSD by my team), a professor at Georgetown Law Center.

I knew Dash well through Washington legal circles. A longtime criminal law professor and former prosecutor, he was universally admired for his dogged pursuit of truth during the Watergate era, when he became a national figure and household name. He had later been a key architect of the original independent counsel statute.

Dash had served as senior counsel to the colorful Senator Sam

Ervin of North Carolina, who had chaired the Senate Select Committee probing the White House scandal. With his twitching white eyebrows, Senator Ervin became an American folk hero. And Sam Dash was always at his side.

With the Watergate hearings featured on national television every day, Dash's incisive questioning of various witnesses, such as Nixon White House counsel John Dean, was still vivid two decades later in the minds not only of lawyers but of the American people. The Washington press corps respected Dash for his unbending integrity.

Dash was very self-possessed; in some ways, he lived in the past. Watergate was almost always on his lips, but at the same time he was well versed in criminal law and practice, more a street prosecutor than a scholarly lawyer.

Dash called me during the early weeks of the investigation and asked to come over to the D.C. office. In our windowless conference room, he got right to the point.

"Ken, you are already coming under fire because of your Republican background. You also haven't been a prosecutor. You'll have tough decisions to make. I would like to help you. I can be a sounding board for the whole staff, including in Little Rock as you come to decisions about whether and who to prosecute."

I enthusiastically welcomed the idea. Dash would serve as our ethics counsel. He would not leave his academic perch at Georgetown, but would jettison all other projects to come alongside my staff both in D.C. and in Little Rock.

Especially appealing to me was the fact that the presence of Tuohey and Dash put the lie to the allegations that the Starr investigation was politically motivated. Insults, condemnations, and outright lies about the Starr appointment were now an everyday occurrence. The meta-narrative had solidified: the GOP had engineered the firing of the nonpartisan Fiske, and gerrymandered the system through Judge Sentelle to insert a Republican loyalist and right-wing hit man to "get" the Clintons.

My motivation in hiring both men was to promote public confidence in the honest administration of justice. With Dash and Tuohey, we created institutional structures or "guardrails" that would guide the exercise of prosecutorial discretion as we tackled important questions.

For example, a proposed indictment would be presented before the grand juries in either Little Rock or D.C. only after undergoing an exacting internal review, what I called the "deliberative process." This process would always include Dash. The roundtable discussion, common in judges' chambers, was painstakingly thorough, with all participants not only welcome but encouraged to speak up.

For the most part, Dash did not work with witnesses, or appear in the grand jury. He was to serve instead as an outside adviser, ethics counselor, and ultimately our independent voice of professional conscience. He asked probing questions, and at times played devil's advocate. He made sure we were careful and our cases were airtight.

And we did have to be careful, since many distractions, in the form of accusations outside our purview, came up. One day at the Little Rock airport, as I was emerging from a connecting flight, I was accosted by an agitated Arkansas resident.

"Mr. Starr, have you looked into the Calico Rock prison deal?" she sputtered. "Crooked as a snake."

"Thank you," I said politely. "I'll alert the FBI to your concern." And I did, right away.

Whether that Arkansas state prison transaction was clean or dirty was not the business of my investigation. That was the responsibility of the U.S. Attorney's Office in Little Rock or the DOJ's Criminal Division in Washington.

But once I took over the Fiske investigation, I realized even more clearly how uncovering evidence in a Whitewater-related crime sometimes led to the discovery of others. Those crimes would fall under our jurisdiction.

With my team largely in place, the Starr investigation got under way. At our first roundtable in Little Rock in the fall of 1994, Dash described the method Watergate investigators had used when tackling the issue of "what did the president know and when did he know it?"

They identified people closest to the targets of the investigation—aides, secretaries, friends, coworkers, lovers—and worked their way out in circles. That's how they first learned of Nixon's secret taping system, which ultimately revealed the president's obstruction of justice.

Over time, the team in Little Rock grew fatigued with Dash's stories. Some would say he was a shameless self-promoter. That wasn't my experience. He tended to pontificate, but I wanted to hear what he had to say.

Hickman had another method of eliciting information: "getting the molecules moving." Say a dirty sheriff had both a wife and a mistress. They'd end up in the grand jury waiting room together, standing by for their turn to testify. We didn't have that particular scenario, but there were periods in our investigation when it seemed molecules definitely were moving.

But that would take time. With Tuohey on board in Washington, we launched our reinvestigation into the death of Vincent Foster. We later brought on three of the nation's preeminent experts in homicide and suicide: Dr. Brian Blackbourne, medical examiner for San Diego County; Dr. Henry C. Lee, an expert in physical evidence and crime scene reconstruction, and director of the Connecticut State Police Forensic Science Laboratory; and Dr. Alan Berman, executive director of the American Association of Suicidology. They began working with a handful of experienced FBI agents dedicated to the Foster investigation.

On December 20, 1993, the White House had confirmed that Whitewater-related documents had been in Foster's office at the time of his death. Why had they disappeared? And did their absence have anything to do with his death?

Our Washington office began interviewing personnel of the U.S. Park Police, White House employees, and Foster's friends and family members. I knew how Washington thinks. Leaving any doubt as to the cause of death by a high-ranking Executive Branch official was a recipe for endless conspiracy theories. I was determined to get to the bottom of Foster's death.

CHAPTER SIX

Whitewater Complexities

T HE NIGHT BEFORE I FLEW TO LITTLE ROCK EACH WEEK, my D.C. assistant, Neille Russell, would call Hickman's assistant, Debbie Gershman, with a message from me:

"Tell Hickman we're going to go get some lard."

That meant breakfast at the Waffle House, that iconic purveyor of high cholesterol fare so familiar in the South.

On December 7, 1994, Hickman and I ate waffles and bacon and drank a vat of coffee while we talked about where the Whitewater investigation stood. Hickman, who had been working on it for about three months, pulled out a yellow legal pad and began sketching an extraordinarily complex diagram.

At the top were the initials BC and HRC—Bill and Hillary Rodham Clinton—with lines connecting them to a web of perhaps thirty associates, foremost Jim and Susan McDougal. Hickman's diagram reinforced the briefing I got from Fiske on that first night in Little Rock.

Bill Clinton had known Jim McDougal for decades. In the late 1960s, both had come into the orbit of Democrat senator Bill Fulbright, an elegant, eccentric man from a wealthy Arkansas family. A Rhodes scholar, Fulbright managed to repeatedly get reelected in his home state despite his vaguely English accent.

McDougal, who was six years older than Clinton, worked as an aide to Fulbright, soaking up stories and Arkansas political lore. McDougal had a reputation as a raconteur and playboy. He adopted Fulbright's sense of style, wearing fine suits and Panama hats. The press could count on him for a pithy quote no matter the situation.

When Clinton returned to Arkansas during a term break as an undergrad at Georgetown, he took over McDougal's job as driver for Senator Fulbright. To McDougal, the twenty-one-year-old from Hot Springs seemed "affable and obviously smart," but that gig didn't last long. Clinton kept up a steady stream of patter and argued with the senator about the Vietnam War and other policy issues. He saw no need for deference to the venerable lion of the Senate. The job didn't turn into anything long term, and Clinton went off to law school.

The connection with Fulbright may not have benefited Clinton much, but the senator's connection would turn out to be pivotal for McDougal.

After Clinton decided to run for office, he and McDougal reconnected and forged a strong friendship. Clinton and another friend, Jim Guy Tucker, a lawyer who at one point was McDougal's roommate, were rising stars in Arkansas politics.

McDougal would be unsuccessful in his own election bids, but he had good political instincts and a deep knowledge of Arkansas political history, thanks to Fulbright. Perhaps even more important, he knew how to find money. McDougal had begun investing in real estate, often inviting friends like Fulbright to invest with him. Despite his family's wealth, Fulbright pinched pennies and was delighted when one of McDougal's land-flipping projects made him money.

Clinton and Tucker often turned to McDougal for advice about fund-raising. He had plenty of experience in delivering "get out the vote" money—strategic payments to community leaders such as pastors who could be counted on to get their people to the polls.

As Hickman's Waffle House diagram showed, these three ambitious men—McDougal, Tucker, and Clinton—had become enmeshed in alleged wrongdoing that would send one to prison, destroy another's political fortunes, and severely damage the other's reputation. Fiske had not been exaggerating when he briefed me on that fateful first day.

As I would learn over the next few months from Hickman and our FBI agents, McDougal was a recovering alcoholic and a complicated, conflicted man. An early marriage failed and he fell into what he called a "dark period." He couldn't get out of his recliner, didn't talk to anyone, just sat and brooded. Years later, he would be diagnosed as manic-depressive.

At one point in the '70s, things got so bad for McDougal that an old friend, former Arkansas Lieutenant Governor Bob Riley, let him live in a trailer on his property and got him a job teaching political science at Ouachita Baptist University (OBU) in Arkadelphia.

One afternoon while in his OBU office, McDougal met Susan Henley, a vibrant and attractive student from a large family, whose ambition was to meet and marry a preacher. After knocking on his door, Susan explained that she had inadvertently locked a teacher's keys in the office next door. Could McDougal help? After trying several keys, McDougal simply kicked down the door.

That was one way to get an attractive young woman's attention.

Jim and Susan got married on May 23, 1976, just after she graduated from OBU. McDougal left the teaching job, and returned to making real estate deals.

His pal Bill Clinton, now married to Hillary, made a successful run for state Attorney General that same year. The two couples sometimes socialized together. The men got along great, but Susan and Hillary never became close. Susan had little in common with the hard-charging Yale Law grad who seemed out of her element in Little Rock.

It was clear that Bill Clinton was going places, but it was hard to keep up with Arkansas's political movers and shakers. According to Jim McDougal, Bill cared little about money, but Hillary had lofty financial aspirations. After Bill became Attorney General, he was making a paltry state salary of twenty-five thousand dollars a year. Presumably hoping to augment that small salary, Hillary joined the Rose Law Firm at about the same time.

One day in 1978, after Bill's first election as governor, the two couples met for lunch. McDougal had joined his administration, but was still pursuing real estate deals.

Jim and Susan raved about a piece of beautiful undeveloped property they had just visited on the White River in north-central Arkansas. They asked the Clintons if they'd like to invest. They'd buy the land, about 230 acres, put in some roads and other infrastructure, then subdivide the property and sell lots to retirees looking for a quiet place in the country.

The Clintons were enthusiastic. Bill had made money on one of Jim's previous deals. By the time lunch ended, they had agreed to buy the land together and split the profits fifty-fifty. In 1978, the couples borrowed $203,000 in a complex, multibank transaction.

History can thank Susan, who came up with the name for the project: Whitewater.

The next year, after Bill was sworn in as governor, Hillary vaulted to partner at the Rose Law Firm. He was now making $33,500 a year, still not much, but the Clintons could move into the Governor's Mansion.

In 1980, Bill lost his reelection bid. That also put McDougal out of work again. He returned to real estate with a vengeance. To fund his projects, he bought a troubled bank, renamed it Madison Bank & Trust, and brought it back to life. He did the same for a failing thrift, calling it Madison Guaranty Savings & Loan. It had $3 million in assets when he bought it; within a year, the S&L had $100 million in assets and $103 million in debts.

Jim saw himself as a deal maker, an empire builder. He began buying properties and flipping them, using his ready access to capital to close deals quickly, build some amenities, then sell them off.

With Bill out of office, Hillary worked hard to support their family, which now included baby Chelsea. She called McDougal, asking for money from what she presumed was the thriving Whitewater project. Jim explained that the project was so remote, lots weren't selling. They needed a model house for prospective buyers to visit, one that might prompt them to picture themselves living there.

The McDougals had been floating the Whitewater loan. Hillary agreed to borrow thirty thousand dollars from Madison Bank & Trust to put a mobile home on one of the lots.

After Clinton returned to the Governor's Mansion in 1982—besting Jim Guy Tucker in the Democratic primary—he borrowed twenty thousand dollars from another bank to reduce what Hillary owed Madison.

The Whitewater project, once so promising, had stalled as high interest rates choked off sales of vacation property.

Despite his recapture of the governorship and Hillary's high-status job, the Clintons' finances were floundering. Per McDougal's later account, early on a hot August morning in 1984, Clinton just happened to jog from the Governor's Mansion to McDougal's office at Madison Guaranty. The governor plopped his sweaty body onto a new leather orthopedic chair. McDougal was irritated but listened as his friend, who had a "hangdog expression," asked him to help Hillary out. She had been advised that she wasn't generating enough business and felt under pressure to recruit more clients for the Rose Law Firm. Clinton hinted that it would be desirable for McDougal to move Madison's legal work to Hillary.

Since Tucker's law firm had been doing McDougal's legal business, that meant McDougal would have to alienate Clinton's friend, fast becoming a political rival, but he agreed.

Within two hours, according to McDougal's account, Hillary visited his office and they discussed the arrangement. McDougal began sending Hillary a monthly retainer fee of two thousand dollars. She began handling various matters for Madison Guaranty and other McDougal real estate ventures.

Meanwhile, the Whitewater project was all but dead, killed off by those high interest rates and its remote location. McDougal exchanged unsold lots with another developer for an airplane and the assumption of thirty-five thousand dollars in bank debt.

Though the Clintons had put little money into the project, Hillary refused to sign over their remaining interest in the property, telling Susan, "McDougal promised that Whitewater was going to pay for Chelsea's education." McDougal insisted he had told her no such thing.

Hillary also, by McDougal's account, improperly took tax deductions for losses the Clintons, as "passive investors," did not actually incur.

Little was going well for Jim McDougal now. He and Susan separated, though they remained in business together. His real estate house of cards—built by juggling loans among various institutions—was collapsing. In 1986, he was forced to resign from Madison Guaranty. Hillary ended her retainer agreement with McDougal, but refused to transfer the Clintons' remaining interest in Whitewater over to the McDougals. Instead she assumed control of the Whitewater investment, perhaps thinking there was still value there.

The McDougals were removed as officers of Madison Guaranty in 1986. A victim of overleverage, bad loans, and outright fraud, the S&L failed in March 1989, at a cost to taxpayers of at least $60 million. Jim McDougal was indicted on charges related to the Castle Grande real estate deal. After a jury trial in 1990, McDougal was acquitted.

When Bill Clinton decided to run for president, he realized they needed to be shed of the taint of Whitewater and any association with Jim McDougal. But Hillary continued to refuse to relinquish their interest. It wasn't until after the presidential election, as Bill Clinton was transitioning to the nation's capital, that Vince Foster, representing the Clintons, signed papers selling the couple's stake in the project to McDougal for a thousand dollars.

During the 1992 presidential campaign, McDougal felt shunted aside, left behind to rot with his failing real estate deals. He was angry at both Clintons, and at Tucker, now lieutenant governor, for their perceived disloyalty. And maybe angry at himself. Even though he'd been acquitted of bank fraud, his legal troubles weren't over. The RTC was probing into Madison Guaranty. Other matters were sure to come out.

He'd held a fund-raising event at the thrift to pay off the debt of one of Clinton's earlier campaigns, skirting campaign finance laws by giving Madison Guaranty's employees money to drop in campaign coffers.

He decided to lash out. As I would later learn, it was at this point in early 1992 that McDougal picked up the phone and called well-known reporter Jeff Gerth of the *New York Times*. He had a story, McDougal said, about a presidential candidate, his wife, and a beautiful place in Arkansas called Whitewater.

CHAPTER SEVEN

Webb

WHEN I TOOK OVER FISKE'S INVESTIGATION, LONG AFTER Gerth had broken the Whitewater story at McDougal's tip, agents had for months been interviewing everyone connected to the 825 loan, which had been designed to keep the Whitewater deal and other McDougal projects alive.

Organizing such a labyrinthine investigation was not easy, but we did what was necessary to sort out the tangle. Each team of OIC lawyers and federal agents was assigned a major segment of the investigation, which they would stay with until it went to court. As Hickman's Waffle House diagram made clear, many but not all of these investigations led back to Bill and Hillary Clinton, either as potential witnesses or as subjects. The president and the First Lady would have to be deposed.

Questioning the most powerful people in America under oath was daunting business.

The earlier DOJ and Fiske investigations had struggled to get documents from the White House. The DOJ issued a subpoena to the Clintons on December 23, 1993, on behalf of the Little Rock federal grand jury, asking for all documents in the Clintons' or their lawyers' possession related to Whitewater Development, Madison Guaranty, David Hale, and his company, Capital Management Services.

Engaging with the White House was like walking in molasses. David Kendall, Bill's personal counsel, was a formidable opponent. Raised in a Quaker household, he had an air of formality about him. He was articulate and prodigiously hardworking, famously dedicated to his clients. Time and again, I would see up close and personal this zealous advocacy.

From the firm of Williams & Connolly, known for its scorched-earth strategy, Kendall delayed, denied, and dragged out responses to requests from the DOJ, Fiske, and from our office. The Clintons claimed to have virtually no documents.

This was frustrating for the Little Rock grand jury, composed of twenty-three citizens drawn from the pool of registered voters. They meet for a term of eighteen months. If necessary, a judge can give them a six-month extension, but then their term expires for good.

Our grand jurors were patient and paid close attention to the testimony. The old canard is that any prosecutor worth his or her salt can get a grand jury to indict a ham sandwich. In my experience, that is a misunderstanding of how the grand jury system works.

But since grand juries meet at most only one or two days a week, the process can drag out, especially with witnesses who delay or refuse to produce documents. It can be maddening. That was the Clintons' strategy.

Fortunately, even if the Clintons did their best to slow down our process, we had other sources of information. For one thing, we had

Hale's testimony. For another, we hoped to get the potentially significant testimony of disgraced Rose Law Firm partner Webster Hubbell, who pleaded guilty to income tax evasion and mail fraud in December 1994.

At six foot five and 310 pounds, Webb Hubbell was a giant of a man with a fun-loving personality. During his days at the University of Arkansas in Fayetteville, he had been a solid student and star football player, destined for fame on the gridiron.

But after his NFL football career was cut short by injury, Webb returned to Fayetteville for law school. He landed a plum perch at the Rose Law Firm and married Suzy Ward; her father was Seth Ward, a wealthy serial entrepreneur who had later gotten involved in several of the McDougals' land deals.

Webb was regarded as an able lawyer, but he soon fell into a deadly financial spiral of living far beyond his means. By 1992, as we later learned, he had stolen hundreds of thousands of dollars from his partners and fraudulently billed several unsuspecting clients, including the federal government. Yet despite his crimes, he somehow passed muster in an FBI background check and joined the Clinton administration as White House liaison to the DOJ in January 1993.

The FBI may have missed Webb's malfeasance, but Fiske and the Rose Law Firm eventually caught on. Lawyers at the Rose Law Firm threatened to bring litigation against their former partner for embezzlement and billing fraud. By the time I came on board, Bob Fiske's investigation of him was virtually complete. Though Hillary reportedly urged him to remain and fight the charges, Hubbell, under mounting pressure, resigned from the DOJ on March 14, 1994. He hoped to reach a civil solution with his firm, but the magnitude of his theft— finally tallied at $482,000—made criminal charges unavoidable.

By December 1994, we negotiated a deal with Webb's lawyer, John

Nields. Webb would plead guilty to two felonies, mail fraud and felony federal tax evasion, and begin cooperating with the OIC. I made it clear that we wanted the facts, wherever they led.

Hickman and others spent considerable time debriefing Hubbell to find out what else he knew about the work the Rose Law Firm had done for Madison Guaranty and the fraudulent Madison Guaranty loans. He was facing stiff time in prison if we didn't recommend "downward departure" from the federal sentencing guidelines, given for full and substantial assistance. We put off his sentencing to see if he would truly cooperate.

The rule of thumb in prosecutors' offices is that even cooperative witnesses, eager to earn a reduced sentence, will give up only 80 percent of what they really know. "Their first instinct is to tell you what they think you already know, and nothing more," one career prosecutor told me.

Webb had an idiosyncratic habit that signaled to our prosecutors and FBI agents when he was not honest with us. Whenever a potentially sensitive question was posed, especially touching on the Clintons, Webb began nervously fidgeting with his wedding band.

Given Webb's physique, his two large hands could not go unnoticed by anyone sitting around the conference room table. When sensitivity levels were manageably low, his hands rested comfortably on the table with occasional insignificant gestures. But when a potentially hot topic was introduced, the wedding band immediately found its way into the fingers of Webb's formidable right hand. Back and forth, up and down, his left-hand finger the ring would move. When the tension returned to normal, the wedding band was once again at rest.

We could only surmise what his attorney grasped about the full state of Webb's knowledge. I felt we were close to a breakthrough. Maybe now we could find the information we needed to corroborate

Hale's testimony, information that had been held back by the Clintons. But it was not to be. Between his friend Hillary, his colleagues at Rose, his wife, and his father-in-law, Hubbell had numerous reasons to keep mum, and yet another Clinton witness delayed our proceedings.

As the months-long debriefing process wound to a frustrating conclusion, I informed Nields that we were disappointed in the level of his client's cooperation, and that we would not be asking the sentencing judge for a reduction of Hubbell's sentence.

The resourceful Nields mustered up an impressive array of supportive letters from the Little Rock community and urged the judge to reduce the sentence based upon Webb's "extraordinary" record of public and community service over the course of many years.

I was impressed with Nields's ingenuity and Webb's admirable community service. Nields asked me if we would oppose or support downward departure.

"John, we'll stand neutral," I said. The judge was impressed with the letters, but seemed disinclined to be lenient. "To whom much is given, much is required," the judge said. Sentenced to twenty-one months, Hubbell reported to a minimum-security prison camp on August 7, 1995.

I wasn't surprised by the outpouring of support for Webb. In my mind, Webb was at heart a decent person. Ironically, Webb's good-heartedness had stifled his income-generating power. The bane of lawyers' professional lives is the billable hour. A huge swath of Hubbell's income-producing hours had been donated to his community, and it didn't seem that the Rose Law Firm had rewarded him for his community and public service. Now, to his own detriment, Webb was remaining fiercely loyal to his friends the Clintons.

We didn't realize it at the time, but Webb was playing it smart. It seemed to us that friendship had trumped basic self-interest, but we later learned that rainmaking efforts had gotten under way in high places. On March 13, 1994, the day before Hubbell said he would resign, White House Chief of Staff Thomas "Mack" McLarty assured Hillary, "We're going to try to be supportive of Webb."

McLarty asked Clinton supporters like Washington lawyer Vernon Jordan to help Hubbell find clients. Jordan, in turn, snagged Revlon as a major account at $25,000 per quarter. The stated purpose of the engagement: "public relations."

The Clinton fund-raising network went into overdrive. Soon, an entirely new set of clients retained Hubbell. California's Eli Broad and Texas's Bernard Rapoport, large-money donors to Democratic party efforts, rallied to Hubbell's cause. In 1994, he earned $450,010. In 1995, after he went to prison, he earned $84,750.

Despite energetic efforts, we were unable to identify any meaningful services actually performed by Webb as the lawyer-consultant for these far-flung clients. Yet he was suddenly making much more money than he ever had as a senior lawyer at the Rose Law Firm.

This pattern—generous payments made at the behest of the White House for amorphous professional services of dubious value—raised the obvious question: Was this hush money?

It certainly appeared to be. I felt snookered when we learned the requests to retain Webb, with lofty fees paid in full up front, had come from the White House, not Arkansas friends and supporters. Our growing suspicions were confirmed by the damning content of transcripts of conversations recorded at Webb's minimum-security prison in Cumberland, Maryland—standard operating procedure in federal prison.

Conversations between Webb and his wife, Suzy, revealed an understanding that Webb was to keep silent about whatever he knew.

At one juncture, Webb remarked, "I guess I need to roll over one more time."

Some of Suzy's comments reflected concern for the security of her own job within the Clinton administration. Suzy was getting a "royal squeeze play" from "Marsha," someone Webb clearly knew. The inescapable conclusion: the Hubbells were protecting the Clintons.

We later learned Webb hid his windfall from the IRS. I was taken aback by his stupidity. Webb had a deep stubborn streak of basic dishonesty that kept manifesting itself in baffling ways.

We eventually launched a second investigation of Hubbell and found enough evidence to go before the grand jury in Washington. I petitioned Reno for authorization. She agreed we should move forward, and if the evidence was convincing, prosecute Hubbell for tax evasion. Webb Hubbell became the Waldo of our work, popping up time and again.

CHAPTER EIGHT

Follow the Money

OUR FIRST MAJOR TRIAL, SCHEDULED FOR EARLY 1996, would cover the complex $825,000 loan. Though the press called it the Whitewater trial, we called it the 825 case, focusing on the dirty dealings that also involved the Whitewater land deal.

Here's a short version of how 825 worked: Thanks to fraudulently inflated appraisals, Madison Guaranty, owned by Jim and Susan McDougal, made a loan for $825,000 to a man named Dean Paul, a nominee or straw borrower. Paul then "purchased" properties controlled by Hale, adding a phantom "profit" of $500,000, which Hale put into his company, CMS. This allowed CMS to get $1.5 million in additional funds. After his chief lending officer expressed concern that it might not get paid back, McDougal told him, "Stop questioning the loan and put it together."

Hale's company then made four fraudulent loans to McDougall's designees, one an entity owned by Tucker. None of the loan proceeds were used for the purposes stated. One tranche of $300,000 went to Susan McDougal.

Hale insisted that Bill Clinton had urged him to make the loan to Susan, to be used in part to bail out the Whitewater project. So far, investigators had been unable to find corroborating documentation.

Slowly the 825 case wended its way through the labyrinth of investigation and into the judicial system in Little Rock. The McDougals and Tucker were charged with financial fraud and conspiracy on August 18, 1995, in a twenty-one-count indictment.

We knew that the 825 trial would make or break other investigations in the pipeline. But would a Little Rock jury, even if convinced of the crimes beyond a reasonable doubt, be willing to convict, knowing their verdicts would ruin the political career of Tucker and possibly send the Clintons' friends to prison? And what would felony convictions mean in terms of getting to the truth of the role, if any, that Bill and Hillary Clinton played in Madison Guaranty and the fraud-infected financing of the Whitewater project?

To have a shot at success, we needed a level playing field. Other than the strength of the underlying case, that depended more than any other factor upon the judge we drew. In my experience, bad judges are rare in the federal system. Unfortunately, Judge Henry Woods, who had been an overnight guest of the Clintons at the White House, was one of them. A Carter appointee, he did not leave his politics at the courthouse door.

As a result of Woods's unprofessional behavior, our investigation suffered significant delays. On September 6, 1995, the judge dismissed our grand jury's first indictment—against Tucker, his lawyer, and his business partner—on grounds that the OIC lacked authority under the Special Division's order to bring the prosecution.

He was dead wrong. We appealed to the Eighth Circuit Court of Appeals in St. Louis, but that took precious time and significant resources. Many months later, the court reversed Judge Woods's ruling in a severe appellate spanking, and ordered him off the case. To my relief, the case was then reassigned to Judge Stephen Reasoner.

The 825 case was assigned to a judge of integrity, Judge George Howard Jr. A Democrat and a Carter appointee, Judge Howard couldn't be dismissed by Clinton and Tucker partisans as a biased Republican in judicial robes. The former civil rights lawyer emerged as a sensitive, caring jurist admirably humble about his considerable power. He reminded me of the sage advice given to new federal judges by a more experienced colleague: "Remember, you were appointed, not anointed."

Based upon our painstaking development of the evidence, we believed that our case against Tucker and both McDougals was airtight. Hale would testify at trial, as would a land appraiser who had entered a guilty plea and was cooperating with our prosecutors. But we knew their testimony would be assailed on cross-examination by defense attorneys.

"Why should the jury believe your testimony? You have admitted committing serious crimes, haven't you?" That line of attack was fair game. How would our linchpin Hale hold up?

So our case had to be grounded on financial documents, introduced to the jury by FBI special agents who specialized in financial fraud investigations. Unless they're doctored up, documents don't lie. Ours were pristine.

Especially damning were the bank records on the loan to Susan McDougal, showing that she'd used a portion of the funds to pay personal expenses, such as tennis club dues, and to redecorate her home. We believed everyone on the jury would understand that kind of theft.

As part of our investigation leading up to the indictments, for the sake of completeness we needed to take the statements of both Clintons.

As an accommodation to the president and the First Lady, we reached the judgment—in consultation with Sam Dash—that the Clintons should not be required to travel to Little Rock to appear before the grand jury. We would interview them in the White House, and as a courtesy would allow their lawyers to be present. This represented a radical departure from customary grand jury practice, because attorneys are not allowed in the federal grand jury room. (Witnesses can excuse themselves and go outside the room to consult their counsel.)

That set up our team's first visit to the White House in April 1995. I was curious to see how Bill and Hillary handled scrutiny under pressure. Bill had long decried the investigation as a witch hunt. Could his testimony save his friends?

CHAPTER NINE

White House Depositions

I SWEAR TO TELL THE TRUTH, THE WHOLE TRUTH, AND nothing but the truth, so help me God."

President Clinton removed his hand from the Bible and sat down in a chair in the Treaty Room of the White House. The OIC team present for the April 22, 1995, deposition consisted of me, Hickman, Mark Tuohey, and Bill Duffey. Several of Clinton's lawyers, led by David Kendall, were there. We'd agreed in advance that the questions would be limited to Whitewater and Hillary's representation of Madison Guaranty; questions on other subjects would be left for another time.

We had first scheduled the depositions for the following day, a Sunday. But the bombing of the federal courthouse in Oklahoma City had occurred the previous Tuesday. Citing the somber mood and the president's need to fly to OKC on Sunday, Kendall had asked us to switch the deposition to Saturday.

Bill Clinton entered with a subdued look on his face; he had just spoken on television about the bombing.

Jim McDougal wasn't cooperating with us, but he had given an interview to a newspaper describing the day when the sweaty governor had jogged from the Governor's Mansion to his office and asked McDougal to throw some work Hillary's way.

Hickman asked him about the "jogging incident." We expected him to say it didn't happen, since he'd denied it during the campaign in writing.

"You know, Mr. Ewing," Clinton said, sounding thoughtful, "I've read that. But I just can't remember."

Hickman later told me that's when he knew the president "was a lying dog."

In claiming he could not remember, Clinton stepped over the line and, in our view, may have committed perjury. It defied credulity that the president would not remember such an unusual episode. This was no ordinary meeting in the state capital. This was a targeted outreach on behalf of Hillary's law practice.

Predictably, the president not only denied any wrongdoing, he denied any knowledge of the financial transactions involving Whitewater. He claimed he was simply a "passive" investor, as was Hillary.

Clinton also denied receiving any financial gain whatsoever from Madison Guaranty. We already knew that a fund-raiser at Madison Guaranty had raised thirty thousand dollars for Clinton in one night, and that Jim McDougal had funneled cash through his employees and other political pals to Clinton's campaign.

We looked ahead with a sense of foreboding. The Clintons would likely be afflicted by purportedly poor memories in all matters related to Whitewater. Our fears were justified. OIC lawyers would eventually question Bill Clinton at the White House five times: twice in 1995, twice in 1996, and once in 1998. Each time, as we saw it, he gave deliberately misleading testimony.

As the deposition ended, the president was all smiles, shaking everyone's hand before he left. Then Hillary arrived. She made no effort to be cordial.

Several minutes into the questioning by Hickman, there was a knock on the door of the Treaty Room. In walked a Filipino Navy steward. He said something quietly to Kendall. Hillary crossed her arms and looked down, her lips tightened in anger. The steward walked over to a closet, removed the president's golf clubs, and walked out.

We all sat in silence for a few moments. The president, despite the somber mood of the country, was going to play golf. That was his business, of course, but the moment was awkward.

As the deposition continued, Hillary repeatedly said, "I don't know" and "I can't recall." She and Bill had entrusted everything about Whitewater to Jim McDougal, though they were jointly liable for the loan. And she denied bringing Madison Guaranty into the Rose Law Firm; a junior associate named Rick Massey had. She performed virtually no work for the thrift.

We were fumbling in the dark because the Rose Law Firm documents were missing; we had only a few internal memos. Suspecting she was involved in keeping those records from us made her non-answers even more maddening. We were convinced there was a lot Hillary was holding back.

On Saturday, July 22, 1995, we returned to the back entrance of the White House to continue our depositions of the Clintons. Each time, I had arranged the meetings with White House Counsel Abner Mikva, whom I knew well because we had served together on the D.C. Circuit.

At 11:30 A.M., I drove my minivan to the White House. Crammed into the back were members of my team, including Hickman, Amy St. Eve, several other prosecutors, and a court reporter. The topics for this session were the 825 loan and Vince Foster's death, a sobering subject. We went upstairs to the Treaty Room a little after noon. President Clinton was already there, along with five lawyers. He appeared a lot looser than during the session in April. While the court reporter set up equipment, he chatted.

"Who was your favorite singer growing up?" he asked Kendall. "Mine was Elvis Presley."

Kendall replied that his favorite was Little Richard. Both appeared to be trying a friendlier approach.

"When I was a kid, I'd cut the grass," Clinton said to no one in particular. "We'd get centipedes and tear them apart and watch them go off in different directions. Hick, I bet y'all did that over in Memphis."

"No, Mr. President," Hickman said, "we didn't do that in Memphis."

Bill was questioned for three hours about Whitewater and the 825 loan by Brad Lerman. He framed a series of "Did you know?" questions. Clinton bobbed and weaved, but was always pleasant as he avoided answering.

When Hillary arrived, it was a different story. No small talk. For three hours, she answered questions posed by John Bates, a career Assistant U.S. Attorney from Washington. John had risen through the ranks to become one of the senior leaders in that shop.

Her responses were so glib, so superficial, they were almost "in your face," alternating on the theme of profound memory loss. In the space of three hours, she claimed, by our count, over a hundred times that she "did not recall" or "did not remember." This suggested outright mendacity. To be sure, human memory is notoriously fallible, but her strained performance struck us as preposterous.

Mikva shook my hand as we left that day and thanked me for handling matters with discretion. "I realize it was not done for this president," he said. "I appreciate your concern for the presidency."

I later learned Mikva had reassured Bill Clinton after my appointment that "Ken and I had good relations on the court and I'm sure it will continue." His cheery view would soon change.

The following Monday, July 24, back in Little Rock, I invited Hickman and several other people involved in the investigation to have dinner at Kirby's Grill & Bakery, across the street from the OIC. We had a two-hour briefing on the depositions over steak and baked potatoes. Hillary's extraordinary lapses of memory—especially for a lawyer and self-described policy wonk—were not credible. Back at our office, we all agreed that we were unimpressed with Hillary's performance. One staff member described her as "affirmatively dislikable."

I asked Hickman what he thought about the Clintons' testimony.

"The president I'd give a C," Hickman said. "The First Lady, an F minus."

I had to agree. I was upset over Mrs. Clinton's performance, and was even considering bringing the matter before the Washington grand jury for possible indictment on perjury.

But proving that someone knowingly lied when they said "I don't recall" or "I don't remember" is extremely difficult, especially if that person is the First Lady. What was clear was that Mrs. Clinton couldn't be bothered to make it appear as if she were telling the truth.

In late 1995, Abner Mikva left the White House. He later gave an interview to the *New York Times* saying his opinion of my character had radically changed after our office summoned Hillary to testify before the grand jury about the missing Rose Law Firm records. As Mikva saw it, we had forced her to go to the courthouse instead of showing deference to her as First Lady.

"The Judge Starr I knew was cautious, deliberate, careful, not zealous and reckless," Mikva told a reporter. "The Ken Starr I see now is not the Ken Starr I knew."

This was a bum rap. We had specifically offered arrangements for Hillary to enter the courthouse unobtrusively through the basement, with no fanfare whatsoever. She chose instead to arrive at the public entrance and march in alone.

"As the First Lady has always said, she is as eager as anyone to resolve questions regarding the billing records," said Mark Fabiani, one of the Clintons' lawyers, "and she will continue to provide whatever help she can finally to resolve these issues."

Hillary made the calculated decision to turn her testimony into a public spectacle—and a public relations opportunity. She wildly succeeded. Tipped off by the White House, the press arrived at dawn to get a glimpse of the historic occasion of a First Lady testifying before a grand jury. As CNN's Bob Franken told Hickman, "This was like the Rose Bowl. You had to get there early to get a seat."

CHAPTER TEN

The 825 Trial

T HE 825 TRIAL OF THE McDOUGALS AND GOVERNOR Tucker began on March 4, 1996. The temperature outside was near freezing. By the end of the trial in late May, Little Rock sweltered in 100-degree heat.

From the beginning, it was a media circus, as if America understood what was at stake for the Clintons. In addition to the Arkansas newspapers, the wire services and national media sent reporters.

The OIC intended to prove that the three defendants had stolen $825,000 by means of an elaborate illegal scheme involving federally insured funds; and that some of the funds had been intended to pay off the McDougals' and Clintons' debts on the Whitewater development.

The prosecution team couldn't have been stronger. Career federal prosecutor Ray Jahn, a Vietnam veteran, had tried the toughest of cases, including the capital murder trial of Charles Harrelson, arising out of the assassination of federal district Judge John Wood in my hometown of San Antonio. (The killer was the estranged father of actor Woody

Harrelson.) At Jahn's right hand was his wife, LeRoy, also a career prosecutor. They were a formidable duo. Ray tried cases in court. LeRoy, the duo's central nervous system, prepped Ray and fed him documents as needed during trial.

Jackie Bennett Jr., a hard-charging former college football player, had risen to prosecutorial fame through the conviction of Congressman Albert Bustamante from San Antonio. He came to Little Rock from the ranks of the Public Integrity Section of the DOJ's Criminal Division.

Also from Public Integrity, Rod Rosenstein was an up-and-coming courtroom litigator, with four or five trials under his belt. Though young, he was extremely well prepared and precise.

Amy St. Eve took on one of the most delicate assignments, questioning a hostile witness, Steve Smith, an Arkansas professor who had pleaded guilty to his role in the 825 loan.

Our youngest associate, Eric Jaso, a Harvard Law–educated attorney whom I recruited from a top corporate firm, took on the challenge of researching and answering a blizzard of defense motions.

One of the first things Robert Hirschhorn, our jury consultant, told us was that the defense would attack the independent counsel at every opportunity. Ray Jahn sat me down and said, "Ken, I'm sorry to say this. The defendants will be pointing fingers in your direction and trying to put you on trial. We have to bench you. You cannot darken the door of Judge Howard's courtroom."

This was a distressing turn of events for me. I had been banned. No appearances in the courtroom, no press statements. For someone who thrived in a courtroom, it was painful to be sidelined. But I couldn't say I disagreed.

I became the OIC's ghost leader. Every day, I waited until the proceedings had gotten under way to drive downtown from our west side offices. I'd park my car in a lightly trafficked lot, sneak through a back door into the federal annex adjacent to the courthouse, and head down the stairs to the basement.

A spacious but entirely nondescript area with numerous cubicles served as our trial headquarters. We kept the office locked tight, with coded access and a skeleton support staff on hand. Festooned prominently on the wall was an enormous, homemade trial banner: "We are honored by our friends and distinguished by our enemies."

I felt a sense of powerless frustration. In my furtive comings and goings, however, I never encountered the press. They were all on the courthouse steps, sitting in the courtroom, or milling around in the hallway.

Hungry for information, I tried to control my impatience but practically pounced on any of our team members who entered our dungeon offices fresh from the trial proceedings upstairs. My most frequent companion from the courtroom battleground was Eric, our prolific wordsmith.

Throughout the trial, the lunch break provided a midday respite from the tension. I was joined by the prosecutors and agents in the windowless conference room. Over sandwiches or pizza, we dissected the morning's events and planned for the afternoon. We studiously avoided the courthouse cafeteria, where, we assumed, the walls had ears.

The trial gamesmanship started even before the jury had been chosen. Governor Tucker arrived on the first day of jury selection with a full retinue of Arkansas state troopers as bodyguards. He marched into the courtroom clutching his wife's hand.

That prompted our jury consultant to ask Ray Jahn why he didn't wear a wedding ring. Ray confessed that he had gained fifty pounds since he and LeRoy had married. His ring no longer fit.

This was socially conservative Arkansas, Hirschhorn told him. Married people wore rings. The next day, Jahn sported a brand-new wedding ring. Like Tucker and his wife, Ray and LeRoy entered the courtroom holding hands. (He still wears the ring.)

Hirschhorn recommended that voir dire—questions for potential jurors—be split between Ray, the tough guy, and Amy St. Eve, the youthful and appealing woman. Amy was anxious; barely out of law school, she'd never participated in voir dire before. Ray told her that he was practically in the same boat. In many federal trials, voir dire is handled by the judge.

Jury selection got off to a poignant start. One older man, told that he had been deemed acceptable by both the prosecution and the defense, was asked by the judge to wait in the corridor. A bailiff came in a few minutes later. The man was crying. He didn't want to be on the jury. He said he couldn't read or write, but was too embarrassed to say so in front of the judge. Understandably, Judge Howard dismissed him.

Then there was the petite female juror who appeared for jury selection dressed in a *Star Trek* uniform. She made it on to the jury as an alternate; our team preferred her to the man who sat next to her.

Several weeks into the trial, she asked the judge if the proceedings could be adjourned earlier than usual. She needed to go home and attach her Spock ears because it was her duty to preside over that night's meeting of the Interplanetary Intergalactic Confederation—or something like that. The judge thanked her for her service and dismissed her from the jury. A headline read: JUDGE BEAMS UP JUROR.

After voir dire, the prosecution's case got under way. Because the trial was so dependent on documents, our team brought in a high-tech projector system that allowed the lawyers to highlight or point to a line of text. The defense immediately objected, saying the court didn't need this "newfangled stuff." But by the end of the day, the defense was asking the prosecutors if they could borrow our equipment.

The White House was closely monitoring the trial. That point was dramatically illustrated when David Kendall appeared unannounced at the courthouse. Our team members kept a watchful eye on him and his colleagues as they sat in the courtroom. Sure enough, during the lunch recess, our staff spotted Kendall counseling Susan McDougal. It was open and notorious.

Susan's lawyer had been taking some hits. Though her defense was that she knew little about the business going on at Madison Guaranty, that Jim handled everything, one witness testified about her standing in the middle of the lobby one day and shouting, "I own this f****** place!"

David Hale had testified that Susan had arrived at his office in a tennis dress, signed documents for the $300,000 Master Marketing loan, then bounced out, saying, "We'll have to do this again sometime soon."

We believed Susan knew a lot about the president. If she testified, she could damage him politically. By remaining silent, she could protect him. Kendall's involvement was understandable, but shameful from a constitutional standpoint. It appeared that Clinton had sent defense lawyers to get his friends and political allies acquitted on charges of looting a federally insured bank. By my lights, this was a mockery of the president's duties to faithfully enforce the law.

The defense tried to brand us as a Republican hit squad dispatched from the banks of the Potomac to do the GOP's dirty work. That tactic worked outside on the courthouse steps. But inside the courtroom, it backfired. Tucker's lawyer got into an embarrassing jam by trying to divorce the OIC from the federal government in the minds of the jurors. At one juncture, Buddy Sutton, Tucker's attorney, leaped up with an objection: "Your Honor, Mr. Jahn says he represents the United States. That's not so. He represents the independent counsel!"

Judge Howard responded with mild righteous indignation.

"Mr. Sutton, your objection is overruled. I draw your attention to the indictment returned by the federal grand jury in this case."

The judge then held up a copy of the indictment, and pointed with his left hand to the caption. "Mr. Sutton, the indictment reads '*The United States of America v. Jim Guy Tucker, James B. McDougal and Susan McDougal.*'"

Roundly cuffed, the defense lawyers didn't try that stunt again.

But to some people in Little Rock, we remained unwelcome outsiders. Even though Arkansas boasted a populist, antielitist culture, complete with a deep-seated suspicion of politicians, hometown pride ran deep. Their governor was in the dock, as were the Clintons' well-known business associates. And, of course, the president had been summoned by the defense as a trial witness. That was big news in Little Rock.

Not everyone felt antagonistic, though.

"This is hard for us," the spouse of one prominent Little Rock businessperson confided to me. "We know the folks you have charged. We go to church with them. We see them around town. They're our neighbors." Then she added in a resigned voice, "We do want to know what really happened. We want the truth to come out."

A small anecdote illustrates our status as invaders. One day in May, I had remained in our west side offices in the morning to attend to other duties. After getting word that Judge Howard had declared a longer lunch break than usual, I took advantage of the additional time and told the trial team: "I'll meet you at Luby's for lunch"—a treat compared to our usual fare.

Hot, muggy weather had already settled in on the banks of the Arkansas River. I met the prosecutors and support team at the entrance to the mercifully air-conditioned mall where Luby's was located.

Grabbing a tray, I went ahead of my colleagues so I could pick up the tab as they made their way through the cafeteria line. As the cashier rang up the charges, a middle-aged gentleman came up to me and smiled.

"Mr. Starr, how's the trial going?" He didn't introduce himself.

Truth be told, that morning had not gone particularly well for us. The jury had seemed bored. After two months, the document-heavy trial was becoming a grind. But I put on a brave face, and responded at a high level of generality that we were pleased to have an able, upright judge presiding over the trial, that the jurors were conscientious and attentive. As my colleagues headed to a large table, I paid the tab and warmly shook the hand of my new Little Rock friend.

"Thanks so much for asking about us," I said. "I really appreciate it."

In a friendly tone, he threw a curve: "Well, to tell the truth, I'm rooting for the other side." That sentiment captured the mood of the town.

Each day after the testimony, the defendants and their lawyers made their way to the courthouse steps to denounce the prosecution. The *New York Times*, the *Washington Post*, many other newspapers, and all the major TV networks gathered on the steps at the end of each day. Some just reported the defense spin, encouraged by Tucker's energetic public relations apparatus and the colorful orations of Jim McDougal.

Our office manager, Debbie Gershman, would take notes of the questions that reporters asked, and if necessary, Hickman would emerge to set the record straight.

The McDougals put on a grand show after each day's testimony. But Jim was visibly aging as the trial wore on. Suffering from several physical ailments, his spark seemed to have gone out.

Despite occasional setbacks and adverse trial rulings, glimmers of hope abounded for the OIC. Judge Howard remained in firm control. He allowed the lawyers, prosecution and defense alike, to try the case. If an objection was raised, he listened to both sides, and then ruled promptly with quiet confidence.

We lost more than our fair share of objections, but the judge always remained scrupulously within bounds. Trials require constant judgment calls, and an effective judge can't dally or take the matter "under advisement." Even so, Judge Howard instinctively leaned slightly toward the defense.

"Mr. Jahn, liberty is at stake," he'd say. "I'm going to allow the defendants a little leeway." In stentorian tones, His Honor emphasized the "lee . . ." in "leeway." It became one of our "clubhouse" takeaways: "Well, the judge is likely to allow the defense lawyers a little leeeee-way today."

We adjusted. As the trial wore on, we made fewer objections, even though we believed we would have been on solid legal ground. We came to know our judge well, and could predict the likely outcome.

One Whitewater trial lesson was this: In the dignity of a courtroom, with all the cacophony raging outside, a United States district judge can become the living symbol of our system of law. Daily, Judge Howard reminded the jurors of their duty.

On March 27, the first real mention of the president came up in the trial. Little Rock judge Bill Watt, who had been granted immunity, said that Hale had told him in 1986 that during an encounter at the State Capitol Bill Clinton had asked Hale "if he would be able to help Jim and him out."

Hale had already pleaded guilty but had not been sentenced. Since he had been accused of making up the allegations about Clinton in 1993 to get a shorter sentence in return for his testimony in this trial, Watt's testimony was important to show that Hale had told him years before then that Clinton was pestering him about the loan benefiting the McDougals.

"Doesn't the testimony today mean that Bill Clinton was a coconspirator?" one TV reporter asked Hickman that afternoon. He declined to comment. The reporter tried again: "Wouldn't a reasonably prudent person conclude from this testimony that Clinton was a coconspirator?"

Hickman again declined to comment, but did say that our team was allowed to put on testimony showing that Hale had discussed the matter well before he was indicted.

Hale testified for eight days in early April and pointed the finger directly at Clinton. He told of a meeting between himself, Clinton, and McDougal at a sales office for Castle Grande, one of Madison Guaranty's problematic development properties. They talked about the Master Marketing loan to Susan McDougal—further confirmation that Clinton knew about the fraudulent loan, despite his denials.

The media's reaction to Hale's testimony was hostility.

"Is Bill Clinton going to be indicted?" Sara Fritz of the *Los Angeles Times* asked Hickman on April 11, at the end of Hale's last day on the stand.

Hickman told her, "I can't comment on that even if I knew the answer." On April 14, Fritz published a very negative article about Hale.

111

She falsely claimed that Hickman acknowledged that the independent counsel's office "sees this trial primarily as a way to obtain more evidence against the president" and that "Starr hopes that, by winning the conviction of Tucker and the McDougals, he can persuade the three to give incriminating evidence against Clinton."

Notes taken at the time by Hickman's assistant showed that he had been egregiously misquoted. We contacted Fritz, who said she stood by her story.

In late April 1996, ABC's *Nightline* devoted its show to Ken Starr and the OIC, featuring Mark Tuohey, my defender, and James Carville, by now my nemesis. Prior to this, he'd denounced me as a "tobacky lawyer," which made it sound like I was dispensing cigarettes to children at schools. In fact, I had simply argued an appeal for a long-term firm client on a constitutional issue involving nationwide class-action lawsuits.

Carville now attacked me as the "dependent partisan persecutor," and added, "Why, his deputy Hick Ewing said that the only reason the trial is going on in Little Rock is to get evidence to indict the President, and that is outrageous."

I had written a letter of protest to the editor of the *Los Angeles Times* and was told they would look into our assertion that Hickman had been misquoted. Audio recorded by another reporter proved that he had indeed. The newspaper did not run a correction until May 18. But from the seed sown by a biased reporter, Carville had already launched a nationally watched attack that was based on a totally fabricated quote.

On Sunday, April 28, our team again went to the White House. In the long-running trial, Judge Howard authorized the defense lawyers to take President Clinton's testimony. Judge Howard remained in Little

Rock, presiding over the testimony by live satellite feed, which was videotaped to be shown later to the jury.

The president sat in a chair in the Map Room at the White House. The OIC team sat at one table on the east side of the room. The defendants and their lawyers sat at another table. Attorneys for the president, the White House, and the DOJ sat at yet another table. This time, we mostly sat and listened, rather than conducted the main line of questioning.

During his testimony, the president denied speaking to Hale and McDougal about the Master Marketing loan to Susan. But under cross-examination by Jahn, he began to show irritation. His complexion turned red, a sign—at least according to those who knew him well—of rising anger.

It's doubtful Clinton's testimony affected the jurors' deliberations, but at least he was now on the record.

Late in the trial, Jim McDougal took the stand. He chose a fool-hardy course, whereas Tucker and Susan remained silent, as was their constitutional right. It was a train wreck. Under withering cross-examination, Jahn destroyed Jim's self-serving testimony.

We suspected the president's attorneys had pushed Jim to embark on this suicide mission. Their strategy to protect the president was easy to guess. Keep the blabbermouth Susan off the stand, and encourage the showboat Jim to testify.

Jim's conviction would stain his credibility in any future testimony against Bill and Hillary. Even if we secured his cooperation against them, he would be damaged goods, a convicted felon who lied under oath.

In late May, after a three-month trial, seven hundred exhibits, and thirty-five witnesses, both sides rested. The jury retired to deliberate the fate of the three defendants. Reporters for the major newspapers began a pool taking bets on how long the jury would be out before we got our heads handed to us.

Occasionally, requests came out of the jury room for particular documents or clarifying instructions. That was a good sign, but the tension was building. After seven days of deliberation, as Memorial Day approached, the jurors asked to see the judge. Some had clearly been crying, others had red faces, suggesting they had been engaged in vigorous debate. Taking the measure of the jurors, Judge Howard— to our chagrin—told them to take the afternoon as well as the long weekend off. The OIC team was apprehensive. We were all suffering from trial fatigue.

I headed back to Northern Virginia. Our neighbors in McLean invited Alice and me to an early dinner on Monday, Memorial Day. I'm usually talkative, but not on that particular evening. I felt empty. My mind kept drifting back to Little Rock. The entire investigation was hanging in the balance. We were predicted to lose. I tried to think of Scripture: *In all things, be content.* At any rate, the result was out of my control.

Although I tried to hide it, when I got up on Tuesday morning I was anxious and concerned. I had a gnawing feeling that the jury would not be able to bring itself to convict the governor. We might find ourselves going one for three, with a conviction of Jim, and acquittals of Susan and Governor Tucker.

I went into my office in Washington. We gathered in a conference room in a state of uneasy apprehension, anticipating a verdict at any moment. Then at midday, we got a call from Hickman about the same time we saw a notice on CNN: A VERDICT IN THE WHITEWATER TRIAL.

Hickman told us the jury found all three defendants guilty on multiple counts. As we listened to CNN, the prosecutors whooped and cheered as each defendant's name and verdict was announced. Jim McDougal had been convicted of eighteen counts of fraud and conspiracy, Susan on four counts of fraud and conspiracy, and Tucker on one count of conspiracy and one count of mail fraud. It was an overwhelming victory. The press's pessimistic predictions had been proved wrong.

One juror told the *New York Times*, "It was the documents we went with. The documents told me more than the testimony did." The months-long burden had at long last been lifted. I had grown weary of the unrelenting assaults and naysaying. Thanks to an honorable judge and a God-fearing jury, justice had been done.

Our office was inundated with calls from reporters. In shirtsleeves, I went out in front of our office and made a short statement: "We march forward from here." I had learned to "feed the beast."

Clinton was subdued in his reaction. A White House statement said he accepted the verdict, and noted he had not been charged in the case. Asked whether his testimony in defense of McDougal had not been believed by jurors, Clinton replied, "You ought to ask them that. . . . I doubt that that's what was going on." Though he was sad for the defendants, "for me, it's time to go back to work, and I intend to do that."

In his later autobiography, *My Life*, Clinton wrote that he had serious doubts about the verdicts: "Jim McDougal's mental illness had progressed to the point where he was probably not competent to stand trial, much less testify. And I felt that Susan McDougal and Jim Guy Tucker might have been caught up in Jim McDougal's downward mental spiral and David Hale's desperate effort to save himself."

Whether the president truly believed this nonsense isn't for me to say. What I can say is that we did not believe that Jim McDougal, although ailing, was mentally incompetent in the slightest. We immediately moved forward with the presentencing phase. We would now seek cooperation from all three convicted defendants. We believed all three would be in a position to know if possible crimes had been committed by Bill and Hillary Clinton, and others in their orbit.

Tucker announced that he would step down as governor on July 15, just a little over one month away. He would have loved to unload on the Clintons, both of whom he had come to despise. Hillary, after all, had peeled away an important client and Bill was his political adversary. But Tucker's indictment for tax and bankruptcy fraud had been reinstated by the Court of Appeals. He thus faced further jeopardy. His cooperation would have to wait for another day.

That left Jim and Susan McDougal, two people who had once loved each other but now found themselves in a strange situation. Though divorced and engaged to another man, Susan had repeatedly professed her affection for Jim. Now both of them faced time in prison. Helping the prosecutors make cases against others who committed crimes could shave significant time from their sentences.

When he testified, Jim had dumped her in the mire. His testimony had laid bare the fact that she had been involved in financial misdeeds at Madison Guaranty, and Susan was furious. We hoped that she would take her revenge on him by talking, but that hope was soon dashed.

Susan's first question for us was not terribly helpful. In the immediate aftermath of the verdict, during a presentencing hearing, Susan's public defender approached our lawyers and inquired what we wanted to ask her in the grand jury. Would there be questions about Bill Clinton and sex?

Ray Jahn told her that wasn't our particular area of interest, but if the issue became pertinent, questions about that subject might be asked. We later learned that the attorney had immediately called the White House.

After that, Susan clamped down. In another meeting, she insisted, "You just want me to lie about the Clintons."

We repeatedly told her that all we wanted was the truth, whatever it was, but that was her mantra and she stuck to it. A subpoena requiring her to testify before the grand jury was issued, and our battle with the indomitable Susan McDougal was on.

CHAPTER ELEVEN

"Get Out the Vote Money"

WITHIN A FEW WEEKS OF FINISHING THE 825 TRIAL, WE were back in court for what we felt was a strong court case related to Bill Clinton.

A different odd couple, two bankers who owned a tiny financial institution in a rural area of Arkansas, had been indicted on campaign finance fraud committed on behalf of Governor Clinton during his fifth gubernatorial campaign in 1990. Bruce Lindsey, national director for Clinton's 1992 presidential campaign and later a senior White House staffer, was an unnamed, unindicted coconspirator. If we got convictions, we hoped the bankers would cooperate and testify about the campaign finance shenanigans that seemed to permeate Clinton's political apparatus.

We were about to get schooled by some good ol' boys who saw the Clintons as heroes and us as interlopers.

Perryville, a small town forty-five miles northwest of Little Rock, was home to a small bank with a modest $45 million in assets. Perry

County Bank (PCB) had two Clinton-friendly owners, Herby Branscum Jr. and Robert Hill. They, through the bank, lent financial support to the Clintons during the hard-fought gubernatorial reelection campaign. The governor needed a big win in 1990 to set the stage for a presidential run in two years.

In July 1996, we entered Judge Wright's courtroom for a six-week trial that opened a window into the fund-raising by Branscum and Hill on Bill's behalf. Branscum and Hill had used bank funds to reimburse themselves for get out the vote money for the campaign. They had instructed young bank president Neal Ainley to intercept and deep-six the reports. We alleged they conspired with Bruce Lindsey to hide the large cash withdrawals from federal regulators.

Though huge sums of money weren't at stake, this was not just political sleaze, it was criminal conduct. That's the way the Fiske team saw it, and that's the way the Arkansas grand jury saw it. The bank's owners had been indicted on eleven counts of conspiracy and bank fraud. If we could obtain their convictions, we might be able to get the men to talk about other campaign finance misdeeds.

During the course of the grand jury investigation, the two bank owners refused to comply with subpoenas seeking various financial records. Branscum and Hill claimed that the independent counsel had no jurisdiction over campaign funding issues. After lengthy wrangling in court, the two bank owners went into civil contempt and sustained heavy fines that were levied for each day they disobeyed a court order to produce the records.

It was either give up the documents or pay ever-mounting fines. The financial hammer worked. We got the documents, which were indeed relevant and damning, and prepared for trial. We had a strong case, a confident and articulate witness in Neal Ainley, who pleaded guilty and agreed to cooperate, and two star prosecutors in Hickman Ewing and Jackie Bennett.

I was still banned from the courtroom, but reports came to me once again in the basement annex. I heard that on the stand Ainley proved to be a disappointment. He appeared nervous, weak, and unsure of himself. He didn't recant any of his testimony, but he was unimpressive.

Hickman was under tremendous pressure. His father was dying. Just prior to his closing arguments, he drove to Memphis and said goodbye to his father. That night he drove back to Little Rock. At 2:00 A.M., on the last day of trial, he was informed that his father had just died. That morning, he rose early and, by all accounts, gave a brilliant, Oscar-winning closing argument.

Rebutting the bankers' contentions that Ainley acted on his own, Hickman argued that "the monkey works for the organ grinder; the organ grinder doesn't work for the monkey."

Our confidence was high. We had the facts and we had the law. But despite Hickman's heroic efforts, Branscum and Hill's bold gamble to go to trial paid off. The jury acquitted them both on four counts, and hopelessly deadlocked on the remaining seven counts.

After the trial ended, with the judge's permission Hickman interviewed the jurors individually. Most were perplexed as to why two of their peers remained stubborn holdouts. One African American juror was convinced Branscum and Hill were guilty on all counts. This went against the consensus that Clinton's popularity in the African American community would result in some sort of jury nullification. We had done our job, the jurors insisted, and the evidence against the two bankers had been overwhelming.

The two holdout jurors were white, blue-collar men. One dismissed the charges with a shrug. It was the owners' bank. They could do what they wanted with the money. And who cared about trivial stuff like filing federal paperwork?

This was bizarre reasoning, and we suspected skullduggery in the form of jury tampering, but we had no evidence to back that up. The other possibility? We speculated that the anti-Starr bias was finally seeping into the courthouse, even though I had remained quarantined in the basement.

I feared this was a harbinger of bad things to come. The political attacks had taken a significant toll. The rich bank owners went scot-free. My only consolation was that their contempt had resulted in accumulated fines exceeding eighty thousand dollars.

We had to decide whether to retry Branscum and Hill. If we did, would we name the person dubbed by the charging document as the "unindicted coconspirator"?

Despite the strength of our case, we decided to call it quits. At this stage, we determined our duty was to prioritize, and to stay focused on the ultimate question of the Clintons' involvement in Whitewater and the illegal use of federally insured funds.

CHAPTER TWELVE

Mysterious Disappearing Documents

O NE DAY IN AUGUST 1995, WHITE HOUSE AIDE CAROLYN Huber, the office manager of the Rose Law Firm when Hillary worked there, by her account spotted a stack of documents lying on a table in the middle of the Book Room on the third floor of the Residence at the White House.

The room was next door to the First Lady's office, rarely used by others. Among the magazine and newspaper clippings, Huber recognized one computer printout as Rose billing records. Showing little curiosity, Huber simply boxed the documents up and took them to her own office in the East Wing, stuck the box on a shelf, and forgot about them.

Strange behavior, since the Rose Law Firm records had been under subpoena since 1992, first by the RTC, then Fiske, then the OIC and a Senate committee. Huber had been tasked with finding the records for all of them.

In April 1994, Mrs. Clinton had responded to the press assaults on her credibility—about Whitewater, Hillarycare, the missing Rose Law Firm records—with what became known as the "pink press conference" for the White House press corps.

Dressed in a pink sweater with black trim, her hair beautifully coiffed and her voice well modulated, Hillary dazzled press and public alike. She cited her "fundamental belief" in privacy, citing unprecedented attacks on their administration. It was a tour de force. But behind the scenes, turmoil was engulfing the Clinton White House. Fiske was digging deep into Whitewater and crimes committed by Hubbell and other associates. The missing documents had not surfaced then. Nor had Huber sounded the alarm in August 1995, despite the intense publicity generated by Hillary's press conference.

Finally, on January 4, 1996, Huber unpacked the box of documents sitting in her office. By her account, she was "taken aback" when she realized they were Hillary's mysterious Rose Law Firm billing records. They had been printed out in Little Rock on February 12, 1992, during the presidential campaign.

Called to testify in front of a Senate committee in January 1996, Huber said they'd suddenly appeared in 1995, but she hadn't recognized their significance.

"I didn't know who left them there," she said. "Somebody did."

Huber's dramatic testimony raised the issue of obstruction of justice. The OIC had been trying to get to the bottom of the disappearing records and other issues related to Whitewater and Madison Guaranty. The pressure had been building.

The White House offered no further explanation. Hillary said she had "no idea" where they came from.

The discovery confirmed Hickman's "the molecules were moving" theory. Destroying the records would have been a federal crime. Hillary needed for them to be "discovered."

These were the only records relevant to a Little Rock criminal investigation to find their way to Washington, then to the White House, then to the Residence. It stood to reason that only three people could plausibly have taken them from Little Rock: Hillary, Hubbell, or Foster. It would be safer to have them in the White House, closer to Hillary. That made Foster the logical thief.

In a statement, David Kendall said that Hillary said they remembered discussing the billing records with Foster and Hubbell during 1992, so she could "accurately" answer press questions during the campaign.

"It is possible they showed her the billing records then, but she does not recall," Kendall wrote. He added that Hillary was glad they had been found because they proved everything she had said about representing Madison was accurate.

Not true.

Her defenders, for once, were muted. Washington, D.C., had been blasted by a blizzard. Columnist William Safire published an Op-Ed called "Blizzard of Lies," marveling at Hillary's many prevarications about the firings at the Travel Office, the FBI files, vanishing records, and cattle futures. Safire dubbed Hillary "a congenital liar." Bill threatened to punch him in the nose.

We believed that the records had been removed from Vince Foster's office after his suicide; that investigation was ongoing. But how did the documents make it to the Book Room in the Clintons' residence?

The OIC demanded that the records be turned over immediately so that they could be examined for fingerprints by the FBI. But Kendall resisted, saying he had to examine and copy them first. That prompted our team to joke that he'd go over them while eating fried chicken.

When we got the records the next day, we saw handwritten notations to "HRC," apparently made by Foster. He had clearly been worried about what the documents revealed about Hillary's legal work for Madison Guaranty. And to add to the mystery, both Foster's and Hillary's prints were found on the records.

The president, of course, rose to the occasion as a character witness for the First Lady. On January 11, 1996, Clinton vouched for his spouse: "I wish all Americans were as honest as Hillary."

CHAPTER THIRTEEN

Flipping Jim McDougal

WITH THE CONVICTIONS IN THE 825 TRIAL, OUR INVESTI-
gation into Whitewater took on new importance. What information might the McDougals reveal to the prosecutors and FBI agents? This
was unprecedented and worrisome, since Clinton's political missteps—
including the ill-fated health-care reform effort led by Hillary—had con-
tributed to the historic Republican landslide in the 1994 off-year election.

Though humbled, Bill Clinton was determined to live up to his
moniker as the Comeback Kid. He was charmingly persistent, resil-
ient, and relentless.

The president's reelection prospects that fall seemed bright. The
nation was at peace, the economy was doing well. International relations were quiet enough, notwithstanding the growing menace of
North Korea and the always fragile boiling pot of the Middle East.
America was happy. Government was divided, with adequate checks
and balances in place.

The president was heeding the counsel of his on-again, off-again political consultant Dick Morris: Show a spirit of bipartisanship, stay humble, and be out and about all over the country.

The president faced a weak Republican candidate, the much-admired but aging Bob Dole. Clinton, the first baby-boomer nominee, had defeated Bush, a World War II hero, in 1992, and now the stage was set for him to dispatch the last presidential candidate from the Greatest Generation. Against that historic shift of political power, Whitewater was seen as an irrelevant episode from long ago and far away.

Meanwhile, in Little Rock, our team's continued success was largely dependent on the cooperation of one of the McDougals. Our goal remained: get to the bottom of the Whitewater deal, especially the issue of any potential culpability on the part of the Clintons, as quickly as possible and be done. I had already devoted far more time than I had originally, and erroneously, anticipated.

In theory, we were operating from a position of strength in the wake of our success in the 825 trial. Yet we knew that a long slog was ahead of us, especially since all three defendants were appealing their convictions.

We went back to Hale, whose sworn trial testimony was damaging to the president. But we still lacked clear documentary evidence to back up his charges.

One Hale-Clinton encounter had taken place at the Capitol. Clinton encouraged Hale to provide funding for the Master Marketing loan. But it was a classic case of "he said" versus "the president said." No reasonable prosecutor would seek an indictment based on that slender reed. The challenge was how to get corroboration, if any existed, to the effect that the Clintons were more than "passive" investors in the ill-fated development project.

Our most promising prospect for collaboration was Jim McDougal. Unemployed and broke, Jim was again living in the trailer on the property owned by Lieutenant Governor Bob Riley's widow, Claudia. With his health failing, Jim was fearful of imprisonment, even in a comparatively humane federal prison, with ready access to good medical care. Jim had a premonition that if sent to prison, he would die there—not from foul play, but from the stresses and strains on his weak heart.

Jim's trial lawyer, Sam Heuer, seemed genuinely to want the best for his ailing client. But Heuer had a close working relationship with the Clintons' defense lawyers. We had reason to believe that David Kendall and his colleagues had drafted some of Heuer's trial motions, and may have encouraged Jim to take the stand. But we had confidence that Heuer would be amenable to encouraging Jim to do an about-face.

The wooing process authorized by Heuer went quickly and smoothly. Our initial ambassadors were Ray Jahn and Amy St. Eve, who made their way to Arkadelphia to visit Jim at home.

Amy had been fearless yet charming in the courtroom. Body language throughout the long trial suggested that Jim had a fondness for Amy. After their first meeting with Jim, Ray and Amy returned to our office enthusiastic about the possibilities. Having fought and lost, Jim was at long last ready to turn state's evidence.

Jim was on medication, but lucid and possessing a strong memory. His new attitude of cooperation didn't seem grudging. He said simply that he could corroborate Hale's account, and thereby implicate the president. Indeed, Jim seemed relieved that he was now free to tell the truth.

Encouraged, I made a trip by myself to Arkadelphia one hot

summer afternoon to sit down with Jim and confirm in person our understanding that we should go forward with a formal cooperative arrangement.

I knocked on the trailer-home door. Jim answered and welcomed me in. Jim's trailer was situated under the shade of towering pine trees. Oscillating fans whirred with little effect on the heat.

Jim was surprisingly friendly and amiable. He invited me to sit down in his simply furnished living room. Two photographs were on prominent display: Winston Churchill and Franklin D. Roosevelt. These iconic men were his two great heroes. To break the ice, I recalled that my parents had high admiration for Churchill, so much so that they had given me the middle name "Winston" in honor of the great man. (They were not so keen on Roosevelt.)

A student of history, Jim relaxed and expressed admiration for the two men who together had saved Western civilization. We talked as Southerners do—friendly, open, relaxed, with a fair amount of swapping yarns. We didn't venture at all into the specifics of Whitewater or Madison Guaranty. We were simply establishing a relationship.

Jim was taking the measure of me, which had to be a challenge for him in light of my professional role and, perhaps even worse, my Republican credentials. To southern Democrats like Jim McDougal, Republicans were snooty country-club types. I didn't fit that profile. For one thing, I had never joined a country club. Nor did I play golf.

Trying to build empathy, I expressed my sincere admiration for another of his heroes, JFK, and shared a poignant story of having been within arm's reach of the president on the day before he was assassinated in Dallas. The president had visited San Antonio to inaugurate the Brooke Army Aerospace Medicine Center. In the crowd, I stood near the president, but didn't get to shake his hand. That evening,

Kennedy traveled on to Fort Worth, and then, fatefully, to Dallas the following morning.

We spent a couple of hours chatting, avoiding all unpleasant subjects. I assured Jim that we were looking forward to working with him. We were only interested in the truth, whatever it was. Nothing was conditioned on Jim pointing an accusatory finger at anybody. The truth, and nothing but the truth, that's what we wanted. Jim seemed to believe me.

I drove back to Little Rock, convened my colleagues, and gave a full report based on my memory of the conversation. We were determined to treat Jim with dignity and respect, so I had deliberately taken no notes, nor had I recorded the conversation.

The formal process began. Most interviews took place in Jim's trailer home, with Hickman, Amy, and FBI agent Mike Patkus doing the lion's share of the questioning. The results were encouraging as we delved more deeply into Jim's financial dealings.

Especially provocative were Jim's revelations about the president. During one of the White House depositions, Hickman had watched Jim while the president answered questions. At one moment during Clinton's testimony, Hickman spotted Jim avert his gaze away from the president, bow his head down, and rest it on his cane.

"Why did you do that, Jim?" Hickman inquired during one debriefing session.

"Because I saw the president of the United States commit perjury," he said, "and he did so in the Map Room." The Map Room, to Jim McDougal, was hallowed ground because of his admiration for FDR. But that sacred soil, so to speak, had been polluted by the self-interested perjury of his hero's successor. Despite his own crimes, Jim was morally outraged by the lies under oath of the Man from Hope.

Jim told Hickman that Madison Guaranty had loaned Clinton

about twenty-five thousand dollars. The loan was intended to pay off another bank controlled by McDougal, which had loaned thirty thousand dollars to Hillary to build the sales office/model home.

"Do you have a loan document?" Hickman asked.

"I don't think so. He was the governor." Even with the duo of Hale and Jim McDougal, a reasonable prosecutor would be deeply skeptical of bringing charges based only on their testimony. We needed more.

We sent federal investigators back to an old garage in Little Rock that stored documents from Madison Guaranty. It looked like that warehouse in the last scene of the movie *Raiders of the Lost Ark*—hundreds of boxes stacked with no rhyme or reason.

One day, they emerged with a piece of microfilm: a check from Madison to Bill Clinton for $27,600. It had been deposited in the bank to pay off the Whitewater loan, but was not endorsed.

That seemed to corroborate McDougal's information. But we didn't have the original check. Back into the records. Eventually agents found a hard copy of another check written on a Madison account in Susan's handwriting for about five thousand dollars. "Pay off Clinton" was written in the subject line. We asked Jim what it meant.

To our chagrin, he said, "You'll have to ask Susan." That did not bode well for getting to the bottom of the Whitewater transactions. The dizzying array of institutions and individuals was baffling. The key point was that in all the machinations, Clinton was determined by hook or by crook to get money into Whitewater. It was deliberately designed to defy detection by sophisticated regulators.

We speculated that if Susan wanted to continue to protect the president, she could say Jim made a loan to Clinton but didn't tell him about it. But Susan McDougal refused to talk to us. Over the long summer of 1996, she rebuffed all our efforts at outreach.

"Starr wants me to lie to get the Clintons," she told the press. "I won't do that."

Absurd. We just wanted her to tell the truth, whatever it was. It soon became apparent that we would secure Susan's testimony only in the formal setting of the federal grand jury in Little Rock.

On September 4, 1996, she stubbornly refused to answer all questions, including queries posed by the grand jurors themselves.

That afternoon, we went before Chief Judge Susan Webber Wright and sought a grant of immunity, so Susan's truthful testimony, whatever it might be, could not be used against her in any later proceeding.

The judge agreed to our request. It was no longer a question of Susan choosing to cooperate or not. The judge had ordered her to. But back in the grand jury room, she defiantly refused.

Susan was again brought before Judge Wright, who ordered Susan to testify truthfully. Susan was respectful in court. Never did she in any way show disrespect for the judge, who gave her the long Labor Day weekend to consider her options: testify or go to jail.

Susan took the opportunity to fly to Los Angeles and go on *Larry King Live*, repeating her mantra that Starr wanted her to lie. The fawning King didn't ask the key question: "You were convicted of serious felonies, weren't you?"

Watching that night, I was outraged. Susan was thumbing her nose at the citizens of the grand jury, showing outright contempt for the rule of law. But I was powerless; there was literally nothing I could do. I simply vented to Alice and my colleagues.

Susan flew back to Little Rock, went to the courthouse on Tuesday morning, and again refused to testify before the grand jury. Federal agents hauled her back to the courtroom of Judge Wright, who remanded her to custody. This was not only appropriate, but standard procedure for a judge to warn a recalcitrant witness that she was required to testify, and if not obeyed, to follow a time-honored process that goes back centuries.

Susan was shackled with handcuffs and leg restraints, a highly demeaning procedure, particularly for a nonviolent, nondangerous witness. However, the shackles are used on everyone taken into federal custody.

In Washington, working on several other aspects of the investigation, I watched the Susan McDougal contempt drama unfold on TV. Susan the convicted felon now became a stoic Joan of Arc resisting the evil powers of Ken Starr, her pitiful photo splashed across the front pages of newspapers around America.

The optics were undeniably negative. But we weren't thinking, "How's this going to play in Peoria?" I thought of it as just another impediment in our quest to finish our investigation.

Under our legal system, when an immunized witness is sent to jail for contempt, the old saying goes that "the witness holds the keys to the jailhouse door." In contrast to a criminal sentence, in civil contempt, all the person needs to say is: "Okay, I give up. I'll testify." The person is promptly released from jail and becomes a free citizen, required to live up to her civic obligations.

Susan adamantly refused.

What followed was a media field day, shamelessly promoted by the president.

He responded provocatively to Susan's claim that Starr's investigators were not really trying to get at the truth: "There's a lot of evidence for that," he told a reporter.

This lie was an insult to Judge Wright, who was simply enforcing long-settled principles of law.

In fact, the irony was that Susan had been remanded by Judge

Wright into the custody of the U.S. Marshals Service, which is part of the DOJ. The marshals report up the chain of command ultimately to the Attorney General, who, of course, was appointed by the president and thus could be fired for any reason whatsoever, including for the mistreatment of federal prisoners.

A simple order from the president could have changed Susan's custodial wardrobe and "jewelry," removing the handcuffs and leg-irons, although he couldn't overrule the chief judge's underlying order holding Susan in contempt.

But Clinton had every reason to encourage her to stand firm. Susan's honest testimony, we felt confident, could strike at the heart of the president's protestations of ignorance. From the president's perspective, no doubt, Susan should go into contempt and remain there at least until after the election, just a few months away.

America loves an outlaw. Susan became, with the president's encouragement, exactly that. We tried without success to employ White House channels to end the stalemate. On five separate occasions, we wrote to the new counsel to the president, Charles Ruff, a respected defense lawyer in D.C. and former U.S. Attorney in the District, requesting that the president encourage Susan to cooperate with the grand jury's investigation.

President Clinton refused.

Susan kept her mouth shut and went to prison. With the OIC team, her actions had the opposite effect of her intentions. What was so important to hide that she would tolerate being imprisoned?

Then we had a little help from a tornado.

CHAPTER FOURTEEN

Raven and the Bad Boys

WEEK AFTER WEEK IN LATE 1996 AND EARLY 1997, HICK-man and Mike Patkus made twenty-five trips to Arkadelphia, forging a strong bond with Jim McDougal. Hickman always made sure to go by McDonald's to pick up an Egg McMuffin for Jim. He seemed isolated and lonely.

Sentenced to three years, Jim was sent to a federal prison in Kentucky in June 1997. I was deeply ambivalent about Jim going to prison. At Jim's request, Hickman lobbied the Bureau of Prisons to move him to Fort Worth, to be closer to friends.

Meanwhile, I was spending most of my time in Washington, while our investigative agents were scouring the Little Rock warehouse and other sources for records pertaining to Madison Guaranty and Whitewater.

In July 1997, we got one of those breaks that seemed like a miracle—or a plot twist in a bad movie.

A deputy U.S. marshal walked into our Little Rock office. "I have something for you," he said.

He dumped a mailbag marked Madison Guaranty on Hickman's desk. Inside had been found the original check for $27,600 made out to Bill Clinton. This was the check we had seen on microfilm. Hickman didn't touch anything. He called one of the FBI's forensic agents.

In the strange but true category, a tornado had blasted through several small towns outside Little Rock in March and hit a lot where an auto repair shop stored vehicles that had been abandoned by owners who decided the repair fees outweighed the value of their cars. The tornado destroyed many of the vehicles. In the cleanup operation, the lot owners looked inside the trunk of one car and found two Madison Guaranty mailbags filled with canceled checks and other documents. A CPA who had worked for the shop owner identified the contents, saw the check, and realized it was made out to Clinton.

"You need to report this to Ken Starr," he told the shop owner.

While the documents were tested, Hickman sent some agents to check out the car, which belonged to a man named Henry Floyd. He had taken the vehicle for repair in 1988 but never returned to pick it up.

Inside the trunk were twenty 45-rpm records in sleeves that said "Raven and the Bad Boys," with the picture of a young black man on the front and a small caption that read: "I want to thank God and the people at Madison Guaranty for loaning me the money to get this record produced," signed by Henry Floyd—the car's owner, aka "The Raven."

The agents tracked Floyd to Austin. It turned out that he had worked as a messenger shuttling mail and other documents between the McDougals at Madison Guaranty and their lawyer, Hillary Clinton, at the Rose Law Firm and the Governor's Mansion. Floyd had abandoned the car, forgetting about the mailbags in the trunk. Floyd was subpoenaed. He complained that he didn't want to fly to Little Rock.

"The Raven doesn't fly," Hickman's secretary reported. "He's afraid to fly."

We sent him an Amtrak ticket. Floyd arrived in Little Rock with a bad attitude.

"Ya'll are just after the Clintons," he said. "I like the McDougals and I like the Clintons. I'm not saying anything. I know my rights." Hickman asked him what rights he was talking about.

"My rights under the Fifth Amendment," he said.

"I'm going to take you up to the judge," Hickman said. "If you don't answer, you'll be in contempt."

"Well, I'm standing on my other rights."

"What other rights?" Hickman said.

"My rights as a Christian," Floyd said. "My daddy's a pastor. You aren't supposed to judge other people."

"Well, you may not believe this," Hickman said, "but I'm a Christian, too. Our main FBI agent is a Christian. So is our IRS guy." He quoted several Scriptures about honoring the king, about telling the truth. Floyd looked perplexed.

"All right, what do you want to know?"

The Raven turned out to be a gold mine of information. He described being at Madison when there was a surprise audit by federal regulators.

"We were scrambling," Floyd said. "The head cashier rented a shredder and we were shredding documents. I remember it well. I lost two ties."

When I heard the story of the tornado, I thought, "This gives fresh meaning to the familiar legal concept of 'an act of God.'" David Kendall was astonished at the news. "It's like saying Elvis is still alive."

We had the elusive check. But the FBI could find no fingerprints on it, and thus no proof Clinton had handled it.

The Raven became a staunch defender of our office, and eventually a witness against Susan McDougal in her trial on criminal contempt charges, saying, "I didn't want to cooperate, but they said they just wanted the truth."

CHAPTER FIFTEEN

Shift to Washington, D.C.

W E APPEARED TO BE WRAPPING UP THE LION'S SHARE OF our business in Little Rock by mid-1997. Most of our attorneys in Arkansas had returned to the private sector or to their DOJ offices, though Hickman remained. I felt the jury was still out on the Clintons. There was much we did not know. Documentation of financial relationships remained a challenge. Above all, we did not have the cooperation of the remaining Big Two: Webb Hubbell and Susan McDougal.

But meanwhile, we had important work to finish in Washington.

We had reopened the Vince Foster investigation in 1994. We released our report on his death in October 1997. We had harnessed a formidable array of experts on homicide and suicide to settle the question of how Foster died.

But our investigation into Foster's death had gotten off to a strange start.

I had hired Miguel Rodriguez, an Assistant U.S. Attorney from Sacramento, in the fall of 1994. He came recommended to me by my law partner Paul Cappuccio, because Miguel, his Harvard Law class-mate, had significant experience handling civil rights cases, which often involved forensic evidence. I assigned him to the Washington office to work the death investigation.

Miguel began bringing witnesses before a Washington grand jury, but raised eyebrows by his accusatory questioning of U.S. Park Police officers and other witnesses. He seemed to believe—before hearing all the evidence—that Foster had been murdered in a different location, then dumped at Fort Marcy Park. This was the stuff of the conspiracy theories that flourished immediately after the reports of Foster's death. We were after the truth and only the truth, yet there was no justification for browbeating or mistreating any grand jury witness.

My D.C. deputy, Mark Tuohey, was outraged by some of the stories he heard about Miguel's strange demeanor and off-the-wall questions in the grand jury room. Even grand jurors were complaining.

One day in early 1995, I spent several hours with Miguel walking around the Mall and talking, trying to understand his viewpoint and strategy. But his answers made little sense, as if he were listening predominantly to pundits, not to the witnesses.

Hickman went with Miguel out to Fort Marcy Park to check out the scene, which Miguel said he knew like the back of his hand. It was icy. Miguel couldn't find the location. Hickman slipped and fell, seriously injuring his back. It was a disaster.

Angry that he was being challenged by his supervisors, on January 17, 1995, Miguel announced that he quit. His irresponsible comments were later spread as "proof" there was a cover-up of a conspiracy reaching to the White House. All nonsense. But some took his stories at face value. Hickman began to receive preprinted anonymous postcards—over three hundred of them—with the words: "Bring back Miguel."

I rolled my eyes in disbelief when I saw the postcards, which seemed to have been promoted by an advocacy group based in Southern California. This was madness, yet another illustration of the paranoid strain in American politics. It was a grim reminder that this investigation had to be comprehensive and complete. We could not afford to leave any stone unturned, but the investigation also had to be conducted professionally, consistent with DOJ policy.

Honest differences of opinions often occur in investigations. That was one reason I stressed the deliberative process, the roundtable discussions that some prosecutors and investigators thought slowed things down. But a rogue prosecutor given free rein in a grand jury can do serious damage to the integrity of the process. I was thankful that of the dozens of prosecutors and agents who worked with the OIC under my supervision, I experienced many differences of opinions, but few serious problems.

We interviewed numerous witnesses in the grand jury, including U.S. Park Police officers, Rose Law Firm colleagues, Foster's wife, the Clintons, and many White House staffers, including Linda Tripp, the last White House employee to see Foster alive.

An exhaustive review of the evidence confirmed what the Fiske team had concluded back in 1994: Vince Foster had taken his own life in Fort Marcy Park while seated on the Civil War berm where his body was found.

Like Rodriguez, conspiracy theorists postulated that Vince had been murdered elsewhere, and his body moved to the remote location. The posthomicide movement of the body, it was further theorized, explained why no blood had been found at the scene. The evidence pointed in a different direction. Foster's body bag, when opened at the morgue, was awash in his blood.

Our findings resulted in a painstaking, thorough, and lengthy report, drafted primarily by Brett Kavanaugh, a key member of our brain trust. In contrast to the skeptical reaction to Fiske's investigation, our follow-up work proved to be the definitive word on the cause of death. Obviously, we couldn't lay entirely to rest far-fetched theories (we could never find the bullet), but we eradicated any reasonable doubt as to the cause of death: suicide by his own pistol.

In addition to investigating Foster's death, we were also able to settle the other matters he'd been involved with—the White House Travel Office scandal and the issue of the FBI files. In contrast to the criminality at the core of the Little Rock cases, both these matters had the makings of arrogance and abuse of power in a political sense. But was there a potential crime lurking in either the Travel Office saga or in the FBI files scandal?

Fiske had first tackled "Travelgate" because of the Vince Foster connection. A formal federal investigation had culminated in an ill-conceived federal criminal indictment by Main Justice of the hapless Billy Dale, accused of misdeeds by friends of the Clintons' who wanted his job.

Eventually a federal jury in Washington acquitted Dale. Jury sentiment flowed to the little guy, who had been cashiered by the high-handed Arkansans at the direction of the new First Lady. The ordeal cost him money and his reputation.

Months of investigations followed, by Congress and the OIC. The biggest challenge facing both the inquiry on Capitol Hill and our own investigation was a monumental lapse of memory. Senior officials of the White House could, oddly, recall little about the Travelgate episode.

One telltale document, a memorandum authored by David Watkins, director of White House personnel, set forth a damning narrative that the decision to fire the travel team lay squarely at the feet of Hillary, egged on by Harry Thomason. There would be, in Watkins's description, "hell to pay" if all seven civil servants' heads didn't roll.

Hillary had her usual amnesia. In the pink press conference in April 1994, she had remembered elaborate details about how she had turned a thousand dollars into a hundred thousand dollars trading in cattle futures by reading the *Wall Street Journal*. This was a preposterous claim, given the way markets work, but at least she "remembered." When it came to official investigations, as opposed to press conferences, Hillary recalled virtually nothing.

Watkins had intended his tell-all memorandum for Chief of Staff Mack McLarty, who dismissed the document as factually wrong. What was not disputed, however, is that the firings were uncalled for, that several employees were soon offered reinstatement, and that the Thomason-inspired allegations of kickbacks and rebates were never corroborated.

Even so, as we surveyed the facts, the mean-spirited behavior by the Clinton White House did not amount to a federal crime. It certainly revealed Hillary's character and her contempt for regular order. But a reasonable prosecutor would consider perjury in this context a hard hill to climb.

We chose, prudently, not to undertake the effort. We were not convinced we could meet DOJ standards to justify bringing possible charges for the grand jury's consideration.

Our involvement in "Filegate" came independent of Fiske's investigation.

On June 18, 1996, Janet Reno assigned the investigation of the Clintons' inappropriate requisition of FBI files to Louis Freeh, director of the FBI. But he realized that his agency had a conflict of interest, that "egregious violations of privacy" had been committed by both the

FBI and the White House. Three days later, he kicked it back to Reno, who assigned the investigation to our office.

We did not welcome the add-on, as it would take time and resources. But we knew that Reno had made a sensible decision to send the matter our way. We had assembled an extraordinarily capable team of investigators and prosecutors, and we were well equipped to figure out if this issue was bureaucratic incompetence or something more sinister.

On the issue of the FBI files, our job was to determine whether a crime had been committed, such as a violation of federal laws protecting privacy, by Craig Livingstone and his aide Anthony Marceca, a White House security worker, in ordering FBI background-check files.

There proved to be lots of smoke but no fire. It was indeed, as the White House claimed, a bureaucratic snafu, occasioned by the Secret Service's use of outdated materials (lists of individuals who had coveted access to the White House complex) and exacerbated by Livingstone's ineptitude. Dependent upon the Secret Service (not the FBI) for the list of employees for whom background-check files were needed, the inexperienced team of Livingstone and Marceca had been led astray.

Then again, they failed to spot the fact that forbidden files from the FBI's vaults had landed in their office. Experienced professionals wouldn't have made the mistake, and would promptly have seen that a file for Republican secretary of state James Baker had no proper place in the Clinton White House.

The ultimate takeaway of this Keystone Kops episode was that the Clinton White House was cavalier in its approach to staffing a hypersensitive position within the Executive Office complex. The Clintons' arrogance was costly. Even in the White House, there are times when it is far better, and more prudent, to entrust certain assignments to career employees who have the requisite training and experience to handle them wisely and professionally.

Instead, replacing long-standing employees with characters who don chicken costumes to disrupt a presidential campaign speech reflected an abysmal understanding of the seriousness of the tasks at hand. In her own way, Hillary admitted as much in her pink press conference, the closest she ever came to a mea culpa.

Exercising poor judgment is exactly that, but it is not a crime.

In contrast to the Travel Office scandal, there was no significant evidence that Hillary or the president had personally been involved in the decision to hire Livingstone. Of particular importance, there was no evidence whatsoever, including the results of an elaborate forensics analysis, that the president or Hillary had ever touched the files.

Unlike Travelgate and Filegate, a third Washington-focused subject matter of the OIC represented a direct connection in the White-water tale of two cities.

It was a tale frequently told, of unscrupulous or imprudent bankers playing fast and loose with federally insured funds, making bad loans, contributing to real estate bubbles destined to collapse, and at times engaging in outrageous self-dealing.

The Resolution Trust Corporation was a special limited-life entity created by Congress within the Treasury Department during the 1980s to address the nationwide debacle of failed savings and loan associations. The hero of the RTC saga was senior criminal investigator Jean Lewis.

Although much maligned by the mainstream media after it became known she was a conservative Republican, and raked over the coals in

Senate hearings, Jean was a thoroughly professional and scrupulously honest investigator.

Based in Kansas City, Jean and several colleagues had pored over Madison Guaranty records and found evidence of criminal wrongdoing. Their conclusions were dismissed by bureaucratic higher-ups, and eventually rejected by the DOJ. The Washington experts concluded that there had only been mismanagement and ethical lapses, but that the record did not demonstrate actual criminality.

They were all dead wrong. Jean Lewis was right. Her insightful analysis was taken seriously by Fiske and his team, then conclusively demonstrated by the 825 trial. The felony convictions of Jim and Susan McDougal provided Jean and her colleagues with the ultimate professional vindication.

Along with congressional committees, we traveled the path pioneered by Bob Fiske and explored with fresh eyes whether political pressure had been brought to bear from the Treasury Department to scuttle the Madison Guaranty investigation.

The appearance of meddling by superior officers gave rise to a furious backlash on Capitol Hill directed at one of President Clinton's close friends, Roger Altman, a Georgetown classmate.

As the number-two person at the Treasury Department, Altman was yet another casualty in the early years of the Clinton administration. His testimony on the issue of political interference with career investigators such as Jean Lewis irritated members of Congress of both parties. In a partisan town, bipartisan sentiment emerged that Altman should resign. He did. The same for Jean Hanson, the general counsel of the Treasury Department.

We determined that the facts were sufficiently elusive, with ostensible judgment calls along the way, that criminal charges, specifically obstruction of justice, should not be sought. The result was a political setback for the Clintons, just as with the Travel Office and the FBI files matters, but nothing worse. All things considered, this was yet another example of the Clintons' political ham-handedness and contempt for the processes of government.

Reputations were being impugned in the early going of the first Clinton administration, and a life had even been lost. But in contrast to the criminal fraud in Arkansas, indictments in the Washington cases were simply not appropriate. We stayed our hand.

CHAPTER SIXTEEN

Pepperdine Invitation

W HAT I HAD INITIALLY ANTICIPATED TO BE A SIX-MONTH sojourn in Little Rock, taking a second look at a "failed land deal in the Ozarks," had turned out to be a long, three-year slog.

Fiske's ominous advice to move—"You're going to be here for a long time"—had proved prophetic.

As the investigations seemed to be winding down in both Little Rock and Washington, I began thinking about the future.

In early 1997, I got a call from David Davenport, Pepperdine University's charismatic young president. David and I had met back when I was serving as solicitor general in George H. W. Bush's administration. Attorney General Thornburgh had asked me to stand in for him as a judge at a Pepperdine law school moot court competition. I was glad to and enjoyed both the competition and the reception before catching a red-eye flight so I could be in my place as a bleary-eyed Sunday-school teacher in McLean the next day.

On that quick trip to Malibu, I had been hosted by the dean of

Pepperdine's young law school, Ron Phillips, a fellow Texan. As we had talked, I had a sense that Dean Phillips was probing a bit beyond natural curiosity. As it turned out, Ron was engaged in succession planning. He knew of my love of teaching, and my keen interest in legal education.

During my days as a Supreme Court clerk, I had interviewed with representatives from different law schools who arrived to recruit potential faculty members. I tried to kick way beyond my coverage back then, including worming my way into an interview with Yale's Dean Harry Wellington, and a faculty member destined to serve on the Connecticut Supreme Court, Ellen Peters. I thought I had done a fabulous job in the interview. The Yale Law School worthies obviously didn't agree with my rosy self-assessment.

At any rate, I had decided that I wanted to be "a real lawyer" before moving into the classroom or college administration. I was mindful of the wisdom of my boss, Chief Justice Burger: Do we really want our medical school professors to be individuals who, no matter how smart, have never practiced medicine? Why should law professors be any different?

The Chief's observation made perfect sense to me, and I had put off pursuing a teaching career. I had not, however, stopped dreaming of it. After the moot court experience, I was invited back to the Pepperdine campus in 1993 to teach a two-week summer course in constitutional law. I enjoyed socializing with the faculty, and balanced practicing law remotely with teaching a two-hour seminar four days each week. It was bliss. The Starr kids used that sojourn in "the 'Bu" as their summer extravaganza vacation, enjoying the university's Carbon Beach pink cottage—next door to Janet Jackson's beach house.

My involvement with Pepperdine dropped off a bit once I was

appointed to the OIC. Yet the dreaming continued. For several years, Davenport and I talked about his intriguing idea to create a public policy school focusing on the interplay of the private sector, including the nonprofit world, with the fashioning of public policy, particularly at the state and local levels.

Then the call came.

"Ken, I would like you to think about becoming the founding dean of the School of Public Policy."

David upped the ante.

"You would also serve as dean of the law school. It's doing well, and you would simply carry on what Ron Phillips has built. But you would at the same time be the founding dean at the new public policy school."

The idea was not only bold, it was extraordinarily creative. I loved the highly ambitious concept. It would mean a return to Southern California, a part of the world Alice and I greatly enjoyed. I thought I could handle the challenge of wearing two administrative hats when I had never donned a single one.

My thoughts ran both to the investigation and my family. Our three school-age children had become "lifers" at the Potomac School. Alice continued to flourish in her successful career in Northern Virginia. All this would be totally disrupted, but the family was fully supportive and encouraging. Here might be a spectacular opportunity for all of us.

I had fallen in love with Pepperdine, with its gorgeous campus overlooking Santa Monica Bay, and deeply respected Davenport. I admired Pepperdine's unapologetic Christian mission. It looked as if our family might be able to live on campus, and thus instantly be part of a vibrant community.

As for the investigation, I reflected on the toll exacted by the constant barrage of personal attacks. I had been too controversial even to sit in court. My *persona non grata* status in Arkansas had stuck in my craw during those long months of 1996. The Perry County Bank setback lingered in my memory. It was time to go.

The Pepperdine opportunity seemed providential, an elegant way to exit the investigation and take on an entirely new challenge. Manna from heaven with a couple of quail to go along with it.

As a bonus, my jogging path would shift from Northern Virginia woods and creeks to Zuma Beach and the most scenic track in the world, right in the heart of the Pepperdine campus overlooking the Pacific.

I confided in a handful of individuals in the OIC, in particular Hickman Ewing. He didn't seem at all surprised and was supportive. While the decision was not mine to make, nor were there any guarantees, I planned to recommend to the Special Division that Hickman be appointed as my successor when I left.

With great excitement, I informally accepted the job. The school wanted me to arrive by August 1, 1997, so all that remained was for me to announce my upcoming departure.

To my shock and chagrin, Tom Dawson, my trial team leader in the Jim Guy Tucker tax and bankruptcy fraud case, marched into my office in Little Rock after my announcement and delivered an announcement of his own: "I signed up to work for you. If you leave, I leave."

I had a minirevolt on my hands. I took his reaction as a compliment, if an unwelcome one. It was a jarring return to my personnel nightmare from the Bob Fiske transition three years earlier, when his lawyers exited en masse.

In retrospect, I should have consulted more broadly with team members before announcing my intention to leave. I had only spoken with the most senior prosecutors in Little Rock and Washington. My task as independent counsel turned out to be deeply personal and relational, not simply institutional. I would continually refer to the Office of the Independent Counsel as an institution, if only a temporary one.

Unfortunately, in the minds of the public and even within our own ranks in Little Rock and D.C., it was the Starr investigation.

I sensed immediately that I was stuck. If I left, the Tucker case would fall through, and as a matter of principle, I couldn't let that happen. I was heartsick, but resigned myself to the situation. The Starrs would not be moving to Malibu after all.

I called Davenport and explained the circumstances. The Pepperdine president wasn't surprised by this turn of events. A minor firestorm had erupted in Washington. It was widely rumored that Republican heavies had put pressure on me not to leave. Untrue. I got not a single phone call or note saying, in effect, that I shouldn't abandon ship. Yet I didn't need any pressure to know that I couldn't shirk my duty.

To my great relief, Davenport was flexible. "We'll postpone this one year," he said. "You'll start August 1, 1998. You need to be here by then to catch 'the wave.'" A clever Malibu reference.

It took only four days for me to announce my change of course. To my relief, Dawson withdrew his threat to go home if I headed off to Pepperdine. Before long, everything returned to a state of normalcy in our two offices. (The cruel irony was that Tucker would plead guilty in February 1998 instead of going to trial.)

I was deeply disappointed but was resigned. I would still get my chance to go to Pepperdine later. And for now, though I was sorry to be stuck being the controversial Republican hit man, it was gratifying to know that my team needed wanted me to stay. Duty had called, and I would honor my commitments, even if it meant remaining in an unpleasant role. After all, it would only be another year.

Little did I know that a storm was brewing beyond the horizon that had nothing to do with my office or role as independent counsel. But it would send another bizarre tornado in our direction and stir up a long nightmare for the Starr family.

CHAPTER SEVENTEEN

Paula Corbin Jones

WHILE THE OIC HAD BEEN PURSUING THE VARIOUS WASH-ington leads, the Clintons had been fighting an unrelated Supreme Court battle called *Paula Corbin Jones v. William Jefferson Clinton and Danny Ferguson,* filed in the Eastern District of Arkansas in May 1994, before I was appointed independent counsel.

Jones, an Arkansas state government employee, had alleged in federal court that she had been subjected to a particularly repugnant form of sexual harassment by Governor Bill Clinton in 1991, and when she rebuffed his advances was subjected to "intentional infliction of emotional distress" and defamation.

While investigating various cases in Little Rock, the OIC never pursued any case of sexual wrongdoing against Clinton. That simply was not in our mandate. At times our agents talked to women who allegedly had been involved with the governor, but as witnesses related to another investigation. And we never came across the path of Paula Jones.

I was uninterested in the facts of her case. I was deeply interested, however, in the issues of presidential power and prerogative.

Jones's lawsuit alleged that during a convention at the Excelsior Hotel in Little Rock on May 8, 1991, Jones and another woman were manning a registration desk on behalf of the Arkansas Industrial Development Commission (AIDC). Governor Clinton arrived to make a keynote address.

After Clinton's speech, Danny Ferguson, a state trooper, approached the desk. Trooper Ferguson was in street clothes but wearing a sidearm. He made small talk with Jones and the other woman and left. He reappeared at 2:30 P.M. and handed a piece of paper to Jones with a four-digit number written on it.

"The governor would like to meet with you," he said, indicating that the number was Clinton's suite at the hotel.

Jones hadn't met the governor. She had joined the AIDC only in March and was making a paltry $6.35 an hour. In essence, she was a very junior staffer, certainly not important enough to meet with the chief executive of Arkansas. She asked Ferguson what Clinton wanted.

"It's okay, we do this all the time for the governor," Ferguson said.

Ferguson escorted Jones to the suite. He knocked, Clinton answered, and Jones entered the room while the trooper remained outside.

Clinton made small talk, asking Jones about her job, mentioning that David Harrington, director of the AIDC and her boss, was his good friend. Then the governor took Jones's hand and pulled her toward him.

She pulled back and retreated several feet. But he continued to move toward her.

"I love the way your hair flows down your back," he said. "I love your curves."

When he attempted to kiss her, Jones moved away.

"What are you doing?" she said.

Jones tried to distract him by chatting about Hillary. She was confused. Here was the governor, whom she had never met, talking about her boss and obviously making a pass.

What transpired, according to Jones, was an uninvited and ugly experience. President Clinton, she alleged, had unzipped his pants, exposed himself, and invited her to perform a sex act.

She insisted, "I'm not that kind of a girl," and said she had to go.

"Well, I don't want to make you do anything you don't want to do," he said, pulling up his pants. "If you get in trouble for leaving work, have Dave call me immediately and I'll take care of it."

Why was he mentioning her boss? As she left the suite, Clinton looked at her "sternly," and said, "You are smart. Let's keep this between ourselves."

Back at the registration desk, a visibly upset Jones told her fellow employee what had occurred. She left the conference, went to the workplace of a friend, and also told her. Her friend urged her to report the incident, but Jones feared she'd lose her job. No one would believe her—and what about her fiancé, Steve? Their relationship was all-important to her. He might think she'd invited Clinton's overtures.

Over the next few days, Jones told other people about the encounter, but she didn't report it to her boss or the police.

One of Jones's duties at her job was to deliver documents to the Governor's Office and other agencies in the Capitol Complex. On one trip, Ferguson approached her again. "Bill wants your phone number," he said. "Hillary's out of town often and Bill would like to see you."

Jones refused to give the trooper her phone number and walked away. On another occasion, Ferguson approached Jones yet again.

"How's Steve?" he asked. Since she'd never mentioned her fiancé's first name, the remark made Jones feel as if she were being watched.

Time passed, and Jones married her fiancé and had a baby. She continued to work at the AIDC. Ferguson was like a bad penny; he kept turning up, making cryptic comments.

"I've told Bill how good-looking you are since you've had the baby," he said one day. Jones felt her activities were being monitored.

One day, Jones was in the rotunda of the Capitol. Clinton walked by and draped his arm around her shoulders and pulled her close and said to a trooper standing nearby, "Don't we make a beautiful couple: Beauty and the Beast?"

At her job, Jones believed she was under negative scrutiny. Her duties were diminished, her advancement stalled, and she received no pay raises beyond cost-of-living increases. She quit her job in 1993 and moved to California.

Her new life was jarred in January 1994, right about the time of Fiske's initial appointment as independent counsel.

Jones was in Arkansas to visit her family and friends when she got a call from a friend who read her a segment from that month's issue of the *American Spectator*. The story, "His Cheatin' Heart" by David Brock, focused on allegations by Arkansas state troopers that they had scouted women for the governor—getting their phone numbers, escorting them to hotel rooms, and in general assisting in his assignations with dozens of women.

One trooper described escorting a woman named "Paula" to a hotel room, quoting her as saying that "she was available to be Clinton's regular girlfriend if he so desired."

Jones was extremely upset and worried that people who knew about the encounter would believe that she had agreed to be Clinton's "girlfriend" while she was engaged. Days later, Paula and her husband happened to be eating at a Little Rock restaurant when Trooper Ferguson, who she believed was the source who told Brock about "Paula," approached them. He said he was sorry her name appeared in the magazine, but he had purposely kept her last name and place of employment out of the story.

"Clinton told me you wouldn't do anything anyway," Ferguson said.

Jones felt the article threatened not only her marriage but her relationships with her family and friends, as well as her reputation. On February 11, 1994, Jones, with her lawyer by her side, made a public statement saying that she was the "Paula" mentioned in the story, but that she had rebuffed Clinton's crude sexual advance and had not asked to be his "girlfriend." She demanded that Clinton—now the president of the United States—acknowledge the incident, state that Jones had rejected his advances, and apologize.

What would have happened if Clinton had apologized? Instead, he attacked, saying the incident never happened, he'd never met Jones, and her account was a "cheap political trick" to hurt his presidency.

"It's just not true," said Dee Dee Meyers, White House spokeswoman.

Worse attacks were to follow.

"If you drag a hundred-dollar bill through a trailer park, you never know what you'll find" was James Carville's pronouncement on Jones.

A few months after the "Cheatin' Heart" story, Paula Jones filed a history-shaping federal lawsuit alleging four counts, including violation of her federal civil rights, retaliation, and defamation. She asked for compensatory and punitive damages in the amount of $175,000 for each count, plus attorneys' fees.

Clinton had the audacity to suggest that as president he should be immune from this kind of lawsuit while in office. Judicial interpretation had already created a cloak of immunity for the president when sued for official actions taken as president. Now Clinton argued that he should have immunity for his private actions, too. After all, lawsuits will distract the president while attending to his important work, regardless of the nature of the underlying dispute. Lawsuits are lawsuits, with all their attendant disruptions.

Unfortunately for the White House, history was not helpful to the new president's cause. Over the span of two centuries, the issue had arisen only three times, all in the twentieth century. Presidents Harding, Truman, and Kennedy came into office with the cloud of civil litigation hanging over their heads.

Harding and Truman quickly settled their respective lawsuits. Responding to two lawsuits emerging out of an automobile accident during the 1960 campaign, JFK requested a temporary halt to the litigation based on a congressional statute that provides temporary relief to our military personnel from litigation demands back home. The trial court turned President Kennedy down, and those two cases likewise promptly settled.

Notably, Kennedy had not asserted a constitutional right to freedom from litigation. He maintained, more modestly, that Congress had spoken to the issue, but the trial courts had rejected that straightforward claim of statutory interpretation.

Ardent admirer that he was of JFK, President Clinton should have taken a page from President Kennedy's story and settled the Paula Jones litigation. He would have had plenty of company; well over 90 percent of civil cases filed in the United States settle before trial. But Clinton wasn't interested in peace; he wanted outright victory. Or perhaps, if his political adviser Dick Morris is right, Hillary would hear nothing of a settlement. As a result, the president embarked on a horribly self-destructive course. Instead of settling the Jones litigation, he asked the Supreme Court to invent new law. That's almost always an uphill battle.

The Court of Appeals in St. Louis disagreed that the president could successfully claim a pass with respect to civil cases until he had left office. Trial judges enjoy considerable discretion in scheduling litigation matters and would doubtless take the high demands of the presidential office into account. But that would be a matter of judicial discretion, not presidential prerogative.

The president litigated the issue to the hilt. Spending hundreds of thousands of dollars, if not more, on attorneys' fees, the president petitioned the Supreme Court to hear his case. Having lost in the Court of Appeals, the president had no further right of judicial review. However, he could, as thousands of litigants do every year, request the Supreme Court to hear the case in the exercise of its broad discretion. The result of the president filing what lawyers call a petition for certiorari was that the case will be forever be known as *Clinton v. Jones*.

The Court agreed and granted the president's request for review. In theory, this did not bode well for the Jones team. The rule of thumb among Supreme Court observers is that the Court does not agree to hear a case just to affirm the lower court's judgment.

Ironically, in early summer 1994, when this issue was the talk of Washington, Robert Fiske contacted me at my law firm to ask what I thought about preparing a friend-of-the-court brief on behalf of his office regarding the *Clinton v. Jones* lawsuit. Without having reached any conclusions, Fiske wanted to leave the door open to possible civil litigation against the president. He was considering filing a brief in the Jones litigation urging the federal courts not to exempt the president from the reach of the law. We discussed the matter briefly by phone. My position on the issue was straightforward: the president was not immune from a civil lawsuit by virtue of his position as the nation's chief executive.

Those conversations never came to fruition. But my firm did approve the filing of a friend-of-the-court brief pro bono on behalf of a nonprofit organization, the Independent Women's Forum. I jettisoned the project when I became independent counsel.

Clinton had a lot of friend-of-the-court briefs on his side. Nevertheless, the president's case was difficult to make. Regardless of philosophy or ideology, the justices take their precedents seriously. Here, literally no precedent could be summoned to support his claim. Equally daunting, no prior president had even asked the American judiciary to create such an immunity bath. That fact alone made it difficult in the extreme for President Clinton and his allies to prevail.

Lacking any on-point Supreme Court precedent to support the president's novel position, his lawyers turned to examples from history. Two loomed large. First was a comment by John Adams that the president of the United States should not be subject to the will of a single judge sitting somewhere in the vastness of our country. That sentiment was expressed, of course, when the country was much smaller and considerably less litigious. The second was Thomas Jefferson's recoiling at receiving a subpoena for presidential documents for possible use in the Aaron Burr treason case in Richmond.

In fairness, President Clinton was not claiming total immunity from civil lawsuits. He simply wanted a time-out. Clinton argued that the presidency carries with it such vast and constant demands that postponing civil litigation—at least a lawsuit not involving life and death—struck the right balance between presidential responsibilities and a litigant's demand for her day in court.

Justice would be delayed, not denied, out of respect for the demands on the president's time and attention. LBJ had recalled that of his 1,886 nights as president, he rarely went to sleep before 1:00 or 2:00 A.M. and then was up by 6:00 or 6:30. In addition, to allow Jones's lawsuit to go forward would potentially open the floodgates to all manner of time-consuming lawsuits.

Yet despite all of this, my position that the president was not above the law remained unchanged. That same position became the eventual ruling of a unanimous Supreme Court in the historic case of *Clinton v. Jones*. Clinton lost on May 27, 1997. His broad reach for outright immunity during the course of his presidential term garnered not a single vote from the nine justices, two of whom he had appointed during his first term. The Court sided with Jones, holding that the president, as the nation's chief magistrate, deserves our respect, but he does not enjoy immunity from the reach of the law. The sexual harassment lawsuit could proceed, and Jones's lawyers could take a civil deposition of President Clinton.

What would happen thereafter was entirely up to President Clinton. He could have handled the case honorably and with integrity. He could have done what his namesake Mr. Jefferson grudgingly did when Chief Justice Marshall insisted that the president obey a subpoena. Like Mr. Jefferson, Clinton could have grumbled but obeyed the judicial command. Indeed, in contrast to Jefferson and Nixon, who were required to turn over presidential materials that each wanted to shield from disclosure, all President Clinton had to do was write a check to Paula Jones and say, "I'm sorry."

Sadly, the president chose the wrong path.

Unaware of the profound implications of *Clinton v. Jones*, in late 1997 the OIC carried on as before. We were examining a massive criminal referral regarding possible conflicts of interest at the Rose Law Firm, in addition to working toward resolution of the Tucker tax case and continuing our increasingly tiresome jousting with Susan McDougal and Webb Hubbell.

Susan and Webb were impossible. Squeezing the truth out of those turnips was maddening, but we felt obliged to use every lawful tool at our disposal to get to the bottom of what happened. Just tell the truth, we told each of them, whatever it is, and get it over with.

However, we did feel obliged to make a decision about whether to seek an indictment of Hillary. Her constant disclaimer of "I don't recall" in her various appearances drew the ire of our entire cadre of career prosecutors, including Sam Dash. This was entirely a professional reaction, because we had lawyers of every political stripe in the OIC. This was prosecutorial intuition and judgment.

No matter the subject, Hillary was a classic noncredible witness. For starters, she was smug and dismissive. Her brittle personality was evident in all our interactions. Just as there was bifurcated Bill (Saturday Night Bill and Sunday Morning Bill), there were two Hillarys. The supersmart, articulate, policy-wonk Hillary; and the private, mean-streak, vulgar Hillary.

In our interactions, Hillary seemed cold and aloof, determined to make herself unlikable. She displayed no empathy factor at all. It was as if she were daring us: "Just try to take me on." In our view, she had lied about her work at the Rose Law Firm, lied about the Clintons' Whitewater investment and her role in it, and lied about the stolen law firm records. We had pages upon pages of her "amnesiac" depositions.

Some of our prosecutors had started out as admirers of the pathbreaking First Lady, who had famously taken on a substantive policy role in the Clinton administration. As important as Eleanor Roosevelt had been in her trailblazing role for presidential spouses, Hillary had set up a functional copresidency.

Yet at a human level, her behavior seemed odd and needlessly counterproductive.

Hillary would have been well advised to spend more time in Arkansas courtrooms, with real people, interacting with flesh-and-blood jurors and nervous witnesses. Courtrooms are places where human beings gather, where humanity is not checked at the door. But our interviews with people had revealed she'd been a mediocre attorney, for the most part. I remembered my early mentors describing their mantras for success in the courtroom. Likability, rock-solid integrity, and honesty: "Jurors will know that every word that comes out of my mouth is true."

Jim McDougal had shed light on the work Hillary had performed for Madison. A close examination of her Rose Law Firm billing records contradicted what she had previously said. We'd recovered more Whitewater documents, including Clinton tax returns that suggested the possibility of fraud. But McDougal had died on March 8, 1998, in a Fort Worth federal prison facility. We had reached a point where we had to make a decision about pursuing any criminal charges against Hillary with what we had to date.

At my direction, Hickman Ewing, as head of our Little Rock operation, led a team, including Bob Bittman and Paul Rosenzweig, that drew up a draft indictment and supporting prosecution memorandum of the First Lady. We wanted to answer the question: Was there admissible evidence to prove beyond a reasonable doubt every element of any alleged federal offense?

Before his death, Jim had tried to persuade Susan to cooperate with the OIC; he thought he knew why she refused so adamantly. He claimed in his memoir, *Arkansas Mischief,* published in 1998 after his death, that on the day when the OIC and defense attorneys met in the White House to take Bill's deposition during the 825 trial, Bill had pulled Jim aside to show him how FDR had used the room to view maps of troop positions during World War II.

"Tell Susan to hang on," Bill told Jim. "It'll be all right." The implication Jim took from that conversation was that Susan would be pardoned.

Jim had complicated relationships with both Susan and Bill. By his account, his marriage to Susan had ended in all but name after he discovered medical records indicating she'd had an abortion while they were married. Jim was furious that she hadn't discussed this profound moral issue with him. He later overheard an intimate telephone conversation between Susan and Bill. He believed they were having an affair. (Susan denied both allegations when Jim's biography, coauthored with Curtis Wilkie, a respected *Boston Globe* reporter, was released.)

But Clinton's implicit promise to pardon Susan made it appear there may have been some truth to his belief.

CHAPTER EIGHTEEN

Disruption

O N MONDAY, JANUARY 12, 1998, PROSECUTOR JACKIE BEN-
nett was working at the OIC office about 9:00 P.M. when he got
a phone call from a woman who declined to give her name.

After trying both the 825 case and the Perry County Bank case,
Bennett had taken over as deputy independent counsel in Washington.
As Bennett was talking on the phone, a new colleague, Steve Binhak,
entered the room. A witty Assistant U.S. Attorney from Miami who
had expertise in prosecuting tax fraud, Binhak had been recruited to
deal with Hubbell's continuing legal jeopardy over income tax issues.

FBI agent Steve Irons walked in and Bennett waved him over.

"So, let me get this straight," Bennett said into the phone. "You've
tape-recorded calls from a woman who had an affair with the president. She's lied about it in the Paula Jones case, and is trying to get you
to lie about it. People are helping her get a job to buy her silence. And
Vernon Jordan is involved in it."

Washington lawyer and power broker Jordan was known to be the president's close friend. Bennett later told me Binhak's eyes were "like saucers."

Jackie asked her a few questions. Then the woman dropped a bomb: "You know me. I'm Linda Tripp. I was a witness in the Vince Foster case."

Tripp had been Foster's executive assistant. Now she truly had Jackie's attention.

Like first responders, Bennett, Binhak, Irons, and Sol Wisenberg, a brilliant career prosecutor from San Antonio who often worked late, jumped into Sol's van and headed to Tripp's home in suburban Maryland, listening to Sol's Ralph Stanley cassette as they drove.

Upon their arrival at about 11:45 P.M., my four colleagues sat and talked with Linda deep into the night. None of them had been involved in the Foster death investigation; thus, they were assessing her credibility for the first time. They found her believable, though they were unsure about her motives.

A veteran of the Bush administration, when she worked in the White House counsel's office, Linda had continued in that role for Vince Foster. From the beginning, Tripp had been appalled at the Clintons' arrogance and treatment of other White House staff. Plus, she was a reminder to everyone around her of Foster's tragedy. After his death, she had been reassigned to a political-appointee job in the Pentagon.

Tripp explained that Monica Lewinsky, who she described as a Beverly Hills child of privilege in her early twenties, had served as a White House intern, starting in July 1995. She had struck up a relationship with the president. The affair had started during the government shutdown in November 1995, when interns manned the phones and delivered documents. Monica, then twenty-two, and Clinton began having sexual trysts in a hallway off the Oval Office. After her internship was over, Lewinsky got a job in the West Wing and continued to see the president whenever possible.

However, after coming under the watchful eye of Hillary's hatchet person, Evelyn Lieberman, Monica had been reassigned in April 1996 to a job across the Potomac. She found herself confined to a desk in the Pentagon's Public Affairs office. She had been trying ever since to snare another job in the White House complex.

Linda became close to the much younger woman, whom she described as emotionally immature for her age. Working at the Pentagon that summer, Monica began confiding in Linda about her divorced parents, and about her anxiety about being overweight. Then Monica began sharing details of her relationship with the president and her ongoing visits to the West Wing, usually arranged through Betty Currie, the president's secretary.

At first Tripp didn't know whether to believe her. But the level of detail, the way her story coincided with White House events, and the gifts that the president had given Monica—including a special edition of Walt Whitman's *Leaves of Grass*—convinced Tripp she was telling the truth.

We later learned it was Tripp who had told Jones's lawyers about Monica's relationship with the president. On December 15, Jones's lawyers had served Clinton with a request "to produce documents related to communications between the President and Monica Lewinsky." His lawyers had been surprised. Who was Monica Lewinsky?

Jones's lawyers sent a subpoena to Monica (named Jane Doe 8) on December 19, 1997, requiring her to appear for a deposition. They had done the same to a handful of other women who they believed had a sexual relationship or encounter with the president, including a woman named Kathleen Willey.

Monica said the president had told her she could get out of the deposition by submitting an affidavit denying any such relationship existed. The president, through Vernon Jordan, had arranged for her to get an attorney. Lawyer Frank Carter drew up the document, which Lewinsky signed on January 7, 1998, affirming: "I have never had a sexual relationship with the President."

Now Monica was pleading with Tripp, who had also been subpoenaed in October because she had witnessed the emergence of Willey from the Oval Office in August 1997 in a flustered state—face red, lipstick smeared, blouse untucked—to file a false affidavit.

Tripp had captured these conversations and more—much, much more—with a telephone recording machine. But she was worried. She had since learned that Maryland had a law making it illegal to tape a telephone conversation without the other party's knowledge. She would turn over her evidence, but only if she could be granted immunity.

Our team agreed that immunity was no problem, assuming the tapes were authentic. They left Tripp's home around 2:00 A.M. and drove back to Washington, not with a sense of triumph but with deepening concern. They found her believable, and if the tapes were authentic, they were powerful proof of an ongoing criminal conspiracy. If what Tripp said was true, not only had Monica committed perjury by filing a false affidavit, the president of the United States was obstructing justice.

I had to fly to Little Rock early that morning to discuss the Hubbell tax case with Bittman and Hickman. We got on a conference call with Bennett after I arrived. At first, I found Tripp's story hard to believe. How could an intern have carried on an affair with President Clinton in the Oval Office? Monica's tale sounded like the feverish fantasies of a Valley Girl. The White House was a goldfish bowl. It would be difficult to have any privacy for a tryst when Secret Service agents were manning doors, and there were cameras and entry and exit logs. It just didn't seem possible.

I wasn't completely surprised by the revelation, however. Jackie had called me the previous Friday, January 9, while I was in Aspen for a conference. He had alerted me that a tip alleging some malfeasance on the part of the president might be coming in—one of those "I have a friend who has a friend" kind of tips that usually go nowhere or aren't worth pursuing.

Bennett had learned of this "source" in a roundabout way, after four lawyers who knew one another decided to have dinner in Philadelphia to catch up on old times and new interests.

Jerome Marcus, who lived in Philadelphia, set up the dinner on January 8. Richard Porter, a young Kirkland & Ellis partner in the Chicago office, flew in from the Windy City. (Richard and I practiced in entirely different fields, he in corporate and I in litigation, and our paths seldom crossed.) George Conway, a New York lawyer, came down on a whim. They were joined by Paul Rosenzweig, a member of the OIC team who lived in Washington. At times, Rosenzweig stayed at my apartment in Little Rock when he needed to be in Arkansas on OIC business.

Porter and Marcus told Rosenzweig that they were helping lawyers representing Paula Jones. They'd come across a source who claimed that President Clinton was involved in an illicit relationship with a young woman and that the White House was trying to get her a job to cover it up and keep her quiet. Would the OIC be interested?

Rosenzweig had informed Jackie Bennett, who at first balked. He told him, "We can't have hearsay." But he realized that if a crime was being committed, the provenance didn't matter. He told Rosenzweig that he was interested, but the information had to come in "through the front door," meaning the source would have to call him directly.

Though I was skeptical, if what Tripp was saying was true, it was a remarkable parallel to the story of Webb Hubbell. An individual who knew of potential wrongdoing was being told to keep silent to protect the president, and was promised that, with the help of the White House, she would be well taken care of.

The president was scheduled to give his own deposition in the Jones case on Saturday, January 17. The issues to be explored would include whether the president had sexual relationships with state or federal employees, or other subordinates, which would tend to corroborate Paula Jones's allegations with respect to what had happened in the Excelsior Hotel. At a minimum, the background evidence would be sufficiently relevant to pursue in discovery and perhaps to be allowed in at trial.

Jordan was helping Monica find a position in New York, where she would be out of the lawsuit's reach; federal courts have limited power over out-of-state witnesses in civil cases.

We couldn't turn a blind eye, but we needed independent corroboration before we could take the next steps. And we had little time. The two women had made plans to meet late that afternoon for coffee at the Ritz-Carlton in Pentagon City.

We knew the stakes were at their highest level in the entire course of our long-running investigation. Potentially the presidency was at stake. Clinton had survived Whitewater, though he had testified untruthfully time and again; but this time in his recklessness he appeared to be carrying on an active criminal course of conduct.

Tripp had planned to surreptitiously tape Lewinsky herself, using amateur equipment. Instead, FBI agents, led by Irons, outfitted her with a microphone and a high-tech recorder that would allow the agents to listen as the women talked. Perhaps to the fainthearted, wiring a cooperative witness is poor form. But wires are used routinely in law enforcement. It's an entirely lawful tool that serves a pivotal purpose in truth gathering. That way, the targets speak for themselves.

The two women met, found a table, and began talking. "This is what my lawyer taught me," Monica said. "You really don't—you don't very often say 'no' unless you really need to. The best is 'Well, not that I recall, not that I really remember. Might have, but I don't really remember.'"

As the FBI team listened in, the Monica-Linda conversation turned quickly to Monica's request that Linda draft and file a false affidavit regarding Kathleen Willey. Monica was counting on Linda's friendship. Her rationale was entirely political: we need to protect the president whom we both serve.

But the device malfunctioned. Suddenly the lead agent couldn't hear what was being said. Hoping that the conversation was still being recorded, the FBI team moved two agents into the restaurant to listen from an adjoining table. They heard enough of the conversation to confirm the topics. After the women's meeting was over, agents removed the wire and learned to their relief that the device had recorded the women's conversation.

Monica insisted that the president didn't consider the false affidavit as lying. "He thinks of it as, 'We're safe. We're being smart.' Okay? . . . It's good for everybody."

After listening to the tape, my initial impression was this was the real thing. Monica described a carefully constructed presidential plan to commit crimes against the fair and honest administration of justice.

In return, Jordan was helping her find a job in New York, perhaps with Revlon-affiliated companies.

We were still investigating the extraordinary payments received by Hubbell from, among other clients, Revlon, and the connection to his unwillingness to provide information to the OIC about certain core Arkansas matters. This was not a perjury trap, this was a perjury game, a calculated plan to prevent the courts from getting at the truth. We saw this as a criminally culpable attitude on the part of both Bill and Monica. But the president was far more culpable. He not only was more than two decades older than she, he was a lawyer and an officer of the court. Even more, he was the chief executive of the United States.

The following day at work, January 14, Monica gave Tripp a three-page document: "Points to make in an affidavit." These included details about Willey's encounter with the president such as "I never saw her go into the Oval Office, or come out of the Oval Office. I have never observed the President behaving inappropriately with anybody." She even suggested that Tripp say, "I now find it completely plausible that [Willey] herself smeared her lipstick, untucked her blouse, etc."

By her actions, Monica was confirming Tripp's information. But that didn't mean Monica had been telling the truth about her affair with Clinton. What if she had a vivid imagination and was regaling her friend with a fantasy story?

Bizarrely, January 14 was the date we had scheduled months earlier to take a deposition of Hillary Clinton on the matter of the FBI files before we made our final determination about her involvement. Shortly after noon, Bennett, Rod Rosenstein, and I went to the White House for the deposition. As we entered, I introduced Bennett to the First Lady as the prosecutor who had tried Tucker and the McDougals. She gave me a peculiar look. I just smiled.

The deposition took only about thirty minutes; Hillary had little involvement with the FBI debacle. At least this time, she didn't repeat her usual mantra of "I don't recall."

Later that day, our team sat around the long conference table and talked about what to do. The Tripp-Lewinsky matter was arguably within our investigative authority under prior grants from the Special Division. We could proceed under the specific umbrella of what we understood to be our "related to" jurisdiction. That is, a witness already known to us from the Foster death investigation, Linda Tripp, had come to us with credible evidence that the president was in the process of planning and committing crimes.

My own view was this: What had been revealed by Tripp—both in her statements to our career prosecutors and in the recording of her conversation with Monica—clearly "related to" our ongoing work and had "arisen out of" our investigation. The factual and logical connection to Foster's death case gave us the necessary jurisdictional hook to carry on the inquiry, at least preliminarily.

This situation stood in stark contrast to someone coming in off the street and urging: "Criminal activity is afoot in the White House, and you should investigate it." That had happened not infrequently in Little Rock ("prison deal at Calico Rock . . . crooked as a snake"). As a matter of course, we simply referred those walk-in leads to the FBI on the second floor of Two Financial Centre.

As we talked, Mike Emmick, a career prosecutor on detail from the U.S. Attorney's Office in Los Angeles, cut to the chase.

"We shouldn't just walk, we should run to the Attorney General as quickly as possible," Emmick said. We not only needed express authorization from Main Justice and the Special Division judges *as a matter of law*, we should go get that authorization *as a matter of prudence*. We

177

needed to be transparent and up front with the Attorney General. Emmick was absolutely right.

Early that evening, Jackie tried to reach Deputy Attorney General Eric Holder. He was at a Washington Wizards basketball game just blocks away, and he put us off until the next day.

I appreciated the seriousness and gravity of the situation. All of us suffered through a restless night.

The Little Rock team, Office of the Independent Counsel, 1995.

Vince Foster, left, is seen in this October 12, 1988, photo with his wife, Hillary Clinton, and then-governor Bill Clinton. Robert Fiske and I investigated Foster's suicide in 1993.

April 22, 1994: First Lady Hillary Rodham Clinton in the State Dining Room, holding her "pink press conference."

Ethics adviser Sam Dash.

Webster Hubbell is sworn in prior to testifying before the Senate Whitewater committee on December 1, 1995.

Hillary Clinton leaving the Washington, D.C., federal courthouse in January 1996, following her testimony before a grand jury on her role in the Whitewater land deal.

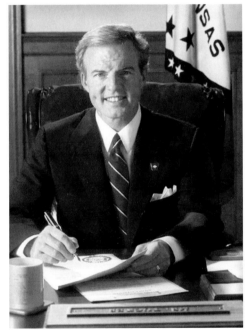

Jim Guy Tucker Jr., forty-third governor of Arkansas (1993–1996). He resigned on July 16, 1996, after his conviction for fraud.

Jim McDougal talks to reporters outside the Little Rock, Arkansas, federal courthouse following his sentencing hearing for Whitewater offenses on April 14, 1997.

Susan McDougal walks to the prisoners' entrance of the Little Rock federal courthouse on May 14, 1998.

U.S. Attorney General Janet Reno testifying before Congress on October 15, 1997.

Linda Tripp talks to reporters outside the D.C. courthouse on July 29, 1998.

White House intern Monica Lewinsky with President Bill Clinton at a White House function. This photo was submitted as evidence in documents by the Starr investigation.

The Office of the Independent Counsel's senior team of prosecutors meeting in their D.C. offices in 1998.

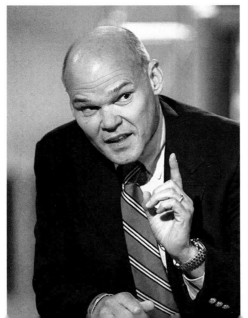

Clinton strategist James Carville launched a public relations war against the independent counsel.

Press conference, January 1998.

Arkansas state employee
Paula Corbin Jones sued
President Clinton in 1994
for sexual harassment.

Senior OIC prosecutors Bob Bittman, left; Mike Emmick, center; and Rodger Heaton.

January 26, 1998: President Clinton angrily denies any improper behavior with a White House intern.

Clinton attorney David Kendall, left, and White House Counsel Charles Ruff, right, prepare for the president's testimony in 1998.

I testified before the House Judiciary Committee for more than twelve hours on November 19, 1998.

House Judiciary Committee chairman Henry Hyde meets with House managers to prepare for the Senate impeachment trial.

April 14, 1999: I'm arguing against the reauthorization of the Independent Counsel Act, citing that it violates the separation of powers.

CHAPTER NINETEEN

Monica

EARLY ON THE EVENING OF THURSDAY, JANUARY 15, JACKIE Bennett, accompanied by Stephen Bates, a Harvard-educated member of the brain trust, met with Eric Holder at his office on the fourth floor of Main Justice. Bennett presented the situation while Bates took copious notes.

Bennett knew Holder well from their service together in the Public Integrity Section of the DOJ. He liked Eric, but thought he was a better politician than prosecutor. Holder assiduously cultivated an image of savvy-lawyer-about-town, often getting photographed for puff pieces that law firms loved to display in their waiting rooms and wave about to clients. Eric had enjoyed a meteoric rise in four years to become deputy AG.

They explained we were happy to pass off the investigation to the DOJ, if that was what the Main Justice leadership deemed appropriate. In fact, on balance, that was what I preferred.

Holder listened carefully, posed a few questions, and went up the private elevator to the fifth floor to talk to his boss.

Bennett and Bates left. Later that evening, word came from Holder. The Attorney General agreed we should continue with the investigation, at least temporarily. She would seek an expansion of jurisdiction from the Special Division judges on an expedited basis. A senior DOJ prosecutor, Josh Hochberg, who I knew well, came to our offices to meet with our prosecutors and review the situation. He listened to the tape from the body wire.

On the morning of Friday, January 16, the judges quickly gave their approval. "The Independent Counsel shall have jurisdiction and authority to investigate to the maximum extent authorized by the Independent Counsel Reauthorization Act of 1994 whether Monica Lewinsky or others suborned perjury, obstructed justice, intimidated witnesses, or otherwise violated federal law . . . in dealing with witnesses, potential witnesses, attorneys or others concerning the civil case *Jones v. Clinton*."

Again, we had to move fast. Tripp was scheduled to meet Lewinsky that day for lunch at the Ritz-Carlton.

Our team dubbed the operation "Prom Night." Fresh from the gym, wearing purple sweats, Monica arrived. After Monica and Linda had chatted for a short time in the lobby, by predesign Steve Irons and several other FBI agents swept in. Identifying themselves, they did not place Monica under arrest, but simply invited her and Tripp to accompany them.

Our team of prosecutors awaited the women's arrival in two adjoining hotel rooms on the tenth floor. I was standing by in my office. When they arrived upstairs, Monica turned on Tripp in a fury. She realized she'd been set up.

In one room, Binhak interviewed Tripp for several hours; she left the hotel at 4:00 P.M.

In the other room, Mike Emmick led the charm offensive with Monica. With FBI agents taking notes, the prosecutors explained their mission. Monica had a choice: She was facing federal charges of perjury and subornation of perjury. She could cooperate and in return receive consideration regarding whether and how we would charge her. The negotiating team was authorized to offer her complete immunity if necessary to secure her cooperation.

For an hour, Monica screamed, she cried, she pouted, and complained bitterly about her scheming, no-good, so-called friend. After a while, she calmed down and began asking questions. The meeting turned into a marathon. At one point, she wanted to call the lawyer who had drafted the false affidavit, Frank Carter. We made it clear she wasn't under arrest. She was free to leave, and she was free to call Carter. We gave her the number of the public defender's office. Our goal was to achieve her honest cooperation. At about four, Monica asked to consult with her mother, who was living in New York.

We immediately agreed. Monica phoned her outside our presence. Before long, Monica announced that her distraught mother was coming to Washington. Since her mother refused to fly, she was taking the next train from Manhattan. She would then find her way as quickly as possible to the hotel.

Wisely or not, we went along. We thought it was a good sign that her mother, Marcia Lewis, was rushing to be at her daughter's side. It was perfectly understandable, but we now faced a long delay. Monica refused to decide what to do without parental input and guidance.

In the company of Binhak, who was the youngest on our team, Monica strolled through the mall, shopped at Crate & Barrel, had a leisurely coffee. The conversation was all small talk. They returned to the hotel to await her mother's arrival. Monica sat in a chair reading the Bible while Binhak tried to find something suitable on TV to watch. He clicked until he found an old movie with Ethel Merman singing "God Bless America."

Jackie Bennett, the former tight end, came in to play the heavy. Monica again mentioned her desire to call her civil lawyer. He shrugged and said okay. They dialed the office number for Carter; he'd left for the day, so Monica left a message.

Not long after that, Monica said she wanted to go out for a walk. Binhak went downstairs with her and told her she was free to roam around the mall. He made it clear she wasn't under arrest. Monica nodded and walked through the lobby. Tired of babysitting her, Binhak turned to go back upstairs. But seeing Monica headed to a bank of pay phones, he held back. He saw her dial, then talk into the phone. She spoke for a few moments, then hung up.

Binhak learned she had called a White House number for Betty Currie and got an answering machine. She hissed "Hoover, Hoover" into the phone, as if she were speaking in code, which she later explained meant the FBI, as in J. Edgar.

She was trying to warn the president before his deposition in Paula Jones's lawsuit the following day. Nobody got the message, apparently— or if they did, they didn't understand it.

From my office, I was on the phone with our on-the-scene team throughout the day. But I ventured nowhere near the Ritz-Carlton. As the afternoon dragged on, the team grew frustrated. We were now at a standstill.

Marcia Lewis arrived about 10:00 P.M. Mother and daughter went out into the hallway to talk. They did not keep their voices down.

Binhak heard Mrs. Lewis urging Monica to cooperate. "You are in peril here," she said. "Give them what they need."

"I will not be the one who brings down this f****** president!" Monica shouted.

We had given Monica lots of time to think it over. She knew what she wanted to do, and who she was determined to protect. Monica overruled her mother. She would fall on her sword rather than implicate the president of the United States.

It was becoming increasingly clear: in thinking she was a naive, starstruck young woman in love who would quickly cooperate, we underestimated her. In her determination to protect the president, Monica kept a team of experienced FBI agents and career prosecutors twiddling their thumbs for much of the day. She was searching for the perfect solution. Monica doubtless calculated that if she could maneuver the situation, she would skate from criminal prosecution and at the same time not turn on the president. Marcia and Monica called Monica's father, Bernard, a highly successful physician in Beverly Hills, who had remarried. Dr. Lewinsky said he would send his family lawyer to Washington right away.

Our high hopes for a quick resolution had been cruelly dashed. Monica had now lawyered up. We could no longer communicate with her directly. Without the benefit of Monica's cooperation, we simply awaited the results of the following day. Who knew what Clinton might do? Perhaps he would come to his senses, and, at long last, settle the long-running Jones litigation "on the courthouse steps."

CHAPTER TWENTY

Explosion

O N SATURDAY, JANUARY 17, NOT KNOWING ABOUT MON-
ica and Prom Night, President Clinton sat down for his deposition in the Jones case accompanied by his personal lawyer, Bob Bennett.

The president did not come to his senses. He did not enter into an
eleventh-hour mediation to resolve the case. Clinton could have done
so, because Chief Judge Susan Webber Wright had flown from Little
Rock at the president's request to preside over the deposition.

But he chose a foolhardy course. He believed he could lie his way
out of it.

After taking an oath to tell the truth, he read a definition of sexual
relations provided by Judge Wright. The definition was thorough and
explicit.

Clinton denied he had any sort of sexual relationship with Monica Lewinsky. But he was alarmed by the specificity of some of the
questions about whether he had ever been alone with Monica, if he had

given her any gifts. Specifically, had he given her a book by Walt Whitman?

It was obvious someone knew a lot about Monica and had suggested telltale questions for Jones's lawyers.

Before the deposition was over, Bob Bennett read Monica's affidavit into the record. The president testified that it was accurate. Bennett then introduced the document as an exhibit. He said his client was fully aware of the contents, and "there is absolutely no sex of any kind, in any manner, shape or form with President Clinton."

Of pivotal importance, the president flatly stated that he and Monica had never been alone together, other than for a possible pizza delivery.

The deposition ended, with Judge Wright directing the parties not to reach out to any potential witnesses. Clinton wasted no time in disobeying the judge's order. He summoned Betty Currie to come to the White House the following day. We later learned that Clinton carefully rehearsed a false narrative with Betty. He also asked her to try to get in touch with Monica, but none of her many calls and pages were returned.

Meanwhile, Tripp had delivered to our office the first batch of telephone conversations she had recorded with Monica. They buttressed Tripp's account of the women's friendship—and Monica's relationship with the president.

On Sunday, January 18, Monica's lawyer, Bill Ginsburg of Los Angeles, arrived at our offices for an initial background briefing with our prosecutors. He quickly became contentious. To our chagrin, we learned that he was a medical malpractice attorney and did not know the ropes. Our prosecutors were unsure that he and they were speaking the same language.

Late that day, Matt Drudge broke the story on his internet platform. The *Drudge Report* said that *Newsweek* had killed a report by Michael Isikoff that Clinton had an affair with a former White House intern, and that recordings of "intimate phone conversations exist."

Ginsburg returned to our office on Tuesday at 5:00 P.M., accompanied by Monica. Moderately heavyset, bespectacled, with a closely cropped salt-and-pepper beard, he went into the conference room with Jackie Bennett and Bittman, while Monica sat in our waiting room and thumbed through magazines.

I was standing by in my office as the final arbiter, allowing the process to run its course. I emerged into the hall, caught a glimpse of her from a distance, and went into another prosecutor's office to carry on. I was naturally curious, but I wanted the career prosecutors to come to their own judgments and recommend a course of action.

My colleagues emerged and told me that while the meeting had not gone well, it wasn't a disaster. The negotiation process would continue. I didn't worry. We were in a position of strength. We had the goods: Tripp's testimony, our own experience with Monica at the Ritz-Carlton, and the tapes. But at the same time, we wanted to secure Monica's cooperation in a professional way and ensure she would be truthful.

Our negotiations with Ginsburg dragged on over the next week. Even with the frustrating delay, we remained willing to grant Monica immunity. But we first needed a face-to-face interview to assess her credibility. Ginsburg offered only a vague and amorphous written statement, and he was exceedingly reluctant for us to interview her.

It became apparent that the brash Ginsburg was in over his head. Criminal law is a specialty, just like malpractice. Why had Dr. Lewinsky, a respected specialist, retained an utterly unqualified if otherwise capable lawyer to handle a case outside his area of expertise and juris-diction? It made no sense.

However, Ginsburg showed no sign of modesty. His cockeyed proposals for securing Monica's immunity in exchange for her cooper-ation were unrealistic in the extreme. No one on our team was buying what Ginsburg was peddling.

Sam Dash was deeply involved in our deliberations. He got visibly agitated in the face of Ginsburg's incompetence. How, in the poten-tially biggest presidential scandal in an entire generation, could a "med mal" lawyer parachute in from Los Angeles and instantly become a high-powered criminal practice attorney in the nation's capital? It was baffling.

As we reviewed his proposals, Ginsburg was in effect asking us to buy a pig in a poke. Monica would get an immunity bath, and we'd get an ambiguous story that was largely contradicted by the detailed reve-lations in the Linda Tripp tapes.

As her lawyer, it was Bill Ginsburg's duty to keep a laserlike focus on her interests, to get a deal to deliver his client out of harm's way. He was balking at the necessary steps to accomplish that. We were left to wonder why. Immunity deals are a part of prosecutors'—and defense attorneys'—daily work. For whatever reason, Ginsburg was not conducting himself in the way criminal lawyers ordinarily do. To our veteran prosecutors, Ginsburg's unreasonable position suggested the possibility that Monica was dictating terms to her lawyer.

The story of "the President and the Intern" erupted into the main-stream press, with a headline that hit the *Washington Post* on Janu-ary 21: CLINTON ACCUSED OF URGING AIDE TO LIE; STARR PROBES WHETHER PRESIDENT TOLD WOMAN TO DENY ALLEGED AFFAIR TO JONES'S LAWYERS.

The White House issued a statement, personally approved by the president, saying he was "outraged by these allegations," and that "he has never had an improper relationship with this woman." Bob Bennett told the *Post*: "This story smells ridiculous, and frankly I smell a rat."

The president continued to deny the relationship to his close aides, including John Podesta, Harold Ickes, Sylvia Mathews, and Erskine Bowles. "I want you to know I did not have sexual relationships with this woman, Monica Lewinsky. I did not ask anybody to lie. And when the facts come out, you'll understand."

Even more outrageously, he blamed Monica for his predicament, according to senior aide Sidney Blumenthal. Blumenthal said Clinton told him, "Monica Lewinsky came at me and made a sexual demand on me." According to Blumenthal, "She threatened him. She said that she would tell people they'd had an affair, that she was known as the stalker among her peers, and that she hated it and if she had an affair or said she had an affair then she wouldn't be the stalker anymore."

It was so unfair, Clinton insisted to Blumenthal. "I feel like a character in a novel. I feel like somebody who is surrounded by an oppressive force that is creating a lie about me and I can't get the truth out. I feel like the character in the novel *Darkness at Noon*."

Though Clinton gave interviews with variations of "there is not a sexual relationship" to NPR, PBS, and *Roll Call*, the story didn't go away. Within days, storm clouds appeared to gather over the White House. All was doom and gloom.

ABC-TV anchor Sam Donaldson opined on January 25 that if Clinton wasn't telling the truth, "I think his presidency is numbered in days. This isn't going to drag out. We're not going to be here three months from now talking about this."

Suddenly, I found myself a target of more than harsh language and lies. U.S. marshals appeared out of the blue at my office to say they were investigating death threats against me. Although I do not know for sure, I suspect the threats were coming by phone or mail to the office of the OIC. From that moment on, for over a year I was under the protection of the U.S. Marshals Service twenty-four hours a day.

I had worked with the marshals and the FBI for years, and I had seen this kind of protection before. While I had been a federal judge, a fellow judge was the subject of death threats and even had marshals living in his home. I didn't inquire about the identity of the bad guys. I trusted that the marshals and the FBI were experts in threat assessments.

They went to our house in McLean and set up a command post in a well-equipped trailer on our street. Detailed from around the country, the marshals took twelve-hour shifts. Occasionally, local law enforcement from Fairfax County would patrol by just to make sure that all was well. Our sleepy Northern Virginia suburb became the safest neighborhood in America.

For me, there was no more jogging through the woods and across runs. I could no longer drive myself to work. While the deputy marshals were uniformly friendly and likable, we had lost our freedom and had to install an alarm system in our relatively modest home. It was intimidating, but Alice and the kids took the marshals' presence in stride. They occasionally came into our house to avail themselves of the bathroom facilities. Though they frequently rotated assignments, we got to know many of them well.

The press arrived bright and early each morning hoping to get a comment from me. I still had not hired a press spokesman, which was foolish. I had to smile and say "no comment," or something entirely innocuous.

For his part, Ginsburg manifestly was not serving his client well.

Monica continued in harm's way, and an immunity deal awaited only one commitment: for her to agree to tell the whole truth and nothing but the truth. Yet as the days wore on, our negotiating positions remained far apart.

Unfortunately, we were continually confronted with Ginsburg's exasperating game of cat and mouse. Ginsburg kept tinkering with the immunity proffer.

We kept coming back to basics. The FBI had confirmed the Tripp tapes were authentic; we corroborated many of the contemporaneous notes Tripp had taken. They revealed Monica's fierce determination to lie under oath. Her written proffer waffled on those key facts. Monica was clearly holding back, just like Webb Hubbell and Susan McDougal had done.

Insisting we had an agreement, Ginsburg went to court to enforce it. Understandable, but what was not understandable, with his client facing legal jeopardy and press scrutiny, was Ginsburg's making statements that did not portray Monica in a positive light.

"I can't tell you what's true and what's not true," he told a journalist on January 21. "She signed the declaration and stands on it at this time. . . . But I'm smart enough after 30 years as a trial lawyer to know that there's always a surprise around the corner. If [Clinton] did have a sexual relationship with a 23-year-old intern, I question his judgment. If he didn't, then I think Ken Starr and his crew have ravaged the life of a youngster."

On January 22, we issued subpoenas for a number of witnesses, including Monica, Betty Currie, other White House staffers, Secret Service agents, and for White House documents. With or without Lewinsky, we were going forward. We would vigorously investigate whether she had lied or obstructed justice.

Ginsburg obviously loved the unprecedented exposure. He extended his newfound notoriety week after week. Had Monica cooperated right away, the investigation would have been over within a few weeks. That precious extra time allowed forces to be mustered to the president's side. Time gave Clinton room to maneuver.

And with Olympian effectiveness, that was what the president did. Monica Lewinsky saved the nation's wily chief executive, who unleashed virtually every weapon in his formidable arsenal against the investigation.

On January 23, Clinton told members of his Cabinet the allegations were false. After the meeting, several Cabinet members appeared outside the White House to fight the rumors.

"I believe that the allegations are completely untrue," Secretary of State Madeleine Albright said. She was backed up by Commerce Secretary William Daley, Secretary of Education Richard Riley, and Secretary of Health and Human Services Donna Shalala.

The next day, Ann Lewis, White House communications director, said she and other Clinton supporters had been given a green light to talk about the allegations. "I can say with absolute assurance that the president of the United States did not have a sexual relationship because I have heard the president of the United States say so," Lewis said on *Good Morning America*. "He has said it, he could not be more clear. . . . Sex is sex, even in Washington, I've been assured."

The Comeback Kid appeared in the Roosevelt Room in the White House on January 26, issuing his strongest denial yet. "I want to say one thing to the American people. I want you to listen to me. I'm going to say this again: I did not have sexual relations with that woman, Miss Lewinsky." He wagged his finger for emphasis. "I never told anybody to lie, not a single time. Never. These allegations are false."

Watching this performance, I was puzzled. He was insulting a young woman who potentially held his fate in her hands. We later learned this had devastated Monica. But she and her incompetent lawyer's televised bloviating sessions continued shielding the president from potential political disaster.

That disaster seemed to be unavoidable. A powerful employer trysting with an impressionable recent college graduate in the nation's most impressive place of employment did not make for a sustainable narrative of presidential innocence. And too many people—especially the Secret Service uniformed officers—knew that their private sessions in the Oval Office were not cerebral encounters.

To his credit, the president performed impressively during his State of the Union speech on January 27. He mentioned nothing of the burgeoning scandal.

But his surrogates did. That same day, Hillary went on the *Today* show with Matt Lauer to defend her husband. "The great story here for anybody willing to find it and write about it and explain it is this vast right-wing conspiracy that has been conspiring against my husband since the day he announced for president."

Representative Charlie Rangel of New York weighed in on January 28. "That poor child has serious emotional problems. She's fantasizing. And I haven't heard that she played with a full deck in her other experiences."

He was referring to a married man from Oregon, who had come forward to sell a story to a tabloid about his long-running affair with Monica while she was an undergrad student at Lewis & Clark University in Portland.

Rahm Emanuel, Clinton's senior policy adviser, told CNN: "Did the president have a sexual relationship with this young lady? No. Did the president ask this young lady to lie? No. That's what matters in a media frenzy about rumor and gossip. [You've] got to get back down to the facts." Then the gossips began their dirty work, with an onslaught of cruel and deeply personal attacks. Monica was a "clutch," a narcissistic stalker, an overweight fantasist who made it all up.

But there was one bright spot for Monica. Back in Little Rock, Judge Wright issued a ruling that Monica's testimony was "not essential to the core issues" in the Jones lawsuit. Her evidence would be excluded. Jones's lawyers immediately appealed.

Free to go and under assault from the press, as well as from Clinton surrogates, Monica had had enough. She left Washington and went home to California to spend time with her father and stepmother.

Meanwhile, the president also regrouped. Two weeks later, he appeared deeply reverent at the National Prayer Breakfast, a Washington tradition launched by President Dwight Eisenhower early in his first term. To show up at that annual event, with Hillary at his side, took some chutzpah. Without mentioning the brewing scandal even indirectly, the president addressed four thousand people scrunched into the Washington Hilton. He spoke movingly to them, and via television, to the nation and the world.

Here was a deeply human president, reaching back to his Southern Baptist upbringing. He spoke to the country's heartland and to the traditional culture that prevailed in his native South. The National Prayer Breakfast is for Little Rock and countless hamlets across America, not Hollywood or Manhattan. Here, on the morning of interdenominational and multifaith prayer, Bill Clinton returned to his spiritual roots, to his days as governor of Arkansas, when he sang in the choir of Little Rock's massive First Baptist Church.

It was the last admirable move he would make for some time. Yogi Berra famously advised: "When you come to a fork in the road, take it." With the public revelation of the Lewinsky relationship, the president had a stark choice. Before him lay two roads: the high road and the low road. Like most successful politicians, Clinton could adroitly motor along both roads at the same time. This time, however, he took the low road and pressed hard on the gas pedal.

Clinton selected this route in the wake of an infamous overnight poll done by Dick Morris. The American people, Morris reported back to the president, would forgive adultery, but not perjury or obstruction of justice.

It was too late. He knew what he had done. He had lied under oath in his deposition in the Paula Jones case. The president's fateful response to Morris: "Well, we just have to win, then."

"Winning" meant employing a multifaceted strategy: First, take care of or at least neutralize Monica, much in the way the White House had taken care of Hubbell. Second, stonewall the investigation while purporting to cooperate. Third, send out surrogates to aggressively attack Starr and his team—and to trash Monica.

Meanwhile, stay focused on the day job. The country was at peace, and it was prosperous thanks to a tech boom and soaring stock market. The danger of being forced to resign had passed, thanks to Monica's self-sacrifice.

But he couldn't dodge the question: Would he consider resigning?

"I would never walk away from the people of this country and the trust they've placed in me," Clinton said on February 6, 1998, during a news conference with UK prime minister Tony Blair.

With no agreement in place with Monica, we began bringing other witnesses in to testify before the Washington grand jury, including eleven friends and family members Monica had told about the "secret" relationship.

The circuslike atmosphere prevailing on the third floor of the courthouse—near the grand jury room—finally led Chief Judge Norma Holloway Johnson, U.S. District Court for the District of Columbia, to call a halt to the disruptive spectacle. She moved the press to a location outside the courthouse. But even so, upon completing their grand jury appearances, witnesses and their lawyers frequently headed directly to curbside on Constitution Avenue, on a spot that was soon dubbed "Monica Beach."

Things got even weirder when Ginsburg went on a public relations blitz. On February 1, he entered news history by making the rounds of all five major American Sunday-morning talk shows. His main message: Ken Starr is the bad guy.

Ginsburg's behavior was appallingly unprofessional and wildly ineffective in terms of serving the interest of his client. He told the press Monica was being "squeezed" by Starr's office and was now a target of the Whitewater prosecution.

Perhaps a bit spooked, Clinton's lawyers began claiming that executive privilege extended to his top aides on these nonpresidential issues. This was a harbinger of hard-fought battles to come over the right of the grand jury to obtain evidence versus endless White House legal gambits to delay and deny.

CHAPTER TWENTY-ONE

Dirt

Early in 1998, we had heard that people were poking about for dirt on individual OIC team members. Laughably, someone circulated the rumor that "Ken Starr had a honey" in Little Rock. A lie. Not content with going after just me, the White House's allies decided to make the so-called cowboy prosecutors the enemy, dredging up personal history and old DOJ investigations to paint them as rogues out to get the president.

I believe one major reason the attacks had ramped up was that we had summoned to the grand jury White House aide Bruce Lindsey, who had helped prepare Clinton for his deposition in the Paula Jones case. We'd been bringing in lower-level witnesses—stewards, secretaries, Secret Service agents—but now we were getting closer to the president. Clinton claimed executive privilege and/or attorney-client confidentiality covered his conversations with Lindsey.

I believed neither privilege applied. Under established law, executive privilege claims are overcome by the specific, concrete needs of the criminal justice system. That was precisely our situation. And Lindsey was a White House lawyer, not the president's personal attorney.

Mystery faxes and anonymous phone calls to members of the press promised spicy details proving that "Ken Starr's office is completely imploding." Not true; our office remained remarkably united. We had terrific esprit de corps.

But I recognized that the Clinton White House had declared war. We moved immediately to strengthen our ranks. Mike Emmick proved to be an effective recruiter, bringing on board Tom Bienert, a career prosecutor from Los Angeles, and Karin Immergut, an Assistant U.S. Attorney from Portland, Oregon. We also recruited new members of the brain trust—especially academics who could counter the White House's onslaught of constitutional claims impeding our investigation. Some were professors from law schools, including Andy Leipold (University of Illinois), Craig Lerner (George Mason University), Bill Kelley (Notre Dame University), Ronald Mann (University of Michigan), and Ron Rotunda (University of Illinois)—quite a collection of legal minds.

The brain trust tackled a pivotally important question: Can a sitting president be indicted? Renowned constitutional scholar Rotunda and his colleagues concluded—contrary to the Justice Department's stated position—that a president can, in fact, be summoned to the bar of criminal justice. The basic reason: in our constitutional democracy, no one is above the law. But we didn't need to act on the brain trust's carefully considered judgment. Congress had provided the OIC with a road map containing highly specific directions for our journey. We were to take our findings to the House of Representatives for possible impeachment, not to a grand jury for possible criminal indictment.

I stopped watching the news. I encouraged my colleagues to do the same. It made no sense to go home after an exhausting day fighting the White House attorneys and, night after night, watch such press luminaries as Geraldo Rivera and White House functionaries like Sidney Blumenthal spew out venom.

My long-suffering wife, Alice, kept up with all the major newspapers and TV news pundits. Of course, criticism of her husband upset her, but she was determined to know what was being said by the White House and other critics. She would let me know when she felt I needed to pay attention to some fresh tactic or allegation against the office. Only rarely did she show frustration. For a documentary for the A&E network, she made a telling comment: "Sometimes, it seems like a nightmare that won't ever go away and I always think to myself, 'It can't get worse than this.' And it does. Every day it seems to get worse and worse."

The barrage of charges was unremitting. A common theme was: Starr found nothing in all his years poking around Arkansas, looking for something, anything, to pin on the Clintons. Now, in desperation, he was probing into the most private of human relationships. Someone should rein in this prosecutor gone rogue.

I turned to those who had authorized me, asking them to weigh in. Attorney General Reno, however, ran for cover. Time and again, I complained that the Justice Department should either rally to our defense, or if I had in their view gone off the rails, Reno should fire me.

Under the statute, the AG could remove an independent counsel for "good cause." If she had done so, I would not have appealed, as the statute provided, to federal court for review of that decision. To the contrary, I would have headed off to Malibu.

Reno didn't fire me, nor did she defend me. Leaving me in limbo, she remained silently aloof. She deliberately sat on her hands while we twisted in the wind, week after week, with no Monica deal in hand. This was moral cowardice, and I said so to my colleagues. Frequently.

To take sides in the White House-OIC confrontation, Reno said, would intrude into the independence of the investigation. Not so. With the threat to the president's survival growing, she cowardly remained on the sidelines.

The AG's agnostic approach stood in stark contrast to the courageous stand of FBI Director Freeh, who at every turn supported the investigation in ways great and small. Freeh had become one of my heroes. Unlike the DOJ leadership, Freeh stood firm in supporting the basic values of the FBI—not only fidelity and bravery, but integrity. We always had the basic personnel—and FBI expertise—that we requested, and Freeh made sure we had the best that the Bureau had to offer. From beginning to end, he was all in to support the rule of law.

The press continued to camp outside our house in McLean. I learned to wave and say, "No comment . . . Have a nice day," as I settled into the backseat of the marshals' vehicle to leave for the office. With regularity, I would mutter harmless bromides such as: "The investigation is active and ongoing." Or: "We're just seeking the truth."

I repeated the "We're just after the truth" statement enough that some thoughtful observers, such as Ben Wittes of the *Washington Post*, concluded that I was tilting too far in the direction of truth-seeking rather than striving for justice. I saw the two as inextricably intertwined. To do justice, we needed to know the whole truth.

CHAPTER TWENTY-TWO

Closing the Books on Hillary

O N APRIL 25, 1998, WE HAD OUR LAST INTERVIEW WITH Hillary in the Map Room at the White House. She responded to all our questions about legal work she had done for Madison Guaranty as reflected in the previously "lost" billing records. The interviewing team was led by Hickman, with assistance from Bob Bittman, Sol Wisenberg, Pat O'Brien, and me.

Hillary seemed well prepared, not surprised by much except the "Pay off Clinton" check and the Hubbell prison recordings. She stuck with most of what she had said in prior interviews, changing some details to fit newly discovered evidence, like documents found in Vince Foster's attic. Again, she answered many of our questions with "I do not recall," but we had fully expected that. It was more of the same.

Two days later, the entire OIC, including Dash, gathered in our D.C. conference room for a full-day marathon. We were there to decide whether to ask the grand jury in Little Rock to indict Hillary Clinton before its term expired on May 7.

We each had a copy of a three-inch-thick binder containing a comprehensive prosecution memorandum prepared by the Little Rock prosecutors. This "pros" memo, written predominantly by Paul Rosenzweig, would be examined in detail. Paul built upon the work of Bob Bittman, Eric Dreiband, and Pat O'Brien.

The memo outlined our findings with respect to Hillary's conduct in the entire investigation. This included Whitewater, the missing Rose Law Firm records, Webb Hubbell, her legal work for Madison Guaranty and other McDougal projects, as well as her "selective amnesia," those convenient but profound memory lapses under oath.

We were continuing to look at the panorama of Arkansas-related events. We had already determined in late 1997 that the entire body of evidence against the president did not meet the exacting standard that Congress set forth in the independent counsel statute with respect to sending a potential impeachment matter to the House of Representatives.

Now we stepped back to look at the overall picture of Hillary Clinton's actions relevant to our wide-ranging investigations both in Little Rock and Washington, D.C.

That morning, we appreciated the gravity of the moment. We felt duty bound to bring her record before the entire group of lawyers for their evaluation and judgment. This was the final step in the deliberation process. What should we do?

By this stage of the investigation, there were no Hillary sympathizers left among our ranks. There were, however, strong feelings by some that it would be a mistake to seek a grand jury indictment. The investigation had been going on a long time, and the unrelenting criticism continued to take its toll. It seemed increasingly unlikely that we would be able to secure a conviction from a fair-minded jury. I remembered vividly the Perry County Bank trial, in which the evidence was overwhelming, but holdout jurors stood stubbornly in the way of justice.

I guided the conversation so that we focused, to the fullest extent possible, on the merits, not the extraordinary context in which we found ourselves. Outside, the world was absorbed with Monica. Inside the conference room, however, our eyes were trained only on the actions of Hillary Rodham Clinton.

Hickman stood on his feet for hours, making the case for indictment like a lawyer presenting an opening argument. About twenty prosecutors, many who had arrived recently to work on the Lewinsky investigation, sat around the long rectangular table.

Using a whiteboard, Hickman outlined the potential charges and the evidence to support them. He was entirely matter-of-fact, never raising his voice or pounding his fist on the conference room table. He was all business, no emotion.

We were of one accord that Hillary was a liar. She had likely participated in financial crimes back in Little Rock. But many records were missing or incomplete. We never found her time sheets from the Rose Law Firm for 1985 and 1986, the years she did work for Madison Guaranty.

The "jogging incident," with Bill asking Jim McDougal to shift his legal work from Tucker's law firm to the Rose Law Firm, was re-examined. Nothing wrong with that in and of itself, but the switch over from Tucker to Hillary opened the door for us to look carefully at her legal work. And the records did show she had worked on the fraud-infected Castle Grande project.

We found Hillary exhibited extreme high-handedness in the Travel Office purge, but arrogance was not an indictable offense. We also looked at false or misleading statements she made under oath, including to Congress.

Most troubling in terms of Hillary's possible culpability was the question of how the long-sought billing records purloined from her law firm suddenly appeared in the Book Room at the Residence. That room was where Hillary wrote her first book, *It Takes a Village*, just in time for the 1996 reelection campaign.

The evidence seemed to us inescapable, if largely circumstantial. To protect Hillary from federal investigators, Vince Foster had stolen the law firm's business records and brought them to Washington. Copies were later found in a briefcase in the attic of his Little Rock home. That was theft, pure and simple, and could constitute obstruction of justice.

Then, in the wake of Foster's suicide, those records had been furtively removed from his office in the West Wing and hustled into the guarded privacy of the Residence. His office should have been treated as a possible crime scene that night and the following day.

However, when U.S. Park Police arrived, White House Counsel Nussbaum kept them from entering. The FBI was likewise kept at bay. But Nussbaum, Craig Livingstone, David Watkins, Hillary's chief of staff Maggie Williams, and others went in and out of his office without supervision. Why was protocol not followed? Lots of round-robin phone calls had taken place that night and the following day among Hillary, her New York pal Susan Thomases, and Williams. But no one in this "circle of grief" had called Lisa, Vince's widow.

This was the one of the most dangerous facts for Hillary. If, after Foster's death, a set of records relating to her Little Rock legal work had been found, the right thing to do would have been to alert her former law firm of this "discovery" and then produce those records to federal law enforcement. The physical movement of the papers to the Residence showed a determination to keep the records hidden from peering eyes.

After careful evaluation, our ultimate assessment was that Carolyn Huber, who had found the papers in the Book Room, was being honest and truthful. She was in no way complicit in an effort to hide evidence relevant to the investigation. But we could not prove that Hillary had orchestrated the removal of the Rose Law Firm billing records to the Residence.

Throughout the long day, our roundtable discussion was lively. However, at the end of our lengthy deliberation, we concluded that we lacked sufficient evidence to go forward to the grand jury with possible charges against the First Lady. Hillary would not be indicted. All things considered, it was the correct professional conclusion. No one, including Hickman, dissented from that judgment. Hillary would walk.

What would have happened if Vince Foster had been alive, if Webb Hubbell and Susan McDougal had been cooperative, we could only speculate. Each doubtless had his or her reasons for holding back. Webb, her friend and former law partner, had been lavished with money; we could only speculate as to Susan's motivation.

We would keep trying, putting the pressure on. But it appeared that the sun had largely set on the Whitewater investigation, with a few cleanup tasks remaining. My original mandate from August 1994 had largely been finished. I had investigated, I had found what information there was to be found, and I had taken the matter as far as it could go with the information we had.

However, as our meeting was drawing to a close, we reviewed the entire record of Susan McDougal's contempt. The contrast was stark. Susan claimed she would not answer our questions because we were out to get the Clintons. Yet Hillary at least *purported* to answer our questions.

Susan had continued to thumb her nose at the entire legal process. We knew she held a key to the Clintons' involvement in the Arkansas financial shenanigans. Our prosecutors were unanimous. We would seek a grand jury indictment in Little Rock against Susan for criminal contempt.

CHAPTER TWENTY-THREE

Monica in Trouble

HILLARY MIGHT BE SKATING FREE, BUT THE CAMERA-hungry Bill Ginsburg had badly overplayed his hand and profoundly disserved his client.

In February, he had insisted that our office had entered into a binding immunity agreement with Monica. I had never agreed to or signed off on any such pact. For months, she remained in legal jeopardy, though I was loath to request a grand jury to proceed against her on various criminal charges, including perjury and suborning perjury. We counseled ourselves to be patient. The only reasonable course for Monica was to cooperate. We would stay the course.

Ginsburg had filed a motion to enforce the purported immunity agreement. In a closed hearing in March, our prosecutor Rodger Heaton squared off against Ginsburg and methodically shredded all his arguments. On May 1, 1998, Judge Johnson upheld our position. There was no agreement. Monica's potential legal shield had now evaporated.

But so much damage had been done. Ginsburg was still reveling in his celebrity, talking about getting his own TV show. He had given Monica spectacularly poor advice, setting her up to pose with celebrity photographer Herb Ritts for a glamour spread in the June issue of *Vanity Fair,* saying that his client's "libido" had suffered and she needed cheering up.

The optics were disastrous. Here was the most famous intern in the world romping on a Malibu beach in provocative clothes and poses evocative of Marilyn Monroe.

"There's something sickening about a young woman who vamps with an American flag, mocking her role as the silent center of a case that could bring down a president," wrote Maureen Dowd in the *New York Times.*

I could only imagine cheers erupting at the White House as the most dangerous witness against the president was being pushed further into the mud by her own lawyer. For that reckless advice alone, Ginsburg should have been cashiered.

We had to decide what to do next. We didn't trust Ginsburg to negotiate in good faith. We could call Monica before the grand jury, but if she lied, would we then charge her with perjury? I had no heart for that option, but asked Steve Binhak to draw up a draft indictment. Monica's window for trading her truthful testimony in return for immunity was slipping away.

Meanwhile, we sent a subpoena to Ginsburg requesting Monica's fingerprints and handwriting samples. As an accommodation, we agreed to handle the procedure in Los Angeles instead of Washington.

We sent prosecutor Ed Page, who had made his reputation in the DOJ by getting a fraud conviction against Linda Medlar, the ex-mistress of Henry Cisneros, Clinton's first secretary of Housing and

Urban Development. Page had such a calm, low-key manner that Sol nicknamed him Mr. Electricity. I had great confidence in Page. Given his experience with former girlfriends, maybe he could work miracles with Monica and her nutty lawyer.

On May 28, a press mob gathered outside the Wilshire Federal Building in Los Angeles. Monica, Dr. Lewinsky, and Ginsburg arrived at 8:15 A.M. "Kenneth Starr is trying to use her as a pawn to get to the presidency," shouted Monica's father to reporters. "This is unfair. This is totally un-American."

Inside, they were met by Page, who escorted them into the fingerprint area. An FBI agent took her finger- and palm prints, then Page took Monica upstairs to give handwriting samples. As Monica wrote out various phrases, using different pens, Ginsburg objected to certain FBI requests, saying he'd allow negotiations to go forward only if he could take handwriting samples from Ken Starr. Ridiculous.

Page was astonished. The tension in the room was overpowering. Then a female FBI agent pulled him aside and pointed out that Monica seemed under the influence of medication. Excusing himself, Page called FBI experts in Washington to ask if drugs could affect a handwriting sample. The answer was yes, it was possible.

Was Monica trying to disguise her handwriting or was she under the influence of medicine? Page asked Ginsburg if his client had taken any drugs that morning. "No," he snapped. Then Monica whispered to her lawyer. Ginsburg changed his tune, saying she had taken medication but it was nothing that would alter her motor skills. (Later, Monica told her biographer she was taking antidepressants that day.)

The session devolved further and was finally called off at 11:00 A.M. An FBI agent handed Ginsburg a subpoena requiring Monica to complete the exam on June 4, this time in Washington, D.C. It was all so unnecessary. But it took one more boneheaded move by Ginsburg to bring Monica to her senses.

Someone showed her an article by Ginsburg titled "An Open Letter to Kenneth Starr," which had appeared a few days earlier in a California law journal.

"Congratulations, Mr. Starr!" Ginsburg wrote. "As a result of your callous disregard for cherished constitutional rights, you *may* have succeeded in unmasking a sexual relationship between two consenting adults."

Since she had filed an affidavit denying a sexual relationship, and the president had adamantly denied "having sexual relations with that woman, Miss Lewinsky," this assertion by her attorney bordered on malpractice.

By Memorial Day, Monica and her parents had had enough. They fired Ginsburg. In early June, Monica interviewed a handful of Washington lawyers and settled on Jake Stein and Plato Cacheris, two highly experienced and well-respected pros. When I heard the news, I thought, "At long last. What an ordeal we've all been through thanks to this goofball." It seemed like divine intervention.

CHAPTER TWENTY-FOUR

Obfuscating the Truth

Unlike Monica, Bill and Hillary had chosen their courtroom warriors well.

Trained by the legendary Edward Bennett Williams, whose fruits of extraordinary success as a lawyer brought him ownership of both the Baltimore Orioles and the iconic Jefferson Hotel, David Kendall and his colleagues from Williams & Connolly were smart and extraordinarily aggressive. Their job was to protect their client from criminal charges and, in the process, to prevent the truth from coming out. They would fight us every step of the way. They came close to succeeding.

Delay, delay, delay. Obfuscate the truth. Attack the prosecutor, primarily through surrogates. The Williams & Connolly no-holds-barred but entirely legal approach was to overwhelm the other side with superior firepower coupled with superb lawyering.

Just as he had done with Susan McDougal in Little Rock, Kendall closely coordinated with lawyers for potential witnesses who were in the line of fire or just sympathetic to the president.

In the meantime, the White House kept up its relentless charge that the bad guys in the unfolding saga were the overly zealous OIC prosecutors intruding into the president's private life, a moral outrage in a free society. In any event, the president had denied any sexual relationship. Case closed.

Kendall was formidable, but he lacked one important arrow in his quiver—the truth was not on his side.

I was dismayed to discover that Kendall laid claim to a powerful new ally: the Department of Justice. My former professional home, which I held in the highest regard, now abandoned all pretense of neutrality.

I had never met Janet Reno. She had little federal experience; her career was spent as a district attorney in Dade County, Florida. She had been gutsy and courageous during the congressional hearings on the Branch Davidian tragedy near Waco, by saying essentially that the buck stopped with her.

But Reno was no longer the highly principled defender of the rule of law. The prior years of support evaporated. All Janet Reno had to do was to say, internally, to the administration: "Stop attacking the Starr investigation. I personally authorized this inquiry into perjury and possible obstruction of justice. This is serious business, so stand down."

A principled Attorney General would have demanded as much, on threat of resignation.

Yet Reno refused. She had come under withering criticism from the administration for authorizing a number of independent counsels, including one targeting Henry Cisneros, a Clinton favorite. Now, it seemed she had decided it was time to close ranks, and the DOJ got in line.

In terms of principled behavior, Eric Holder likewise left the straight-and-narrow path. For years, he had been a stalwart ally, beginning with his supportive service as a line attorney in the Public Integrity Section, which had detailed my colleagues Jackie Bennett and Rod Rosenstein to the OIC.

Later, as U.S. Attorney for the District of Columbia, Holder had readily agreed to the temporary assignment of a key leader, John Bates, who had questioned Hillary at a deposition, to join the investigation. For all Holder's help along the way, I was most grateful.

That was then, this was now. Reno and Holder, perhaps tired of fighting other battles within the administration, persisted in claiming, lamely, that for them to stand up and be counted for the cause of the honest administration of justice would somehow compromise the OIC's "independence."

This was nonsense. By their inaction, Reno and Holder allowed the White House—and its myriad surrogates—free rein to carry out daily attacks on the OIC's integrity.

Word came to us that Holder was now frequently seen at the White House. If true, that could be entirely legitimate, or it could also mean that the Deputy Attorney General had joined the defend-Clinton squad. We assumed the latter.

But whether the Deputy AG was an active collaborator or not, Clinton's determination to win at all costs significantly compromised the Justice Department's hallowed independence from politics. Just as Richard Nixon compromised the DOJ, so did Bill Clinton.

I first understood that the rug was actively being pulled out from under us by the DOJ when we subpoenaed certain Secret Service personnel to testify to the grand jury about their knowledge of Monica's visits to the White House, including the dates, her extraordinary efforts to gain access to the Oval Office, and times she met privately with the president. We believed they knew a lot.

The Solicitor General's office helped block the subpoenas, presenting an argument that was preposterous on its face, namely, that Secret Service agents should be shielded from testifying before the federal grand jury.

The administration's lawyers had come up with the novel idea that Secret Service special agents could not be required to testify under a previously unheard-of "protective function privilege."

But no such privilege had been recognized over many centuries of Anglo-American law. Congress had never provided for such an evidence-cloaking measure at the federal level. No state had recognized it. This was a phantom doctrine, one cleverly invented solely for the occasion of preventing federal law enforcement agents from doing their sworn duty in the perjury and obstruction of justice investigation into Bill Clinton's actions. Not even Richard Nixon's lawyers had come up with such a bizarre notion.

This frivolous legal argument was unfortunately cloaked with legitimacy by able DOJ attorneys. I urged the department to reject the heretical doctrine. Even if there were such a privilege, it could be waived. To no avail.

This was classic Clintonian maneuvering. Just as he had urged the courts in the Paula Jones sexual harassment litigation to fashion an unknown doctrine—presidential immunity from civil lawsuits against him personally—the president was now advancing through the formal apparatus of the DOJ a dubious constitutional doctrine animated entirely by self-interest, for individual, not institutional, reasons. He was once again using the law to try to shield his personal peccadilloes. (He would later whine about the expensive legal bills he had incurred with all this pointless litigation.)

There were no logical limits to the president's blunderbuss position. The asserted privilege would attach, by way of hypothetical example, to what Secret Service agents overheard the president saying to Webb Hubbell on the golf course about taking care of his financial needs at a time when Hubbell was supposedly cooperating with the OIC's investigation.

For all its weaknesses, the Secret Service's "go silent" approach effectively served the president's overarching strategic objective: buying time. Monica's long period of noncooperation had given Clinton and the White House spin machine ample running room. With time, the prosecutors would likely commit unforced errors. Perhaps they hoped we would go too far, and then find ourselves as subjects of the criminal process. We could, in the meantime, be hammered relentlessly in the press.

Unwittingly, I played right into the White House strategy.

In the preceding three years, I had turned down interview requests time and again. But in late spring of 1998, when journalist-entrepreneur Steven Brill approached me, I considered his request. My relationship with Steve went back well over a decade. We had kibitzed when he launched the highly successful *American Lawyer* magazine in the early 1980s. I viewed him as trustworthy in part because he made a big deal out of not allowing his reporters to use anonymous sources.

He called me from his office in New York and made a pitch to this effect: "Ken, I'm launching a new publication. I'm calling it *Brill's Content.*"

That self-promoting handle should have alerted me that this was an unlikely platform for objective journalism. But as a personal favor to Brill, I agreed to an in-depth interview for his inaugural issue. Tired of being bashed, I hoped that he would do a fair and balanced treatment of the investigation to date.

I reported the Brill request at our regular morning meeting. My colleagues were dubious. Their views of Brill's bona fides were decidedly negative.

"Are you sure you want to do this?" one prosecutor said. "Brill is known to be a snake."

Charles G. Bakaly III, our new press spokesman, agreed that it was a bad idea. I had hired Bakaly on April 13, 1998, at the urging of several friends, and especially my wife, Alice. He was to help stem the hemorrhaging we were experiencing in the court of public opinion.

Stubbornly, I stuck by my agreement. I had nothing to hide. I was also being encouraged to get out and defend the investigation and my own conduct. I failed to consult with Sam Dash.

Instead, I went ahead and sat down with Brill at the OIC office. We talked for well over an hour. Throughout the conversation, I made it clear time and again that I was limited in what I could say. While I believed my role as independent counsel included a responsibility to provide the public with appropriate information, I could not get near, much less cross, an important line, namely protecting grand jury secrecy.

Brill took what I had to say and spun it. The resulting twenty-nine-page article, titled "Pressgate," in the much-ballyhooed June 1998 first issue of *Brill's Content* made it appear as if I were spilling grand jury material to an outsider.

The magazine's editors sent an advance copy to our office in the middle of the day on a Saturday. Wisenberg read it and immediately paged me. "We thought it would be bad," Sol told me. "But it's worse than we could have imagined."

Relying heavily on unnamed sources, Brill's organizing theme in the piece was: The Lewinsky scandal was a scam, manufactured to get Clinton. Starr and his cronies were cultivating and spinning the national press, resulting in unfairly damaging reports with respect to the president and Hillary.

Brill's slanted reporting constituted a blatant distortion of what I had said. I briefly mulled over the idea of filing a defamation action, but knew immediately that was a nonstarter, with a long line of Supreme Court jurisprudence vigorously protecting America's free press. Liability would rest on my being able to demonstrate "knowing falsity" or "reckless disregard of the truth" on Brill's part. The facts were on my side, but the law was decidedly against me.

I surmised that Brill had been put up to this hit job by the Clinton White House or their friendly surrogates. Perhaps not; maybe he was just following his own left-leaning predilections. Later I learned that Steve's latest journalistic venture was being bankrolled by, among others, the left-wing billionaire George Soros, a major Clinton supporter. Either way, thanks to my misplaced trust in Steve Brill, terrible damage had been done to the investigation.

Brandishing the heavily promoted story, the president's legal team marched into court, and accused me of violating basic precepts of grand jury integrity. If guilty, I had committed a crime. I was confident that no grand jury material had actually been disclosed. But we were in for a rough period, distracting us from getting the job done.

Initially, the president's lawyers found a receptive judicial audience in Chief Judge Norma Holloway Johnson, who supervised all matters pertaining to grand juries operating in the federal courthouse. Judge

Johnson was entirely honest and honorable, but she held to a sweeping definition of grand jury secrecy, which was later rejected by the D.C. Circuit. In doing so, this diligent, hardworking judge inadvertently played into the president's hands.

Judge Johnson responded promptly to the alleged grand jury secrecy violation by conducting a conference behind closed doors at 4:00 P.M. on Tuesday, June 16. It went poorly for us. Bittman and Paul Rosenzweig said that David Kendall and his team were nothing short of giddy. Starr's team was going down. The judge expressed her extreme disappointment, essentially accepting Brill's story at face value.

I was on the Metroliner going from New York to Washington, returning from cohosting a conference of appellate judges in New York, when I heard a report of the hearing. Judge Johnson authorized Kendall to take depositions of both Jackie Bennett and me.

I was heartsick. My misplaced confidence in Steve Brill and my belief in my own integrity had led to potential disaster for our entire effort.

At our next morning roundtable, I apologized to my colleagues for my naïveté and stupidity.

"I have no excuses," I said. My colleagues found my blunder difficult to understand. After all, I was an old Washington hand. How could I have been so misguided, especially since I had been forewarned? I had no good answer. The accurate response was that I had been too obliging, too eager to counter the president's attacks, and naively assumed good faith on the part of an ambitious, aggressive journalist.

We had to fight back, to forestall those depositions at all costs. We immediately went to the Court of Appeals. In addition, we responded to Brill's story with a nineteen-page letter rebutting his misstatements and misrepresentations point by point. We heard from Sue Schmidt and Mike Isikoff, who complained that Brill had misquoted them. Glenn Simpson of the *Wall Street Journal* was also misquoted. Brill conceded error after learning that Simpson had tape-recorded the interview.

The appellate court reversed Judge Johnson's order allowing Kendall to take our depositions. But she then appointed a special master, a highly respected retired judge from the District of Columbia local court system, to investigate—all as a result of phony reporting and my own disastrous decision.

There were other blows. I was asked to resign from the Alibi Club, a private group that included the leading lights of the nation's capital. I was miffed. These people had known me for years.

Then my law firm sent a partner to "suggest" I take an unpaid leave of absence. I was too radioactive. Clients were asking questions. Although I knew it was the right and smart thing for the firm to do, this was a grievous blow to my paycheck and my sense of self.

I remember attending church one Sunday during this period. Through the previous weeks, Lon Solomon had been very pastoral, sending notes and reaching out. That day, he preached about bad things that can happen to good people, especially loss of reputation. As we left the church, Lon shook my hand.

"Ken, did you relate to what I was saying?" he asked.

I was so overwhelmed by emotion, I couldn't answer. Silent, unable to form words, I saw my reputation crumbling. I realized I was very prideful, too concerned about what people in my world thought about me. It was a dark moment.

In the drama now swirling around us, Judge Johnson's penchant for secrecy proved, ironically, to aid our ability to move forward. At her direction, the special master conducted his work behind a heavy curtain of confidentiality. Assured of a fair-minded process, we proceeded with our investigation.

To her great credit, Judge Johnson did not stand in the way of our ongoing work, which was focused entirely on the grand jury's truth-seeking endeavors. Day after day, witnesses came streaming in. Many seemed honest and forthright. Others, not so much. But through it all, we were systematically building our case, with the crimes of perjury and obstruction of justice at the core of what we understood, ever more thoroughly, the president had committed. What was becoming clear: The president had blatantly lied in the Paula Jones deposition by insisting he and Monica were never alone, and in the process obstructed justice. But as the pieces came together, we increasingly saw a broader evil at work. The president was abusing his power to protect himself from his own folly.

As if the personal attacks on our team weren't bad enough, then the "leak war" erupted. Embracing the concept of condemning the other side for something your side was doing, Kendall accused the OIC of leaking grand jury information. Untrue.

Only the prosecutor and the grand jurors themselves are legally obliged to maintain absolute secrecy about what happens inside the grand jury room. The prosecutor cannot disclose what the grand jurors are thinking, what the grand jury's ultimate decision may or may not be, or who the prosecutor or grand jurors may want to call as a witness, much less what a witness testified to.

In contrast to these severe and proper limitations on the prosecutor's and grand jurors' ability to speak, a witness can walk out of the grand jury room and describe, accurately or otherwise, what had transpired. So, too, can the witness's lawyer.

Furthermore, in a joint-defense arrangement, lawyers for various witnesses can team up, debrief the grand jury witness or the lawyer for the witness, compare notes, and formulate a joint strategy to fend off the prosecutor.

They can leak the information to the press without attribution. A common tactic for defense lawyers is to describe their sourcing as "sources close to the investigation," which naturally sounds as though the prosecutor (or the FBI) is leaking.

Even more exasperating, the witness, or his lawyer, can outright lie to the press about what happened in the grand jury room. We, on the other hand, had to remain mum about grand jury matters. We just had to take it.

Oddly enough, a huge practical impediment to maintaining confidentiality was the physical location of the D.C. grand jury. In the early phase of our work, as key witnesses were coming and going in their respective grand jury appearances, members of the press were not only allowed inside the courthouse, they were permitted to roam around on the same floor where the grand jury was in session.

Milling around in the courthouse hallway, a witness could neither get in nor get out of the grand jury room without being seen and therefore being subjected to press questioning.

We had one court-authorized method for secreting witnesses in and out, but this required special arrangements with the courthouse security personnel. We were reluctant to make use of that avenue, save for the most sensitive circumstances. We had offered that alternative to David Kendall in connection with the grand jury appearance of the

First Lady. They declined, and she marched dramatically into the courthouse through the front door. The symbolic message: "I have nothing to hide." Smart.

In the face of the alleged leaks, I went stonily silent. We retreated from carrying out what I viewed as an entirely lawful function of providing appropriate information to the public.

The special master, whose identity had not been officially revealed, quietly carried on his work. The Williams & Connolly warriors had been silenced by the confidential process now being played out. The appointment, all things considered, proved to be a blessing in disguise, with its calming effect on the hysteria.

Even though we necessarily adopted a bunker mentality, we continued day by day to make significant progress on the merits. The growing body of evidence was pointing entirely in one direction: Bill Clinton had committed perjury and obstruction of justice in connection with his Paula Jones deposition, and he had been encouraging others to lie. He was also taking affirmative steps to cover up the truth. In doing so, the president was abusing the powers of his office.

We were moving toward a head-to-head confrontation with the president. There was no doubt in the minds of any of my colleagues in the investigation, including those who had voted—twice—for Clinton. Perjury, we believed, constituted a "high crime or misdemeanor" within the meaning of the Constitution. Clinton's obstructionism simply added additional weight to our growing conviction of his criminality.

If he had nothing to hide, if he hadn't committed perjury during the Paula Jones deposition, then why wasn't he forthcoming? Why was he invoking executive privilege? Our office was moving steadily toward a unanimous conclusion. The president of the United States appeared to have committed crimes worthy of possible impeachment, and possibly of criminal prosecution.

Especially damning was the statement of the highly credible Betty Currie, the president's secretary.

In the wake of his deposition testimony in the Paula Jones case on Saturday, January 17, Clinton had summoned Betty to the White House the following day, when Betty always went to church. She testified that the president rehearsed the circumstances of Monica's frequent visits to the Oval Office: "You were always there when she was there, right?" he suggested. "We were never really alone." A lie. The two had actually been alone time and again. Betty knew this full well.

"You could see and hear everything, right?" he said. "Monica came on to me, and I never touched her, right?" The president was not only lying, but he was engaged in witness tampering. He was also blatantly violating Judge Wright's specific directive that he was not to be in contact with other potential witnesses.

Likewise incriminating: The president urged Betty to contact Monica and retrieve various gifts he had showered on her over the course of their long relationship. Betty did as she was directed. She recovered approximately eighteen gifts from Monica and tucked them under her bed.

To her credit, Betty, a person of deep faith, admitted all this. In contrast to her mendacious boss, Betty took the oath to tell the truth seriously.

CHAPTER TWENTY-FIVE

Breakthrough

EVEN AS MY REPUTATION WAS TAKING CONSTANT HITS, things were looking up for the office. We had won a series of important judicial rulings. I was particularly pleased that Judge Johnson determined we had neither violated Monica's constitutional rights on Prom Night at the Ritz-Carlton nor violated any ethical requirements.

And we batted down the president's attempt to claim the bogus protective function privilege regarding the Secret Service.

The outlandish White House arguments over privilege had gotten so crazy that one day our prosecutors arrived at the office to find a memo from the White House arguing the "culinary protective privilege," shielding waiters and cooks in the Residence from testifying about matters observed while serving at state dinners. Pretty soon everyone was laughing at the joke, crafted cleverly by one of our more creative legal writers so that you had to read it all to realize it was phony.

We had tired of jousting with the White House over interviewing

President Clinton. Bittman had sent Kendall six letters asking for his client to be made available for a voluntary interview. The answer was no, or maybe later.

Perhaps we'd have a breakthrough now that Monica had jettisoned Ginsburg. I trusted Jake Stein and Plato Cacheris; both were outstanding criminal defense lawyers of integrity. They'd take care of their client.

By June 1, the OIC was in a considerably stronger position against Monica than we had been in February, when Ginsburg was making nutty demands. We had taken the statements of many witnesses in the grand jury, including Vernon Jordan. We had retrieved the president's gifts to Monica. But we suspected she had another piece of evidence: the blue dress.

On the Tripp tapes, Monica talked about wearing a dress from Old Navy when, during a sexual encounter with the president, it had been stained with semen. Upon the execution of a search warrant, the FBI had recovered a blue dress and had tested it, but it had no such stains. Perhaps the dress had been cleaned, or had been thrown away, if it ever existed.

In early June, Jake and Plato met with me, Bob Bittman, Jackie Bennett, and Sol Wisenberg in a conference room in Washington. Plato did virtually all of the talking, as he usually did when Jake and he worked together. We negotiated the immunity deal, and Plato pulled out his trump card. "We have material evidence that would strongly corroborate her testimony," he told us. We suspected he meant the dress, but he refused to say.

It took time to work out all the details. But we agreed that Monica would be made what prosecutors call "queen for a day," granted temporary immunity. In return we'd be able to ask questions to explore her potential testimony and credibility. I offered a location: my stepmother-in-law's apartment in midtown Manhattan, away from prying eyes in D.C.

I said to Grandma Joan, "Mum's the word." She readily agreed. Although excited about stepping into an odd chapter in history, Grandma Joan was true to her word.

On July 26, I put on casual clothes, donned a baseball cap, and took the train to New York. I tidied up the apartment and spent the night there. The next morning, I went out for bagels and orange juice for our unusual guests.

Monica would be debriefed by Dash, Bittman, Wisenberg, and Mary Anne Wirth, a New York prosecutor with our team who had broad experience in sexual assault cases. I wanted a woman there. A devout Catholic, Mary Anne's nickname in the office was Hallmark, for her warmth and empathy. She was pivotal in our work with the grand jury, and in building the case. Wisenberg, who by this time was a deputy independent counsel, led the day-to-day operations of the grand jury.

I didn't intend to be seen, much less present for the interview. Because Stein was known for his punctuality, I left fifteen minutes before they were scheduled to arrive. I made my way to the nearby Fitzpatrick hotel, where several other members of our team were standing by.

I was gone when a cab drove up. Monica, wearing a blond wig and glasses, got out along with Plato Cacheris, Jake Stein, and Sydney Hoffman, a female associate with Plato's firm. They went upstairs to talk to our team.

The hours wore on, and finally the word came to the Fitzpatrick.

"She's completely believable," our colleagues announced. Sam Dash was effusive in his praise of Monica's powerful memory and winsome manner. With his vast experience, Sam saw her as a credible and sympathetic witness. I was relieved and thankful. At long last, the end was in sight.

Within days, we had worked out immunity agreements for Monica and her mother. On July 30, Monica's lawyers delivered a navy-blue dress to our office. We sent it to the FBI for testing.

Hallmark and another female prosecutor in our office, Karin Immergut, began meeting with Monica at her Watergate apartment, interviewing her in detail over two weeks about her long-standing relationship with the president. Karin had once served as an Assistant U.S. Attorney in Los Angeles; she understood the Beverly Hills landscape in which Monica had been raised. Tall, athletic, and very pregnant, Karin came across as Scandinavian cool. The three women made a strong connection. Soon Monica began knitting something for Karin's baby.

Monica disclosed that she and the president had had ten sexual encounters, which she faithfully documented on a calendar. But the relationship included fifty or so late-night intimate conversations that sometimes included phone sex. She had given him about thirty gifts, including carefully chosen ties. He wore these at various events knowing he'd be photographed, telling Monica later the tie was a message that he was thinking of her. The president had tried to terminate their relationship on February 19, 1996, but they resumed the sexual contact on March 31, 1996.

After each interview session, I talked with the two prosecutors to see where we were. I had already been impressed with Monica's intelligence, as she had run circles around us and our experienced prosecutors on Prom Night. Now, I was astonished at Monica's prodigious memory. Monica remembered who the president had been talking to on the phone during some of their sexual encounters, and what the subject was. She created an eleven-page chart that chronologically listed her contacts with the president, including meetings, phone calls, gifts, messages, and notes.

I sensed a genuine affection and rapport had existed between Monica and Bill Clinton. Their relationship was complex, sparked by physical attraction, but deepened by other human touches.

But for the shutdown of the government, the love affair might never have happened. Monica had become a friend and intimate of the president of the United States due to unusual circumstances. It might have ended when all normalcy returned. Instead, it continued. Bill seemed drawn to Monica, as illustrated by their long late-night chats.

I remembered Clinton's earlier denial that he had not had a sexual relationship with "that woman, Miss Lewinsky." She must have felt a deep hurt and a sense of outright betrayal at a time when she was facing legal jeopardy. Yet he was twice her age and her employer.

Monica told Wirth and Immergut that the president did not ask her to lie, but he didn't have to; he just led her in the direction he wanted her to go. She knew what he wanted and needed to happen. Most of all, she wanted their relationship to continue. But she now knew, thanks to his public statements, that would never happen. Clinton and his surrogates had tried to destroy her reputation. Harming the president was, she said, "the last thing in the world I want to do." But she had to tell the truth. She could lose her immunity if evidence showed she lied.

We made arrangements for Monica to testify before the Washington grand jury. As Hickman would say, the molecules were moving again.

CHAPTER TWENTY-SIX

The President Testifies

W E ARRIVED AT THE WHITE HOUSE FOR PRESIDENT CLINton's grand jury testimony on the afternoon of August 17, eight months to the day after he had given his deposition in the Paula Jones lawsuit.

After months of presidential stalling, we had backed Clinton into a corner. After learning the FBI had confirmed Monica's dress was stained with semen, I asked Bob Bittman to send a letter to Kendall saying that "investigative demands" required the OIC to seek a blood sample from the president.

Though we provided no other information, he would surely guess it was for a DNA test. On August 3, by return letter "to be opened by Mr. Bittman only," Kendall agreed that the White House physician would be made available to draw the president's blood that night.

Bittman and an FBI technician were escorted into the Map Room at 10:00 P.M. Ten minutes later, Clinton, who was hosting a White House dinner that night, appeared and perfunctorily shook the visitors' hands.

A female doctor drew his blood; Bittman noticed the president's face and neck turned bright red.

A day or two later, the FBI gave me the news. The president's DNA matched the semen on the dress. I told no one but Bittman and Hickman. The FBI ran a more sensitive second test; it also matched Clinton's DNA.

Now the day had come for President Clinton to testify before the same grand jury that had been taking evidence from White House staffers. So far, it had not leaked out that we had a deal with Monica— or that she had begun testifying before the grand jury.

After months of no cooperation, I had sent Kendall a subpoena for the president's testimony. I was tired of playing the White House's games. We sparred with Kendall over the terms. He insisted that Clinton would testify, but wanted us to withdraw the subpoena so the White House could say he was presenting himself to the grand jury voluntarily. This was a bad joke, because Kendall had been refusing our polite letters for months, while telling the press they were cooperating fully.

I had some sympathy for the president's situation. Unlike most witnesses, he could not plead the Fifth Amendment; that would likely destroy his political career. But once we withdrew the subpoena, what was to compel him to follow through with his end of the deal? After years of lies, we had no trust he would do the right thing.

Kendall wanted to bring the grand jury from the courthouse to the White House, the president's turf. We declined, realizing that the majestic trappings of his office would be distracting. Kendall refused to have it videotaped. We insisted, because one grand juror could not attend. Finally, it was agreed the president would testify via a live two-way video feed to the courthouse. That allowed the grand jurors to ask questions, as they did with other witnesses.

We prepared for days on end, holding moot court sessions with Hickman playing the role of Clinton. Our prosecutors—Bittman, Wisenberg, Bennett, and me—would each ask the president questions on different topics. We would have four hours. Here was our chance to try out our game plan. Almost everybody in our office attended to render their opinions.

Hickman, who had deposed Clinton, watched him at trial; studied his speeches, television appearances, and body language; parried our best efforts in a drawl that was a dead-on impersonation of the president at his most charmingly southern.

Sol asked if he had ever given Miss Lewinsky gifts.

"Why, Mr. Wisenberg, we are generous in the South," Hickman said. "We may not have much money, but we are always giving gifts. At Christmastime, your aunt might keep some extra gifts on top of the washing machine." On and on.

Asked by Bob Bittman if he had ever hugged Miss Lewinsky, Hickman laughed.

"Now, Mr. Bittman, I'm from the South. We hug in the South. We hug everybody. That's just who we are down South. So yeah, I could have hugged her once." On and on.

Lesson: Don't ask Clinton imprecise questions or he'll run circles round you. It would be hard to cut him off politely.

Hickman drew out his answers, running out the clock. His performance was brilliant, maddening, and disquieting. Two of our newest prosecutors congratulated him at the end of our last mock session. After seeing how well his "President Clinton" had performed, they were skeptical we had a chance.

"You're better than Clinton," one said.

The leaks from the White House started a few days before Clinton was due to give his testimony. Bob Woodward reported in the *Washington Post* that Clinton planned to admit sexual activity with Monica and trusted that Starr would accept his retraction "magnanimously," without trying to humiliate him with "intrusive sex questions."

"Starr wins," a Clinton confidant said. "And we hope he wouldn't feel it necessary to drag the body around the arena."

Clinton's people were approaching Sam Dash, trying to feel him out about what level of disclosure would appease Starr. Keep the embarrassing details to a minimum. Spare the president and his spouse humiliation. Dash told me of these overtures. But we were long past gamesmanship. I remained noncommittal. Yet out of respect for the presidency, I took a leap of faith and directed that the subpoena be withdrawn.

The night before the grand jury testimony, the White House pulled another stunt. Attorney Cheryl Mills called and vetoed the grand jury phone line, as well as our plans to record the president's session with a video camera. No two-way feed to the courthouse meant the grand jurors couldn't ask questions. Our missing juror wouldn't see it without video.

A career prosecutor, Jay Apperson, a relatively new member of our team, didn't buy it. He had dealt with Mills in the past. He believed it was just another White House gambit, designed to force our office to call it off. We pushed back, eventually coming up with a phone line work-around.

I later learned Kendall had just gotten a copy of the sealed video deposition of the president in the Jones case. It wasn't flattering. Now he was trying to call off our agreement to tape the testimony; next he was demanding that we destroy the tape after the missing grand juror saw it. Ad infinitum.

Finally, the day arrived.

Anticipation hung in the air. Washington, D.C., was talking of little else, even though grand jury appearances are supposed to be secret.

On the drive to the White House, I was lost in thought. Bittman told me his father, who was a renowned lawyer, had offered him some advice born of experience. "Don't worry about how you do," he said. "You're just going to have every litigator in the country picking apart your performance for the rest of your life." That made me chuckle. I was feeling that tension all too keenly.

A chair was set up in the Map Room. We noticed the TV lights had a rosy glow. We speculated that, because the president turned scarlet when upset or angry, the rose-colored light was intended to mask his anger for those seeing him on camera.

Our team set up ahead of time, making sure the phone lines worked and the grand jury was ready at the courthouse ten blocks away.

Kendall and his team of lawyers arrived, including Nicole Seligman, Charles Ruff, and Cheryl Mills. Kendall asked me to go outside the room to speak privately. The president would make a statement, and would answer all the questions asked of him. But "to preserve the dignity of his office," he would refuse to go into details about his relationship with Monica.

"You can't ask the president deeply personal questions," Kendall said in a menacing tone, "or I'll fight you to the knife."

I was taken aback. This I had not expected. I returned to my team and told them what Kendall had said. Everyone looked at me in astonishment. They took it as an outright threat.

I had never been spoken to like that by an opposing attorney. That threat undoubtedly reflected the president's deep anger at me personally, and the investigation more generally.

Then I thought, "This is one great defense lawyer." In that instant, I realized he had a pretty empty toolbox. He was doing the best he could.

Kendall was using the image of sharp edges. In his strange warning, I heard the voice of the great litigator Edward Bennett Williams, his firm's founder. It was Williams's philosophy: Gut the opposition. They were doubtless thinking, "We've made Starr's life miserable. Let's keep beating him up and threatening him. He'll make a deal."

But Kendall and the president had nothing to offer. We wanted the truth.

At this point, of those on the OIC team, only Hickman, Bittman, Wisenberg, and I knew about the results of the DNA test. That information had not been shared with Clinton's legal team, but they could guess the results. I now shared the news with the rest of the team, which included Apperson, Bennett, and Mary Anne Wirth. We had the dress. We had less to prove. That lifted some spirits. All we had to do was get President Clinton on the record.

The president arrived and greeted everyone, cordial but somber. Apperson had previously advised Wisenberg, our leadoff questioner: "Ask him what he thinks taking the oath means. What does telling the truth mean to him?"

Genius. Remind him of the seriousness of the oath at the front end. The American people would forgive adultery, as Dick Morris had told the president, but they wouldn't forgive perjury.

That afternoon, President William Jefferson Clinton placed his left hand on a Bible, raised his right hand, and swore to tell the truth, the whole truth, and nothing but the truth.

After Wisenberg's opening, Bittman wasted little time on niceties: "Were you physically intimate with Monica Lewinsky?"

Clinton put on his reading glasses and pulled a piece of paper from his pocket. As unusual as this was, we had expected this—yet another accommodation we had made to his office.

In his prepared statement, he admitted to "inappropriate contact" with Monica, but said, "These encounters did not consist of sexual intercourse, they did not constitute sexual relations as I understood them to be defined at my January 17, 1998, deposition." More important, he admitted he *was* alone with Monica. That seemingly innocuous statement was an admission that he had obstructed justice in the Jones deposition.

He folded the paper and said, "This is all I will say about the specifics of these particular matters."

We called for a short break. Here was the parsing Clinton, just as Hickman predicted. He was admitting to "inappropriate contact," but not lying under oath. Now he was defying us and the grand jury. Our choices were limited. We could play his game and ask no further questions about Monica and their sexual relationship. We could pack up and walk out, giving the White House a victory, because we could not talk about what had occurred. Or we could press on. If Clinton refused to answer, Bittman had a fresh subpoena in his pocket for that exigency.

My decision was to press ahead, to evaluate the situation as it unfolded, but not to play the president's game.

Monica's affidavit, introduced by Clinton's lawyer in the Paula Jones case, had stated she had no sexual relationship with the president. Asked if that affidavit was true and accurate, Clinton had testified it was "absolutely true."

Wisenberg pointed out to the president that he just acknowledged being physically intimate with Lewinsky. Why had he allowed his attorney to tell a federal judge, "There is absolutely no sex of any kind"?

"Well, in the present tense that is an accurate statement," Clinton said.

Wisenberg pinned Clinton down. "That statement is a completely false statement. Is that correct?"

"It depends upon what the meaning of the word *is* is," Clinton said. "If *is* means is and never has been, that is not—that is one thing. If it means there is none, that was a completely true statement."

We were all astonished. Even Hickman had never soared to this level of parsing the English language.

"Do you mean today that because you were not engaging in sexual activity with Ms. Lewinsky during the deposition, that the statement of Mr. Bennett might be literally true?" Sol said, picking up on a note handed to him by Apperson.

"No, sir," Clinton said. "I wasn't trying to give you a cute answer. . . . I was trying to tell you that generally speaking in the present tense, if someone said that, that would be true."

At any rate, he claimed he hadn't been paying attention to what his lawyer was doing in that deposition and had little to offer. Untrue. They had taken a break to discuss this strategy in great detail. He had believed that Monica Lewinsky could offer a truthful affidavit about the relationship. Their "inappropriate contact" had ended, so therefore it was true.

A phone call came from the courthouse. The grand jurors wanted the president to be more specific about the "inappropriate conduct." Clinton danced around the question, explaining how painful and embarrassing it all was, complaining that his enemies were trying to "criminalize my private life."

Another question from the grand jury. Was oral sex included in the definition provided to him by the judge in the Jones deposition?

"As I understood it, it was not, no . . . if performed on the deponent," Clinton said.

He later followed up with a clarification. "Let me remind you, sir, I read this carefully. And I thought about it. I thought about what 'contact' meant. I thought about what 'intent to arouse or gratify' meant. And I had to admit that under this definition that I had actually had sexual relations once with Gennifer Flowers." He was referring to the nightclub singer in Little Rock who had claimed they had a twelve-year affair. "Now I would rather have taken a whipping than done that."

Under Clinton's delusional view, Monica had sex with Clinton, but he didn't have sexual relations with her. His dissembling and outright lies were unconvincing.

I asked the president a few questions about whether he had authorized his aides to invoke executive privilege. Yes, he said, but just out of "an honest difference of constitutional principles" between the White House and our office, not because he was worried about what they would say.

Talking to Clinton was like nailing spaghetti to the wall. He rambled on about the "witch hunt," arrogant and challenging. At the end of four hours, Clinton stalked from the room, clearly furious. But he returned five or ten minutes later to shake our hands, saying he knew we had a hard job. Classic Bill Clinton.

As we left around 6:30 P.M., some on our team were discouraged; he had thoroughly bested us. But I thought we had managed to get the president on the record making significant admissions and telling demonstrable falsehoods. As we went through the transcript later, his lies were magnified. The bizarre statement that "it depends upon what the meaning of the word *is* is" revealed Clinton's contempt for the truth.

At 10:00 P.M., members of the OIC gathered around a television set to watch the president's speech to the American people. Sitting in the Map Room, he looked cool and collected, in stark contrast to the way he'd left the same room earlier that day.

Good evening. This afternoon in this room, from this chair, I testified before the Office of the Independent Counsel and a grand jury. I answered their questions truthfully, including questions about my private life, questions no American citizen would ever want to answer.

Still I must take complete responsibility for all my actions, both public and private. And that is why I am speaking to you tonight.

As you know, in a deposition in January, I was asked questions about my relationship with Monica Lewinsky. While my answers were legally accurate, I did not volunteer information. Indeed I did have a relationship with Miss Lewinsky that was not appropriate. In fact, it was wrong.

It constituted a critical lapse in judgment and a personal failing on my part for which I am solely and completely responsible.

Then came the blame shifting and the prevarications.

But I told the grand jury today, and I say to you now, that at no time did I ask anyone to lie, to hide or destroy evidence, or to take any other unlawful action.

I know that my public comments and my silence about this matter gave a false impression. I misled people. Including even my wife. I deeply regret that.

Now the lip biting.

I can only tell you I was motivated by many factors. First, by a desire to protect myself from the embarrassment of my own conduct. I was also very concerned about protecting my family. The fact that these questions were being asked in a politically inspired lawsuit which has since been dismissed was a consideration too.

Clinton's demeanor underwent a subtle shift, from apologetic to angry. Time to turn the tables.

In addition, I had real and serious concerns about an independent counsel investigation that began with private business dealings twenty years ago—dealings, I might add, about which an independent federal agency found no evidence of any wrongdoing by me or my wife over two years ago.

Not exactly; just because a prosecutor doesn't indict doesn't mean there is no evidence of wrongdoing.

The independent counsel investigation moved on to my staff and friends. Then into my private life. . . . This has gone on too long, cost too much, and hurt too many innocent people.

Which could all be laid at the feet of the Clintons and their law-yers. He moved on with an appeal to the Almighty.

> Now, this matter is between me, the two people I love most, my wife and our daughter, and our God. I must put it right. And I am prepared to do whatever it takes to do so. Nothing is more important to me personally, but it is private. And I intend to reclaim my family life for my family. It's nobody's business but ours. Even presidents have private lives. It is time to stop the pursuit of personal destruction and the prying into private lives and get on with our national life.

Spoken by the same man who had sent his minions out to demean, attack, and intimidate women who had tried to call him to account.

> Our country has been distracted by this matter for too long, and I take my responsibility for my part in all of this. That is all I can do. Now it is time, in fact it is past time, to move on.

Nothing to see here. Move along. He would return to his labor for the American people.

> We have important work to do, real opportunities to seize, real problems to solve, real security matters to face. And so tonight I ask you to turn away from the spectacle of the past seven months, to repair the fabric of our national discourse and to return our attention to all the challenges and all the promise of the next American century. Thank you for watching and good night.

Though advised to apologize, to give an unabashed mea culpa, Clinton had once again let his anger get the best of him. He came off as insincere, upset because he got caught. Despite Clinton's political skills, what came shining through was his disdain for others, his self-indulgence, his willingness to lie. The reaction from the political elite, who now discovered he'd been lying to them all along, was withering.

August 17, 1998, had not gone well for the president. He had sealed his fate.

CHAPTER TWENTY-SEVEN

The Referral

WE HAD COME TO A CROSSROADS ON AUGUST 18. DO WE seek an indictment of the president for various crimes against our justice system? Or do we turn the matter over to Congress for possible consideration of impeachment? The first question raised profound constitutional questions under our system of separation of powers. I quickly set aside the earth-shattering issue of an indictment. In the independent counsel law, Congress had specifically directed us to advise the House of Representatives of any "substantial and credible information" that may constitute "grounds for an impeachment."

We had that level of information in abundance. Our duty was clear under the law: we were to complete our work and submit the matter to the People's House. The sooner the better.

I was deeply concerned about accusations of potential interference with the upcoming midterm elections in November. Though the statute gave us no firm deadline, I believed the imminent campaign season should be able to absorb this new reality and move on from there. I set a flexible deadline: as soon as humanly possible after Labor Day.

To complete the record, we brought in Monica for a return visit to the grand jury after Clinton's testimony. We began piecing together the Lewinsky narrative, supported at every turn by significant evidence developed during the still-unfolding grand jury inquiry—we were determined to be thorough in telling the story, irrefutably proving every element of our case. Sending up a skeletal outline of the record to Capitol Hill would be irresponsible. The document had to be comprehensive and bulletproof.

Clinton's grand jury testimony proved to be the last link in the evidentiary chain. At long last, we had his story. In our morning meetings, we pored over the evidence and worked through drafts of the different components of the report, which we dubbed the "referral."

In that respect, Monica's memory proved to be invaluable. Her recollection of their romps coincided perfectly with White House records of her numerous visits to the Oval Office. Other witnesses corroborated her stories: Betty Currie, Secret Service agents, and other White House staffers.

A core question arose: How detailed should we make the descriptions of their various sexual encounters? A reasonable reader might ask, Why all this salacious detail?

The female prosecutors, Mary Anne Wirth and Karin Immergut, who had worked most closely with Monica, insisted we had to include these explicit details. The president had insisted he had no sexual relationship with Monica because it did not include intercourse. He had relied on his own peculiar, convoluted definition of what constituted sexual relations during his testimony in both his Jones deposition and his grand jury testimony.

By his own mendacity, and then by his continued dissembling, the president had forced our hand. The facts were relevant to the president's guilt. We would set forth those facts, fully and fairly, and face the inevitable criticism that we had gone too far and said too much.

After Clinton's nationally televised temper tantrum, Capitol Hill was uneasily anticipating receiving an impeachment referral from the OIC. Clinton had stubbornly rejected bipartisan advice to come clean before the grand jury. He trusted his own communication powers, knowing he had the considerable benefit of a country at peace. All in all, the electorate was happy. And the Clinton spin machine had transmogrified the puritanical Starr into a hyperobsessive Inspector Javert.

Yet the facts were the facts. As the young lawyer John Adams had argued to the Boston Massacre jury, "Facts are stubborn things." They invariably rise to the surface and demand their own day in court. For the next few weeks, we continued our assiduous review of grand jury transcripts, of White House records and other relevant evidence.

After thorough evaluation of the Whitewater material, we decided not to include anything related to that inquiry. We were unpersuaded that we had the necessary evidence to satisfy the standard of "substantial and credible" information on Whitewater. We deliberately set the standard high—which is what we concluded Congress intended.

Members of our staff, including Sam Dash, were of one accord.

Our research made clear that what constituted impeachable offenses—high crimes and misdemeanors—was ultimately a political judgment entrusted to the unfettered discretion of the House of Representatives.

We wrestled with the number and order of counts of impeachable offenses to include in the referral. Clinton had committed perjury, tampered with witnesses, and obstructed justice in many ways. We began with the clearest charge—the president's perjury, in both the civil deposition and before the federal grand jury.

With Brett Kavanaugh as chief wordsmith, the set of charges proceeded in a logical manner, from the first to the eleventh (and final) count—abuse of power. This last charge represented our judgment that, in various ways, the president had improperly employed the powers of his office—including meritless invocations of the doctrine of executive privilege and the ginned-up invention of the phantom protective function privilege.

Sam Dash sat around the crowded conference-room table as we worked our way through each count. Count 11—abuse of power—created the conceptual link to Watergate. Sam agreed with every count, especially count 11.

On Wednesday, September 9, at 1:30 P.M., I signed the referral letter, saying, "Many of the materials in the referral contain information of a personal nature that I respectfully urge the House to treat as confidential."

Our staff piled a mountain of materials, including relevant grand jury transcripts and exhibits, in a rented white van and drove up to Capitol Hill. With a phone call to alert the officials of its arrival, the 445-page referral—later dubbed "The Starr Report" to my chagrin—was delivered to the sergeant-at-arms of the House of Representatives.

Two days later, on Friday, September 11, the House voted 363–63 to release the report, sight unseen, on the internet. They wanted to "give folks something to chew on over the weekend," said Henry Hyde, chairman of the House Judiciary Committee. "We probably should redact some personal stuff, but it would be too hard to do it."

When we learned the entire report would be posted *without redactions,* or indeed without even a single person reading it, we were perplexed by the House's rushed decision. This possibility had never occurred to us. Congress deals with classified and sensitive material, such as the Bob Packwood diaries and national security materials, all the time. We had expected the House to review and redact. Indeed, the grand jury report in the Richard Nixon impeachment had never been made public.

CNN reported that the Starr Report generated unprecedented internet traffic as government sites were swamped.

"An analogy for what this would be like is to have a local grocery store that supports ten cars in its parking lot. And then, all of a sudden, you are asking it in two days to build a parking lot big enough to support a free day at Disney World," Ken Allard of Jupiter Communications told reporters.

The format of the file uploaded by the House allowed people to search for certain terms, like "dress." As people read, many were scandalized. Why had this salacious stuff been thrown into the public domain with no warning? Even movies have ratings to provide guidance. This document had been released willy-nilly by Congress with no thoughtful consideration given to its effect. For the first time, AOL added several government sites to its list of sites blocked by parental controls.

Down Pennsylvania Avenue, the president changed his tune. At a prayer breakfast the same day the report was posted on the internet, he finally expressed contrition.

"I don't think there is a fancy way to say I have sinned," he said, apologizing to his family, staff, and Cabinet, to Monica and her family, and to the American people. Tellingly, however, his "repentance" was entirely directed at the illicit relationship, not his status as a duly sworn witness obliged to tell the truth under oath.

The *New York Times* issued a scathing editorial on September 12, titled "Shame at the White House."

> Until it was measured by Kenneth Starr, no citizen—indeed, perhaps no member of his own family—could have grasped the completeness of President Clinton's mendacity or the magnitude of his recklessness. . . . A President who had hoped to be remembered for the grandeur of his social legislation will instead be remembered for the tawdriness of his tastes and conduct and for the disrespect with which he treated a dwelling that is a revered symbol of Presidential dignity. . . . By using that great house for sad little trysts with a desperately starstruck employee, by skulking around within sight of nervous Secret Service agents, by conducting erotic telephone games while traveling without his wife, Mr. Clinton has produced a crisis of surreal complexity. . . .
>
> In framing the question in the Jones case, Mr. Clinton's interrogators specified exactly the kinds of intimate activity that Ms. Lewinsky described under oath. By relying on this kind of destructive legal counsel from Mr. Kendall for so long, Mr. Clinton has managed to create one of the most disastrous personal situations in the history of the Presidency.

Then, if possible, it got worse. Judge Johnson authorized the release of his videotaped grand jury testimony. On September 21, the world saw him arguing over the definition of sexual relations, and the meaning of the word *is*.

David Kendall issued a seventy-eight-page rebuttal, calling the referral "little more than an unreliable, one-sided account of sexual behavior."

By this point, our prosecutors were a high-powered central nervous system prepared to assess and evaluate any serious charge of error of fact or interpretation. That powerful set of minds, consisting of some of the most highly experienced prosecutors ever assembled on a single case, were girded for battle. Kendall's missive was a blast from a popgun.

On September 30, Bob Bennett sent a letter to Judge Wright, who held it under seal. He admitted a misrepresentation to the court. Without corrupt intent, he had participated in misstatements to the judiciary. As a matter of honor and professional responsibility, Bennett wanted to set the record straight:

"Pursuant to our professional responsibility," Bennett wrote, "we wanted to advise you that the Court should not rely on Ms. Lewinsky's affidavit or remarks of counsel characterizing that affidavit."

Better late than never.

CHAPTER TWENTY-EIGHT

Stress on the Family

IN MID-SEPTEMBER, OUR DAUGHTER CAROLYN, NOW EIGH-teen, headed off to Stanford University, accompanied by Alice and me, as well as two of my ever-present deputy U.S. marshals.

My children had not been insulated in McLean from the craziness of the Lewinsky phase of the investigation. Even though we had a close supportive community and church, their friends' parents sometimes told my children they disagreed with what their father was doing to the president.

There was a certain unwelcome notoriety in being a Starr. I was on the TV news almost every night. The media was camped out on our street most mornings; the marshals' command post was at the curb.

Carolyn took the disruption, the awareness that her dad's life had been threatened, very much to heart. She could see the pressure I was under. It was difficult not to be able to discuss the investigation freely. But I couldn't. I tried to be upbeat, to focus on what was going on with their schoolwork, extracurricular activities, and friends.

After graduating from high school in May, Carolyn spent the summer in England, where no one knew who she was. In early September, the press reported that my daughter would be attending Stanford, along with a famous young woman, Chelsea Clinton, now a sophomore. Suddenly Carolyn came under attack.

A newspaper columnist for the *Guardian* wondered how Chelsea would react to "the daughter of her father's tormentor" arriving on campus. Comedian Jay Leno made a joke on his late-night show about Carolyn going to the West Coast to spy on Chelsea.

The prevailing theme was: "Who does Carolyn Starr think she is? There are four thousand colleges in America? Why can't she stay out of Chelsea's way?"

But Carolyn had decided she wanted to go to Stanford during her sophomore year in high school, when she attended a weeklong Japanese language and culture orientation on the Palo Alto campus before heading to Japan. When she was selected for early admission to Stanford, she thought we would be living in Malibu by the following year.

Flying to the West Coast with my deputy marshals to get her enrolled and moved into a dorm required us to board the airplane from the rear, before the other passengers, and to wait until everyone else had departed to get off. We arrived in Palo Alto on September 16 and checked into the Cardinal Hotel, our base for three days, along with the ubiquitous marshals.

Stanford had experience dealing with famous students. The school newspaper was prohibited from reporting on the offspring of well-known people except in their capacity as students, limiting intrusive gossip. At the convocation for the seventeen hundred incoming freshmen in the Quad, the president of the university was giving his welcome when aides stood up to block photographers from taking pictures of Carolyn.

That afternoon, we had an outdoor lunch with the other parents and met Provost Condoleezza Rice. "We have many friends in common," she told us with a smile, referring to my days in the Bush administration.

Alice and I left the campus like normal parents after getting Carolyn settled in the coed dorm. However, the second night, campus police gave her one of those huge cell phones, as they were concerned about her safety. During orientation, she accidentally left the gadget behind and two men in dark suits tracked her down. "Where were you? Where's your phone? We couldn't get in touch with you."

Carolyn explained, but the officers were not mollified. Within hours of her arriving on campus, the threats had started. One agent told her, "You're not going to be alone anymore, young lady."

The deputy marshals read to me one vivid, nasty letter promising to do Carolyn bodily harm, written by a professional man living in an affluent community in East Bay. When FBI agents interviewed him, the man was devastated and his spouse appalled.

The marshals informed us that they considered the ominous threats serious. From now on, our daughter would have individual protection by deputy U.S. marshals, like Chelsea Clinton, who was protected by the Secret Service.

Carolyn's deputy marshals were all young and tried to blend in with the students. The detail included twelve agents—six for each twelve-hour shift—with two stationed in the hallway of her dorm, two in a command post in the parking lot of her dorm, and two off duty. Four marshals accompanied her to classes, football games, even went on dates with her.

There were tears. Each month I was briefed on the continuing threats against her. Alice and I couldn't give Carolyn what she wanted the most: to be a normal student.

My son, Randy, had it a bit easier, but he worried about how his mom and dad were withstanding all the stress and negative press. By now a sophomore at Duke, only his closest friends knew who his father was during the Whitewater phase of the investigation. But in January 1998, he was coming back to his dorm when a senior asked him if he had seen the news on CNN.

"Hey, Starr, I think your dad is going to impeach Clinton," he said. Now everyone knew.

Randy also received eight to ten threats and nasty notes in his mailbox, probably not from Duke students, based on the grammar. He wasn't worried. He was living in a fraternity house with sixty other guys. The marshals apparently didn't think the threats were serious enough to warrant protection. Even so, it seemed like every few days he had to defend his dad.

He later told me it upset him that his father was deemed to be some right-wing zealot, unfairly targeting "a gregarious, brilliant, if a bit flawed (in a wink-wink sort of way) president."

Things heated up for Randy even more when the Starr Report was released by Congress. Seeing his last name, Starr, literally everywhere, on every TV screen, was truly tough. He became a more private person, and after graduation in 2000, moved to New York City to work at Salomon Smith Barney, where he could become anonymous again.

In mid-October, a few weeks after we got Carolyn settled in at Stanford, I was back home in McLean. One morning, I was climbing into the backseat of the U.S. marshals' town car when an eerie group of shrieking actors clad in black-and-white Puritan garb suddenly emerged from a van parked on our suburban street. One man wielded a bound copy of "The Starr Report" as a group of women ran around the car, banging on the window, hollering about witch hunts.

The actors yelled and screamed epithets in the direction of our Brady Bunch house. As the marshals and I pulled out of the driveway, with cameramen filming all the while, I spotted filmmaker Michael Moore, dressed in his customary slovenly way.

"That's Michael Moore," I said to my deputy marshal friends. "Contact the Fairfax County police. See if he has a license to demonstrate on the streets of McLean, causing a ruckus and blocking the driveway."

The word quickly came back from county law enforcement authorities. Moore had no license. But he had something better. The First Amendment. The Fairfax County authorities wouldn't interfere for hours. That amateurish—and erroneous—analysis was put to the test by our concerned neighbor, Donna Hogan, who confronted Moore.

"You should be ashamed of yourself," said Donna, who had three school-age offspring. "There are children on this street!"

It was, in fact, time to hustle kids off to school, and Alice couldn't leave the house. To avoid Moore's hired disrupters, my thirteen-year-old daughter, Cynthia, in junior high, was forced to exit our home by the back door, climb through the wooded backyard, hop over two fences, and run through two neighbors' properties to reach safety. Donna Hogan picked her up and took her to school.

Sobbing, Cynthia arrived at school two hours late. Her adviser—known for being the strictest teacher in the school—took her into his office and comforted her. He promised she didn't have to remain in school that day, and brought Cynthia's homework to her. It was an act of kindness she always remembered.

After Moore's actors eventually abandoned our street, they headed to Capitol Hill, invaded congressional offices, and some got arrested. Moore no doubt felt he was just aggressively doing his job, but his stunt was very upsetting to the families in our neighborhood.

A few kids in Cynthia's class made mean comments (as you would expect with teenagers), but most were just curious and supportive, thinking it was cool to have an "infamous" father. It helped that she went to Potomac School, where her teachers and adviser were acutely aware of the situation and would not tolerate bullying.

I would come home late almost every night, but still tried to be a loving, upbeat father and husband. I never brought work with me or discussed what happened that day or in the news. That was frustrating for Alice and the kids, but home was for family and for relaxing after a stressful day.

And "stressful" was the only word for my life at that point, though the tide was turning in our favor.

CHAPTER TWENTY-NINE

My Testimony

IT QUICKLY BECAME EVIDENT THAT EVEN WITH DAVID KEN-dall's rebuttal, the House had no interest in retrying the facts.

David Schippers, a hard-nosed Chicago lawyer brought in as special counsel to the House Judiciary Committee, visited my office several times to explain that the OIC's role was not limited to the referral. The Judiciary Committee would hold hearings—after the midterm elections in November—and there would be only one witness: the independent counsel. I was to fly solo in the witness box.

This was dispiriting. In effect, I would be on trial, not the president. Pushing back, I told Schippers that our work had been done thoroughly. Our labors had been completed in the face of many White House roadblocks and attacks. We had held nothing back from the House of Representatives.

Schippers was polite but firm. The OIC had done its job thoroughly and well. However, in the committee leadership's view, the optimal approach going forward was for the "author" of the report to come up to the Hill and testify in open session under oath. I would be sworn in, and be obliged to tell the truth, the whole truth, and nothing but the truth.

It was abundantly clear that Schippers wasn't just politely sounding me out to get my reaction, nor was he looking for my guidance. He was telling me what was going to happen. Lacking enthusiasm, I agreed without saying or even thinking about the combative option: "Send me a subpoena." Weighing in my assessment was this: it was apparent that Dave Schippers was firmly on our side in terms of the strength and reliability of our submission. Whether impeachment should follow or not as a remedy for the president's long course of misconduct was a question for the House.

The stage was set for the nationally televised confrontation with the Democrats: Starr, appearing alone, in front of the entire committee. I knew the Judiciary Committee room well from my days as chief of staff to Attorney General Smith during the Reagan years. It was the squawky roost of the most liberal voices in the entire House of Representatives, including Chuck Schumer, who had just been elected to the Senate from New York, and Detroit's John Conyers, destined to be drummed out of the House two decades later due to his own sexual-harassment improprieties. But the die was cast. I would testify. We bade farewell to Schippers and prepared for the onslaught to come.

Meanwhile, the special master conducting the leak investigation emerging out of the *Brill's Content* episode concluded his elaborate review of our office in October. He rejected the proposition that I or any of my colleagues had improperly disclosed grand jury information.

I felt the weight of the world had been lifted from my shoulders. But I realized I had brought this on myself and my colleagues. We had been dragged through a painful and lengthy process. The sense of vindication was tempered by my own foolhardiness in the first place, but we could press ahead without that terrible sword of Damocles dangling over our heads.

No sooner did I move on from that chapter, though, when the hopelessly politicized DOJ leadership came after me.

Shortly before my scheduled testimony, I went to the fifth floor of Main Justice for a meeting with Janet Reno. I wanted to discuss the escalating criticism that I had failed to disclose contacts and communications years earlier about the issue of presidential immunity from suit. I viewed all of this as wildly irrelevant political rhetoric. But I thought it wise to alert the Attorney General that I had been contacted by my predecessor, Bob Fiske, who explored the possibility of his office preparing an amicus brief addressing that issue.

Bob Bittman and I entered the Attorney General's conference room aware that we were not there to receive Justice Department awards. We had been under assault, and the department's leadership had not stood up for the office. That eroded confidence in the honest administration of justice.

Reno sat at the head of the long rectangular table. I was on her left, and Holder at her right hand.

I explained about Fiske. She asked a few questions but seemed uninterested—or distracted. Then she read a set of talking points from a single sheet of paper. A number of allegations of OIC misconduct had been brought to the department's attention. There were demands from Capitol Hill that "Starr needs to be investigated."

She stared fixedly at the paper, not looking up. It was not a conversation. It was as if she were reading a judgment and making sure she got each word exactly right. There was no expression of empathy or concern. She conveyed an attitude that said, "This is the way it is. Life is tough." I glanced at Holder, who gazed benignly at the AG. The thought shot through my mind: he wants her job.

A blood sport was now being played on the fifth floor of my beloved Justice Department. I speculated what was behind this ill-timed assault.

During Reno's first term, she had appointed numerous independent counsels to investigate matters in the Clinton administration. But in her second term, she steadfastly refused to appoint one to investigate extraordinary allegations of potentially illegal foreign campaign contributions. In the face of a recommendation by FBI Director Freeh, Reno stubbornly refused to seek the appointment of an independent counsel. When it came to independent counsels, the Clinton administration had had its fill.

The news that the OIC was under investigation was a gut punch, and I received it with ill grace. I was deeply angered by what I viewed as an ultimate sellout. I knew I could not get up and storm out, that I had to remain calm. I did, but I spoke with firmness and determination.

This was a challenge to the independence of our office, I said. It was up to her to remove me or not. But I was not going to allow the DOJ to go poking around our files, interviewing our people, and the like.

After all, Reno reported to the president, and here she was announcing an investigation of the president's so-called tormenter. Nothing in the independent counsel statute suggested that the Attorney General had such authority.

Indignant, as I was leaving I coldly remarked that the fact of this meeting better not leak. But by the time Bittman and I got back to the office, Mike Isikoff of *Newsweek* had called to inquire about the DOJ's investigation of the OIC. Holder was able to report to the Clinton White

House that Reno had authorized an investigation into Starr's operation. I later learned that she viewed my reaction that day as "sanctimonious." Fine by me. I was standing firm.

We drafted an opening statement. My written testimony needed to put the Lewinsky phase of our four-year investigation into the broader context of Arkansas, the Madison Guaranty trials, and the rampant criminality that had occurred in Little Rock. It needed to be clear, comprehensive, and readily understandable.

By now, the fourteen convictions in Arkansas were a distant memory in the national consciousness. However, though we believed Jim McDougal and David Hale, and were convinced that Bill Clinton had lied, we could not say that we had "substantial and credible" evidence that he had committed fraud or perjury in the Arkansas phase of our work.

Schippers had made clear that I could take as long as I wanted, including reading the entire statement rather than the usual summary, with the written statement submitted for the record. By Chairman Hyde's ruling, I would not be interrupted during the opening statement, however long it might be, but then the onslaught would begin. It reckoned to be a long day.

Lawyers prepare carefully for oral arguments, and I viewed this appearance as the oral argument of a lifetime. At the urging of several friends, I called my dear friend from Reagan days Merrie Spaeth, in Dallas, for help. Merrie had been a White House Fellow assigned to the FBI with Director Bill Webster, and media relations director for President Reagan; she was married to my DOJ colleague and fellow Texan Harold ("Tex") Lezar. Her public relations firm, Spaeth Communications, boasted an impressive array of corporate clients, but Merrie hadn't forgotten her friends back in D.C. I asked her to put me through the always-humbling moot court paces, with the video camera rolling.

To be effective, the moot court inquisitor needs to come at you hard. Along with her colleague Judi Nardella, a longtime friend from Northern Virginia who ran Merrie's D.C. operation, Merrie posed all the tough questions, and then some.

From the outset of our long practice session on November 16, Merrie attacked, role-playing a clever Democrat on the House Judiciary Committee. At every turn, she egged me on. Her unrelenting bearbaiting assault eventually resulted in my erupting in ugly righteous indignation. I was practically sputtering. "How dare you challenge our motives? Instead of playing partisan games, Congressman, why don't you look at the overwhelming body of evidence. The facts you're conveniently ignoring cry out that the president is guilty of serious crimes against our justice system!"

Merrie showed me the videotape. "Do you like that person, Ken?"

My face was contorted and furious. I knew immediately I had to control my temper. I could not afford to lose it during my testimony. I steeled myself for another round.

As Merrie's brickbats continued, I grudgingly restrained myself and remained calm. Thanks to Merrie and Judi, I had gotten the venom out of my system. It was a reminder that a flare-up of temper, especially when I got tired, would be horribly self-defeating.

I knew that the Democrats—even though many of whom loathed what the president had stupidly done, especially his cover-up—would play to the cameras and to their home base. I didn't expect any Democrat to express concern in the nationally televised hearing about the president's lawlessness and arrogance.

The congressional midterm elections in early November had not been a GOP bloodbath, but it was a spanking. The American people were not keen on impeachment and they voted accordingly. The president was once again flying high. He had recovered from the dog days of August and his pitiable performance on national television in the wake of his ill-fated grand jury testimony.

All seemed forgiven. The president was not only the Comeback Kid, he was also Mr. Lucky, as the country remained prosperous and at peace. Now here came the judgmental Republicans and their hit man Starr.

CHAPTER THIRTY

The Hot Seat

T HE JUDICIARY COMMITTEE HEARING, CHAIRED BY RE-publican Henry Hyde of Illinois, convened at 10:00 A.M. on November 19.

I entered and sat down alone at the witness table, situated close to the more junior members of the committee. I hadn't remembered how intimate the sprawling hearing room could be when filled to capacity. Behind me were a half dozen members of the OIC staff, including Sol Wisenberg, Brett Kavanaugh, Bob Bittman, Charles Bakaly, and Julie Myers, a young lawyer from private practice in Chicago who had joined the OIC in early 1998. I wanted my senior prosecutors and contributors to the referral there to symbolize the solidarity of our team.

Now, with standing room only, the chamber seemed to close in on me. I felt as if I could almost reach several of the representatives if I stood up and extended an arm to shake hands. I raised my right hand and took the oath to tell the truth, and began my opening statement at 10:48 A.M.

From the outset, I laid out the case carefully and methodically. I sought to make it clear that we were providing the committee with evidence and legal analysis. It was entirely up to the committee what to do with our submission, including tossing it in the trash can.

With the Starr Report in the hands of the American people, my prepared statement followed closely the structure of the referral. With no dissent within our ranks, my colleagues and I believed the ten counts of perjury and obstruction of justice were rock solid. Those built step-by-step to what we viewed as the capstone, the eleventh accusing the president of abusing the power of his office. He had employed the powers of his high office to stand in the way of justice and the rule of law. For self-interested reasons, the president had invoked executive privilege, a privilege entrusted to protect the presidency in our system of separated powers.

His months-long hiding behind the phantom shield of the Secret Service's make-believe protective function privilege was an especially egregious abuse of presidential power, and wasted the time and resources of both our office and the DOJ. The president had also influenced members of the Cabinet, who were confirmed by the Senate to occupy their high offices, to go before the American public and lie to protect him. Clinton had directed a White House employee, Betty Currie, to gather and hide the gifts to Monica, all of which were relevant evidence. Even worse, the president had indirectly encouraged Currie and others to lie, just as he had encouraged Monica by his own example.

In short, the president had employed the official levers of power to escape the basic demands of America's system of justice. Abuse of power stood at the center of the president's behavior; his other crimes would send an ordinary citizen to jail.

The president had not just indulged in a lengthy illicit relationship with a subordinate in the workplace, and then continually lied about it under oath. He had gone far beyond "lying about sex." The president had summoned up his powers as the nation's chief executive to obstruct—month after long month—the orderly process of justice.

The grilling went on hour after hour. As the day proceeded, I scanned committee members' faces for reactions. Lawyers do that with judges and juries, reading body language and drawing inferences. Am I connecting? You can usually tell.

I believed, from her facial expression, that I was making a basic emotional connection with one of the most partisan members on the minority side of the aisle, Representative Maxine Waters from Los Angeles. From her perch on the bottom row of the multitiered committee room, we were physically quite close to each other. In contrast to her nearby colleague from Texas, Sheila Jackson Lee, who scowled at me throughout the day, Representative Waters's face seemed surprisingly gentle, at times even empathetic. Then came her turn to question me.

She skewered me with gusto. I saw her previously soft features harden into a fixed, menacing stare. "No justice-loving American can respect the ill-gotten, ill-conceived, convoluted allegations based on the investigation of a private personal sex-related affair," she said. "Mr. Starr's obvious bias and dislike of the president, his investigatory tactics and his flimsy case, does not meet the constitutional standard for impeachment."

I had badly misread the situation. Or perhaps Representative Waters got back into character. She lashed out with venomous enthusiasm. She did not take kindly to the sex patrol's intrusion into the personal life of America's "first black president" (as Clinton was called) and blamed the shock and horror that had been visited on his family on me.

The chairman finally cut off her intemperate rant. Her astonishing "flimsy case" broadside demonstrated that she had simply closed her eyes to the evidence.

I made the point in different ways, time and again, saying, "We found the facts. We didn't make up the facts. It's now up to you to decide what, if anything, to do with those facts."

Our team followed my testimony on TV back at the office. Late in the day, they were alarmed to see that Sol, in plain view behind me, was nodding off as millions of people watched. Someone paged a short message to another prosecutor in the room: "Tell Sol to wake up!"

The Republicans, to a person, were empathetic and open to hearing what I had to say. The headwinds created by the disappointing election returns earlier in the month seemed, at least for the time being, to have gone away. The GOP members focused on the facts and their implication. Every single member seemed to treat the record we had furnished to the Hill as essentially undisputed and authoritative.

The most intriguing comment came deep into the hearing from Representative Lindsey Graham of South Carolina. With his charming southern style, Lindsey observed that he had been asking himself whether this entire episode was *Peyton Place*, a sexy TV drama of a prior decade, or was this the stuff of impeachment. As he continued, without consulting notes, Representative Graham's eyes shifted over to the Democrats. He was talking to them, not to me or the cameras.

Graham, a trial lawyer, got their attention. The audience sensed something different was happening. Camera shutters snapped away. After my long testimony, everybody was electrified. Would Graham break ranks with the GOP and join the rock-solid Democrats arrayed in opposition?

Teeing up the issue, the homespun country lawyer Lindsey Graham then brought his Hamlet-like speech to a conclusion. He rendered his judgment: The case was not about sex and *Peyton Place* philandering. It was about a president flouting the rule of law, committing perjury and then encouraging others to lie. Lindsey Graham got it.

Concluding for the Republicans was Mary Bono of California, widow of former entertainer Sonny Bono, who had tragically died on a ski slope. A nonlawyer on a lawyer-dominated committee, Bono represented constituents in the Southern California desert who were probably unenthusiastic about the impeachment drama under way across the continent.

But she seemed determined to do the right thing, as opposed to taking the politically expedient course. Press reports had placed her in the "undecided" camp, but as her formal statement unfolded she was clearly taking her responsibilities seriously. To Representative Mary Bono, this was not *Peyton Place*. This was about the solemn legal obligations of the nation's chief executive.

Toward the end of the day, the time finally arrived for a much-anticipated confrontation with the president's lawyer, David Kendall, whose tactics and scorched-earth litigation had dragged out our investigation for many months. Under the committee's protocol, Kendall would interrogate me after all the members had taken their shots.

Just before the showdown began, my friend Paul McNulty, on Chairman Hyde's staff, sat me down in the chairman's offices off the hearing room and said, "Ken, I know you must be very tired. But you have to summon all your energy and strength. The square-off against Kendall will be watched by the entire nation. You've got to be at the top of your game."

Oddly enough, I was not disturbed. I felt entirely at peace. At the same time, I wondered if the combined litigation armada of the White House and Williams & Connolly had found any chink in our armor. Had we gotten some material fact wrong? I had no reason to doubt the accuracy of our referral, but the fleeting thought occurred: Has Kendall found something?

The hearing resumed at 8:30 P.M. Kendall, seated at a table to my right, began his questioning. I expected a full-blown Williams & Connolly onslaught to try to poke holes in the record. To my surprise, Kendall did not even try to deconstruct the mountain of damning evidence arrayed against his client. Instead, he trained his guns on the investigation itself. He was going after our methods, not our conclusions.

That was a smart move, as the hours of hostile questioning from Democrats had entirely failed to draw the evidence into serious question. And, at a public relations level, I was potentially vulnerable to defense-lawyer hammering, since the caricatures in the press were highly negative. Halloween masks of scary Ken Starr worn by trick-or-treaters the prior month sent a strong message about my image across the country.

Defense lawyers are wont to say, "If you have the facts, pound the facts. If you have the law, pound the law. If you don't have either the facts or the law, pound the table and attack the prosecutor." That's precisely what Kendall did.

Even though I had remained on the hot seat for over twelve hours, I felt strangely energized during Kendall's barrage. This was lawyer against lawyer, one-on-one. This was no longer high-stakes politics and posturing for the constituents back home, or seeking to curry favor with the White House. This was a superb Washington lawyer practicing at a high level, with me as his sole target.

Not in the least fatigued, I felt in command and in control. Kendall did well, but at every turn I parried his thrusts with reasonable success. Listening to myself, as lawyers are oddly able to do, I sounded confident without coming across as either obnoxious or overbearing. Throughout Kendall's interrogation, I kept reciting Scripture to myself for strength and comfort. Abruptly, the exchange with Kendall was over.

Chairman Hyde, who had remained unruffled and dignified throughout the stormy proceedings, brought the hearing to a close with some kind words about the guy sitting, still all alone, at the counsel table.

To my pleasant surprise, the audience rose and gave me a standing ovation, joined by many of the Republican representatives. The Democrats remained glumly seated. The day had not gone well for them.

I later learned that the public opinion polling shifted throughout the day from a solidly negative, anti-impeachment position to a significant majority polling in favor. By the time the hearing concluded, the decision had been made. The House Judiciary Committee agreed to debate several counts of impeachment.

With my years in and around courthouses as a lawyer and judge, I felt that throughout the hearing I remained judicious and restrained. I had walked a fine line, trying to answer the questions honestly, but not turn myself into an advocate for impeachment.

When the chairman adjourned the hearing, it was around 11:00 P.M. I went into the committee offices and plopped down. Well-wishers came in to express congratulations about my performance throughout the long day.

I felt profound relief. I said a silent prayer of thanks. My strength had held up. I had never requested a recess or break, but now I was mentally exhausted.

The marshals ferried me home quickly. I made it to McLean around midnight. Alice had beaten me there. She had the television on; the news commentary was flowing freely. It was clear the day was being taken seriously and not simply dismissed.

The next morning, I was still at home when CBS reported that Sam Dash had resigned.

I had, in Sam's view, transformed myself during the course of the hearing into an advocate for impeachment, not simply a lawyer presenting facts and providing answers. I strongly disagreed, as did our entire legal team.

I was stunned, yet not really surprised. Sam had come under unrelenting pressure from his Democrat colleagues. He didn't call me in advance. He just did it. His resignation made page-one news in every major newspaper across the country. His resignation stung, sending a message that my ethics counselor was so outraged by my actions he had no choice but to resign.

I didn't call him up to complain; in fact, we never had occasion to speak again. To this day, I very much regret that. Sam was such a large figure, at times controversial and not well liked by some of my colleagues, but I appreciated what he had brought to the investigation. I tried to take the longer view of these events. How significant was it that Sam Dash had resigned? I viewed it as a personal rebuff, but not a challenge to the integrity of our work.

Sam and I had strongly agreed on count 11, presidential abuse of power. That would be largely set aside during the House's deliberative process. The reaction of the abuse-of-power skeptics—including Republican members of the House—surprised me. This wasn't an obscure legal doctrine. This is what had brought Nixon down. The president employed his power and prerogatives to further an enterprise aimed at shielding himself from the rule of law.

My sense was that in the avalanche of facts, many of which were salacious, House members were unable to adequately reflect on the significance of the president's misuse of constitutional protections. This was the constitutional lawyer in me. I felt the structure of the entire referral led to the mountaintop of count 11. Instead, the members got lost in the forest of facts along the way. The debate that ensued was the poorer for it.

CHAPTER THIRTY-ONE

Media Madness

W HEN I EMERGED FROM THE HOUSE IMPEACHMENT
hearing, I looked forward to doing a long-discussed, elaborately
negotiated interview on ABC News's popular program *20/20*. Finally,
I would be able to communicate publicly in detail the goals and methods of our investigation.

A senior network producer, Chris Vlasto, had interacted with our
colleagues over the years, including in Little Rock. Chris had developed friendships among various folks swept up in the Little Rock phase
of the investigation, Jim McDougal among them. In my simple taxon-
omy, Chris was squarely in the media camp of truth seekers. The Clinton White House hated him, as it did other truth-seeking press people,
especially Sue Schmidt of the *Washington Post*.

We sifted through various invitations, as virtually every media
platform on the planet was eagerly seeking an extended on-camera interview. Prior to the November hearing on Capitol Hill, Chris had
worked up the concept of an hour-long, taped interview with one of

ABC's most respected reporters and anchors, Diane Sawyer. Trusting Chris, we agreed to the ABC proposal. The taping would follow soon after my Judiciary Committee testimony, and then be aired during Thanksgiving week.

I should have turned around and walked out the door when we showed up at the designated place for the taping, which turned out to be a nondescript building far removed from ABC's downtown D.C. studios. In contrast to the regular network operation situated across the street from the Mayflower Hotel in Washington, a makeshift studio had been set up, creating a cold, forbidding atmosphere of gloomy darkness. It was ridiculous. With no preliminaries, and in a frosty atmosphere, I sat down, got miked up, and Sawyer launched an assault.

The announcer set the stage: "The tables are turned. Now it's the prosecutor's turn to be grilled."

Jettisoning her usual Kentucky charm, Sawyer immediately went on the offensive. She lambasted me for producing "demented pornography, pornography for puritans." On and on. When she asked me about the tone of the referral, I was matter-of-fact: "Diane, don't fault career prosecutors for telling the truth."

A rhetorical question from Sawyer: "Are you part of a right-wing conspiracy?" I had the presence of mind to answer: "No. I don't know that there is one." That was all Hillary-generated nonsense, intended to avert the nation's gaze from her husband's crimes. She was a systematic enabler, in the White House no less, just as she had been in Little Rock, viciously attacking the various women who came forward to say they were Bill's paramours, including Monica Lewinsky.

About the president, I offered my honest opinion. Clinton was "extraordinarily talented, wonderfully empathetic." But I believed then, and now, that he was a terrible example for others called to testify truthfully in our legal system.

"I think perjury—lying under oath and encouraging lies under oath—does go to the heart and soul of what courts do," I said. "And if we say we don't care, let's forget about courts and we'll just have other ways of figuring out how to handle disputes. Let's abolish the judiciary. But as long as we have the courts—I think any judge worth his or her salt would say, 'We cannot tolerate perjury.'"

Sawyer asked if she had the right to ask me if I'd cheated on my wife. As if adultery were the issue.

"I have not been unfaithful to my spouse," I said. "I'm not trying to pat myself on the back, but I've tried to live by what I believe is my obligation and my responsibility."

After about an hour, I left the makeshift studio feeling as if I had been set up. There was not the slightest hint that Diane was even vaguely aware that the president had forced our hand. She ignored the fact that Clinton had denied under oath the key element of the Bill-Monica relationship, which in turn was the pivotally important fact in assessing whether the president had committed perjury both in the Paula Jones deposition and then again in the federal grand jury.

Sawyer and her editors brushed past all that. She wanted to taunt me and demean the investigation. She wanted the opportunity to attack the guy who revealed the facts, a bit of an irony for a journalist. Unwisely, we gave her a golden opportunity to do so.

Instead of shock that the president, during one of his sessions with Monica, had employed his cigar in a grossly demeaning way, Diane was outraged that the referral would dare even mention the degrading incident.

My family and I watched Diane's *20/20* show on November 25, over Thanksgiving weekend at the welcome retreat of the Grand Floridian at Disney World. My fears about Sawyer's bias were proved justified. Some of her questions were doctored up in studio after the interview was over, which I viewed as manifestly unprofessional. The producers had even added ominous special effects to enhance the forbidding setting.

Although I was taken aback by the almost silly, menacing background music, I was all in all surprisingly satisfied with my answers. Diane had embraced the White House narrative that the investigation represented a gross intrusion into personal privacy, but my responses came across well, I thought. I was honest and straightforward, or at least I tried to be. Maintaining my cool, I didn't look, as I had feared, like the hapless deer caught in the headlights.

Family members agreed with my rosy assessment of ABC's attempted ambush. Sawyer came across, ironically, as the bad guy, using third-degree tactics to browbeat her guest. The emotion of the one-on-one struggle seemed to flow in my rather unlikely direction. But as with Steve Brill, I had learned my lesson. That was it for formal, taped press interviews.

Even with round-the-clock security, whose ranks were augmented by Disney security personnel, I was determined to have as "normal" a Thanksgiving break as possible. It was my father-in-law's favorite holiday, one of his last, and I was eager to be a typical, carefree Disney World visitor enjoying the company of close family.

I was pleasantly surprised by the number of fellow Disney World vacationers who came over to our Thanksgiving table, or to the buffet line at the Grand Floridian, to say hello and extend their warm wishes. Anonymity was now a thing of the past. In any event, at Disney World, no one cares. They're having fun with their families, not looking around for newsmakers.

During that getaway, I began thinking anew about bringing my public service to a close. Sadly, the Pepperdine opportunity had gone away. My extended deadline of August 1998 to report for duty on America's most gorgeous college campus had come and gone. Davenport, Pepperdine's patient president, was obliged to move in a different direction, naming an interim dean of the law school. The missed Pepperdine opportunity represented a truly grievous loss. Miraculously, it would unexpectedly return. There would indeed be a second chance, thanks to the decision of Pepperdine's new president, Andrew Benton, not to renew the contract of founding dean Ron Phillips's successor. To Malibu I would go—five years later.

CHAPTER THIRTY-TWO

The House Votes to Impeach

F OR THE REST OF THAT LONG YEAR, I FOLLOWED THE
House impeachment proceedings on television and in the press.

I had no contact of any kind with House members. The ultimate question of presidential fitness to serve was now entrusted to the people's elected representatives. But the Judiciary Committee did not have the benefit of our experience in the Little Rock phase of the investigation.

We believed the president had committed perjury both at the Whitewater trial and in several of his sworn interviews with our office. House Republicans were obviously disappointed that our referral was limited to the Lewinsky phase of our investigation, but we simply lacked what the independent counsel statute set forth as the standard: "substantial and credible" information that an impeachable offense may have been committed. Whatever our views might be on the president's earlier acts of perjury, we did not believe we could meet the necessary benchmark.

We were cognizant of the frustrating difference for a prosecutor's office between what they know, or at least believe, and what they can prove by admissible evidence beyond a reasonable doubt. Our duty was to remain silent, save for the final report when the OIC officially closed down its operation.

As the impeachment debates raged within the Judiciary Committee, and then on the House floor, I was reassured by the ready acceptance of the proposition that the president had committed serious crimes against our system of justice.

Chairman Hyde, in various ways, made the case that the issue implicated our foundational values of the rule of law, of basic honesty and integrity in the justice system.

At the same time, I despaired that the entire constellation of presidential crimes, coupled with the unleashing of Oval Office power to block and impede the investigation, was not widely perceived as an abuse of power.

The events that followed proved to be a tale of courage on the part of the Republican members of the committee. They knew full well that the American people strongly disfavored impeachment and removal of the deeply flawed but eminently likable president. Not only was he likable, he was teachable, as his midcourse policy adjustment during his first term of office demonstrated.

The postelection polls were crystal clear: Scuttle impeachment. Even with the temporary pro-impeachment bump during my daylong hearing, the American people at day's end wanted stability and continuity.

They had drawn a line—lying versus encouraging others to lie—but that, too, was now blurred. Just forget the whole thing.

The vote in the Judiciary Committee proceeded entirely along partisan lines.

Of the four proposed articles of impeachment, the vote was 21–16 for impeachment on three counts; as to the fourth, which charged perjury in the Paula Jones case, the vote was 20–17. As to that count, Lindsey Graham of *Peyton Place* fame voted nay. Graham gave the president the benefit of the doubt due to what he, Graham, saw as a confusing definition of sexual relations fashioned by Judge Wright. That was generous of him. But even granting the point, there was no ambiguity infecting the grand jury's definition.

The House pressed forward. I imagined what might have been if the Judiciary Committee hearings had taken place while Congress was in full session, rather than during the postelection rump session. The inside-the-Beltway political dynamic would perhaps have shifted sentiment to a no-vote position to reflect prevailing national sentiment.

But with the full House in recess, the Judiciary Committee members were entirely absorbed with the overwhelming body of evidence before them, not having to race from pillar to post in the usual manner of overly busy representatives.

Back home, the almost four hundred other House members could watch the proceedings at a safe distance and listen to their constituents up close.

And Republicans in particular typically got an earful from morally outraged folks back home. Committed Republicans, especially in heavily GOP districts, would not have looked kindly on their member of Congress waving a white flag of surrender and countenancing what was viewed in conservative ranks as profoundly unacceptable presidential misconduct.

Despite polls testing the general sentiment of the American people, impeachment was not a national plebiscite. Just as with the presidential election and the electoral college, the nation wasn't voting. Instead, individual representatives of 435 widely varying districts, each with its own peculiarities, were the electors.

Ultimately, as the old saying goes, all politics is local. Especially on such a monumental question as continuing presidential tenure, members of Congress had to keep their fingers on the pulse of their districts, regardless of what CNN's or other national polls might be reporting. And many districts all across the country were adamantly pro-impeachment.

Might something short of impeachment suffice? Constitutional scholars fretted that a resolution of censure, especially one coupled with a fine or other monetary sanction, might well be a constitutionally forbidden "bill of attainder," that is, Congress singling out a named individual for punishment. The Constitution set forth a formal mechanism for dealing with presidential misconduct, and that was the route that must be followed.

I had a different view. As I interpreted our founding document, the specified removal procedure of impeachment was elaborately provided for, but there was no express or implied prohibition on employing, in Congress's considered judgment, a less draconian procedure.

Imagine a situation in which, as with President Donald J. Trump, the chief executive engages in a pattern and practice of castigating and denigrating highly respected individuals.

The example of President Trump belittling Senator John McCain of Arizona springs to mind, or his alleged disparagement of immigrants from "shithole countries." By my reading of the Constitution, nothing prevents one or both Houses from formally expressing their disapprobation of the president's ill-mannered statements or inappropriate conduct through the mechanism of a resolution of censure.

In fact, the far less dramatic procedure of censure was once employed by Congress to express its vehement objection to the blatant lawlessness of President Andrew Jackson.

In the situation of President Clinton, a resolution of censure, possibly combined with a sanction, would likely have enjoyed overwhelming bipartisan support.

But even without a sanction, the censure resolution would simply express the views of the two houses of Congress. I saw nothing in the text, structure, or history of the Constitution to foreclose the resolution of censure alone, with no accompanying penalty. But no one asked me.

Constitutional issues aside, a stark political fact was this: Why would Republicans want to remove a popular lame-duck president, render him a martyr at the bloody hands of what would be assailed as right-wing zealotry, and then usher Vice President Al Gore into the Oval Office with less than two years remaining until the 2000 presidential election?

With the nation continuing to enjoy peace internationally and technology-driven prosperity here at home, newly installed President Gore would likely be a shoo-in for election in his own right. Electing the more stable, less controversial former senator from Tennessee would likewise serve as a form of vindication for the ousted President Clinton and reward the nation's forty-second president with an informal "third term" of the Clinton-Gore administration.

All these calculations were doubtless on the minds of politicians and pundits across the country.

The vote in the House, held on December 19, exactly one month after my testimony before the Judiciary Committee, was not quite as close as I had expected. Thirty-one Democrats joined the almost unanimous ranks of Republicans in sending two articles of impeachment to the Senate for trial.

The first article—perjury in the grand jury—passed muster 228–206. The second article—obstruction of justice—garnered a much closer 221–212 vote. Along the way, the proposed article on abuse of power fell by the wayside.

The stage was set for the nation's first impeachment trial in the Senate since the era of Andrew Johnson immediately after the Civil War.

CHAPTER THIRTY-THREE

The Senate Trial

CHIEF JUSTICE WILLIAM REHNQUIST, BEDECKED IN HIS odd Gilbert and Sullivan–inspired judicial robe, took the chair in the Senate on January 7, 1999, as the presiding officer in the first presidential impeachment since the 1860s.

I knew the brilliant but quirky Rehnquist well. He had been a judge for decades. He usually wore a sport coat and Hush Puppies, not a suit, beneath the robe.

His opening comment was entirely perfunctory. Nary a word about the gravity of the proceedings. Rehnquist blandly informed the House managers that they had twenty-four hours to present their case. For the rest of this historic proceeding, the Chief Justice presided but did not direct. He allowed the Senate to work its will. He later opined, "I did very little, and I did a good job of doing very little."

From the get-go, the thirteen House impeachment managers found themselves in a hostile work environment. The Senate leadership would honor the House's action only in the most formalistic way. There would be a "trial," but no witnesses, a rather unorthodox approach to a trial—perhaps the first in the English-speaking world. But the Senate is the master of its own house.

Majority Leader Trent Lott, a grizzled politician from Mississippi, saw no future in going after the Comeback Kid. Clinton had weathered the storm in public opinion polls, the ultimate arbiter of important questions for career politicians like Lott. Their realpolitik task was to dispense with the mess as quickly as possible, with an eagle eye trained on the 2000 presidential election.

Even with their party's standard-bearer under the dark cloud of impeachment, congressional Democrats were once again riding high. The House managers were the skunks at the garden party. Everyone promptly forgot about the thirty-one Democrats in the House who had joined in sending the articles of impeachment over to the Senate.

In response to an inquiry by Senator Tom Harkin, a Democrat from Iowa, Chief Justice Rehnquist ruled that the senators—although sworn in to judge the "grand inquest" of impeachment—were not limited in coming to their respective judgments to the evidence put in the record by the House managers. The senators were not jurors. To the contrary, their duty as statesmen transcended that of the American jury bound by the facts as adduced at trial and the law as instructed by the judge. They were, rather, to serve as representatives and voices of the people, now called upon to exercise the ultimate judgment of life or death of a particular presidency.

The Chief's ruling was entirely correct. Elected in their respective states, senators were duty bound by their oaths to listen to what the House of Representatives, through the impeachment managers, had to say. But the senators could listen with stopped ears. All that was needed was for their warm bodies to be in their seats as the impeach-ment case unfolded and then to vote yay or nay.

The Rehnquist ruling was obviously unhelpful to the House man-agers. Rehnquist's opinion "from the bench" took the senators totally off the evidentiary hook. They could, as a matter of principle, conclude that the president had committed perjury, encouraged others to lie, obstructed justice and all the rest, and still vote to acquit.

The trial promptly experienced hiccups.

First, the House managers wanted to take depositions of certain key witnesses. One might wonder, why didn't they do that over on the House side during the impeachment inquiry? The managers wanted to call witnesses to testify at the trial. Ditto. They had allowed that chance to pass them by during the Judiciary Committee hearings. As a compromise, the Senate trial was adjourned to permit deposition tes-timony of a handful of witnesses, including Vernon Jordan, who had masterminded the job search for Monica.

Second, encouraged by the Clinton defense team, Senator Robert Byrd, the West Virginia Democrat, filed a motion to dismiss. This was a bold move, designed to cut the entire proceedings off and take the solons off the hook. If a supermajority to convict and remove the presi-dent was lacking, as it indeed was, why go through the motions of a trial?

But the Senate obviously felt bound to proceed to its inevitable conclusion. The vote was lopsidedly in favor of going forward: 56–44. One Democrat, Russ Feingold of Wisconsin, came across the aisle to vote with the Republicans. The proceeding would continue.

Faced with the prospect of a witness-free trial (or at least live testi-mony), and thus unable to create drama in the "courtroom," the impeach-ment managers were determined to do everything they could to seek

Monica's "testimony." That happens all the time in the real world. In the course of a civil trial, a court may call a recess or simply direct that a deposition be taken after court adjourns for the day or over a weekend.

The managers wanted to interview Monica. They assured her lawyers that it would be friendly, with no court reporters. She refused. Hyde called our office with the request that we direct Monica through her lawyers to do so.

This was so unwelcome by me and my colleagues as to defy description, though I empathized with the House managers. Under Senate procedures, they could call no witnesses to testify at the trial. I sensed that curiosity was playing no small part in the request to arrange for her interview.

The House already had access to the testimony from Monica's appearance before the federal grand jury. She had held nothing back. She was not the typical 80-percent-cooperating witness, hiding the ball as to the 20 percent that she suspected the prosecutors would not be able to figure out.

What's the point in having her go before the Senate? we wondered. We scratched our heads, but upon review of the immunity agreement, I concluded that Monica had committed herself to cooperating with duly authorized inquiries. Chairman Hyde's request reflected the most democratic of authority in our constitutional order. We went to court and got an order directing her to cooperate. Though I knew we would get hammered by our usual critics, that went with the territory.

The press went crazy. So did the Democrats. Here was their totally biased take on the situation: Starr was once again cozying up to the zealots hell-bent on overturning the 1996 presidential election. Off base, as usual, but fervently held and aggressively espoused. My take on the press as a whole was reaffirmed: frequently wrong, never in doubt.

I did what I thought was right, period, and in this instance, what was plainly within the contemplation of our written agreement with Monica. No lawyerly stretching or twisting of contractual language was needed. To the contrary, the natural reading of the immunity agreement meant that Monica must cooperate or be in breach—and suffer the unwelcome consequences, including possible prosecution.

Her lawyers well knew by this time that Monica was not simply the victim of Saturday Night Bill's flatter-filled, gift-giving charm. She had served as the perpetrator of a determined effort to keep the truth long hidden. By this time, she had also been savaged by Clinton partisans, in the playbook mode for dealing with Bill's dalliance partners. When we came to judgment on the question, Monica's lawyers quickly relented, and didn't seek relief from a higher court, which would have been a tall order.

The interview proceeded, with enormous press fanfare, in a suite in the Mayflower Hotel. Our office did not participate. In light of the venue, I was reminded of our encounter with Monica in the Ritz-Carlton one year before and the pivotal assessment interview in Grandma Joan's Manhattan apartment. Monica sat for sensitive interviews in exceedingly comfortable venues.

As we expected, the encounter proved to be a media circus, but little else. The interviewing subcommittee of three House managers emerged from the two-hour informal session with lukewarm praise for what had transpired. They sounded like diplomats dealing with an implacable foe. The utter irrelevance of the makeshift enterprise was demonstrated by the House impeachment manager who had risen through the ranks to be—other than Henry Hyde himself—the Churchillian figure in the drama. California's James Rogan absented himself from the Monica-interview circus and, dutiful dad that he was, took his two daughters to the zoo. Rogan had definitely put his time to better use.

The trial marched on, but now spiced with video testimony from Monica, Vernon Jordan, and Sidney Blumenthal. Though the nation had practically tuned out, Blumenthal's testimony was arresting. He acknowledged that the president had savaged Monica as "a stalker." This was yet another lie.

By and large, the facts had long since been reported in detail, and all that was needed was an up or down vote.

However, the closing arguments riveted the nation's attention. Hyde was magnificent, but both sides performed admirably. The president was well served by his defenders, White House Counsel Charles Ruff and Dale Bumpers of Arkansas.

Although he had recently retired from the Senate, Bumpers now served as President Clinton's lawyer. It was a masterstroke. Bumpers was respected on both sides of the aisle as a thoughtful moderate Democrat. A highly successful trial lawyer back in Arkansas, he wowed his former colleagues with his stirring and whimsical argument for the defense on January 21, 1999.

"H. L. Mencken said one time, 'When you hear somebody say, "This is not about money"—it's about money,' and when you hear somebody say, 'This is not about sex'—it's about sex," Bumpers said. "Pick your own adjective to describe the president's conduct. Here are some that I would use: indefensible, outrageous, unforgivable, shameless. I promise you the president would not contest any of those or any others."

The final vote on February 12, 1999, came with little drama. The Senate went into secret session for several hours. A vote to open the proceedings for the debate was rejected 59–41. Interestingly, the closed session echoed the confidentiality of jury deliberations. The Senate obviously wanted it both ways, the freedom to speak without the burden of accountability other than the bottom line, yay or nay.

Various senators later released statements as to what they had said during the secret session. Intriguingly, no Democrat joined in that process.

Once again, the Chief Justice was parsimonious in his comments as the decisive vote drew nigh. He simply invoked the Senate rule prohibiting demonstrative outbursts. The first article (perjury) was voted down 45–55. The second article (obstruction of justice) failed by a tied 50–50 vote. The eccentric Republican senator Arlen Specter of Pennsylvania cast what he dubbed the "Scottish verdict"—"Not proved." He made clear, however, that he was not persuaded that the president was actually innocent. That jump-ball tie reflected the prevailing national mood. Everyone just wanted it to be over.

The perfect record of presidential gauntlet-running remained intact.

Chief Justice Rehnquist drew the proceedings to a close with a verbal bouquet: "I have been impressed by the quality of the debate in closed session on the entire question of impeachment as provided for under the Constitution. . . . I leave you now a wiser but not a sadder man."

The impeachment-or-bust strategy proved to be a boon to the president's already soaring popularity. As portrayed day after day, Clinton was the victim. He was trying to work hard for the American people. The House managers were the obstructionist pariahs.

After the Senate vote brought the long national ordeal to closure on the birthday of Honest Abe Lincoln, a solemn President Clinton spoke to the nation from a podium in the Rose Garden.

"Now that the Senate has fulfilled its constitutional responsibility bringing this process to a conclusion, I want to say again to the American people how profoundly sorry I am for what I said and did to trigger these events and the great burden they have imposed on the Congress and on the American people."

Leaving the podium, with eyes on the ground, he then did an about-face, returned to the podium, and made a final plea for forgiveness.

"I believe any person who asks for forgiveness has to be prepared to give it," Clinton said.

That's the way the drama ended. Few paused to consider this: If the president had simply told the truth before the grand jury the prior August, and then apologized to the American people for his mendacity, all this could have been avoided. The president, and he alone, was squarely to blame for the long national ordeal.

I am frequently asked if I was disappointed that the Senate didn't convict him. No, I'm not. Eventually Clinton would be called before the bar of justice by my successor to answer for his long trail of contempt.

At the end of 1998, *Time* magazine put Clinton and me on the cover as "Men of the Year." Under the circumstances, it was tantamount to being awarded "Skunk of the Year."

CHAPTER THIRTY-FOUR

Winding Down

IT WAS TIME FOR OUR LONG-RUNNING INVESTIGATION TO begin winding down. A few items of business remained, including the odd case of Julie Hiatt Steele. An on-again, off-again witness, Steele allegedly spoke with another asserted Clinton sexual assault victim, Kathleen Willey, who had emerged from the Oval Office disheveled and in an agitated state after an unwelcome encounter with the president many years earlier.

By Steele's early account, Willey had told her on the day of the alleged episode about the aggressive and unwanted physical encounter with Clinton. But Steele's story waxed and waned. Finally, under oath, Steele claimed that Willey had pressured her to lie about what happened. Our prosecutors believed Willey's account.

Steele was indicted in Virginia for obstructing justice and making false statements. In a hard-fought criminal trial in Alexandria in the spring of 1999, Steele was acquitted on the obstruction of justice charge, but the jury deadlocked on the issue of who was lying, Willey or Steele. We let the case go.

Remaining on our docket was the ever-appearing Waldo, Webb Hubbell. Putting together a criminal tax prosecution arising out of his failure to report hundreds of thousands of dollars of compensation for purported consulting work, our office subpoenaed various financial records from the former DOJ official and Rose Law Firm partner. He was indicted on November 13, 1998, for tax evasion.

To my surprise, we created a minor constitutional law landmark when the district court, upheld by a divided D.C. Circuit in January 1999, accepted Hubbell's claim that the documents he produced under subpoena could not be used as evidence against him. Without those documents, the prosecution was at best a very long shot. (The Supreme Court eventually sided with Hubbell.)

That left Susan McDougal. In March 1999, Susan was once again in the Little Rock courthouse to stand trial on charges of criminal contempt and obstruction of justice before an Arkansas jury. Our terrific team of Mark Barrett, a career prosecutor from Denver, and Julie Myers knew they had a tough case to prosecute, given the venue.

Susan was represented by the colorful Los Angeles attorney Mark Geragos. He had defended her in Santa Monica on California state charges of embezzling $150,000 from Nancy Mehta and her husband, the famous conductor Zubin Mehta, while she worked for them as a personal assistant in the early 1990s. She was acquitted in November 1998 on all charges. The high-profile case put Geragos on the map.

The trial had an unusual twist. Hickman Ewing was called as a witness, not by the prosecution but by the defense. The purpose of this unusual gambit was to suggest that the OIC generally—and Hickman in particular—was simply out to get the Clintons. Hickman was examined at length by Geragos, in connection with his early draft of a possible indictment against Hillary. The indictment, of course, was never presented to a grand jury for its consideration.

But Geragos skillfully employed the defunct draft to try to discredit our entire investigation in the eyes of the Little Rock trial jury.

Susan's trial also witnessed a vicious public attack on Hickman's faith journey. Hickman and his wife, Mary, became devout Evangelical Christians early in their marriage. Hickman taught Sunday school and regularly made mission trips to Mexico. As a sign of the growing secularism of American culture, Hickman's beliefs came under public assault in the media. It echoed James Carville's mocking of my own penchant for singing hymns in the Northern Virginia woods. The assaults represented a sad commentary on the coarsening culture.

After a four-week trial, Susan was acquitted on the obstruction of justice charge; on criminal contempt, we ended up with a hung jury. Susan had protected Clinton until the end. Her contempt for the system had paid off. She no longer had to respond to basic questions about her own stewardship of Madison Guaranty, and the possible culpability of her business partners, the Clintons.

At the same time, the recurring nightmare of alleged leaks—and ensuing investigations—had continued into 1999. My colleague and friend Charles Bakaly was caught up in a leak-related investigation by the FBI concerning the OIC's possible consideration of criminal charges against the president. Although, to my sorrow, Charles had to leave our office, he was eventually fully vindicated. Our office's squeaky-clean record in properly handling grand jury information remained intact.

In the fullness of time, I would voluntarily step aside. On October 18,

1999, I turned the office over to Robert Ray, an experienced prosecutor on our staff who was chosen by the three-judge panel as my successor. I had had enough.

I had been eager to leave the office for a long time. The protracted experiences in Arkansas provided a grim reminder that attacks on the prosecutor inevitably take a toll—a toll that grows with time. I remembered all too vividly being banished from trial courtrooms in Little Rock. Literally for years, my personal integrity and professionalism had been subject to a well-organized, relentless campaign of character assassination. Quite apart from personal and family considerations, I was strongly of the view that the investigation needed a fresh face.

In light of all the accusations, going back to my appointment in August 1994, I would not be the one to make the fateful decision on what action, if any, to take against William Jefferson Clinton, private citizen, when that time finally came.

To my great satisfaction, on the day after I left office, I received a magnificent letter from FBI Director Freeh. In his generous way, Freeh kindly praised what he called my "persistence and uncompromising personal and professional integrity" and passed along thanks from the FBI's lab scientists.

Ironically, Clinton had settled Paula Jones's lawsuit against him for $850,000 on November 13, 1998, just before my testimony to the House Judiciary Committee. For the president's misconduct in that case, Judge Wright issued a stern rebuke on April 12, 1999, finding him in contempt of court. She accompanied that with sanctions, including a fine of $96,000.

This was imposed, Judge Wright ruled, to cover some of Ms. Jones's legal expenses. But Her Honor also invoked the goal "to deter others who might consider emulating the president's misconduct."

To rub salt into the wound, Judge Wright directed the president to pay her travel expenses to Washington back in January 1998, when she had journeyed to the nation's capital for the sole purpose of presiding over the president's civil deposition. She had done so at the president's specific request, a highly unusual procedure taken entirely out of judicial respect for the presidency. He had perjured himself in her presence. That slap in the court's face constituted an egregious instance of contempt.

The sanctions for his contempt of the rule of law kept flowing in.

In a symbolic imposition of a quasi–death penalty for the profession, the Arkansas Supreme Court began proceedings to revoke or suspend his law license. True, Bill would soon amass a fortune speechifying and writing his bestselling memoir, *My Life*. He didn't need to hang out his shingle and start hustling clients. But the legal authorities did what they deemed fully within their power to say, in effect: "What you did was contemptuously wrong. As an officer of the court, you deserve stern punishment."

Back in his natural habitat, Chief Justice Rehnquist—along with his eight colleagues—administered the ultimate sanction for a lawyer. The Supreme Court removed Clinton from the rolls on October 1, 2001. He could never practice there again. The judiciary—both in the federal courthouse in his native state and the highest court in the land—had spoken with a clarity and firmness that triggered a lame response of "inappropriate" from David Kendall.

But what was "inappropriate" about slamming shut the courthouse door to a perjurer? Not even his fawning supporters in the press suggested that the federal judiciary had behaved precipitously or imposed an "inappropriate" punishment in light of what were now firmly established facts of record.

CHAPTER THIRTY-FIVE

Legacy of Contempt

WE WERE NEVER ALONE." BY THOSE SIMPLE WORDS, William Jefferson Clinton knowingly and deliberately entered the legal landscape of contempt. By those words, Chief Judge Susan Webber Wright authoritatively adjudged the president of the United States as guilty of obstruction of justice.

That judgment, never appealed, stands forever in the annals of American jurisprudence.

Over the years, on three separate occasions, I have been asked by influential individuals whether I would be willing to meet with President Clinton in the spirit of reconciliation. Each time I answered the same: "Yes, of course. Anytime, anywhere." Nothing ever came of it.

My last significant act as independent counsel was to testify on April 14, 1999, before the Senate Government Operations Committee chaired by Senator Fred Thompson, Republican of Tennessee. The issue was whether to reauthorize the independent counsel law.

Placed under oath, I testified that the law should be allowed to expire. Senator Dick Durbin, Democrat of Illinois, was incredulous. He wasn't unkind, but he was perplexed. How could I, of all people, be opposed to the law's renewal? In response, I took the senator quickly through the long history of DOJ opposition, by both parties, until the arrival of Janet Reno.

I recounted the DOJ's strenuous disapproval of the law, going back to the early 1980s, during my first tour of duty in the department. Much of that stormy history had been lost in the fog of incessant political warfare on Capitol Hill. But too much blood, on both sides of the aisle, had been spilled.

To my relief, Congress allowed the independent counsel law to expire later that year with existing ICs grandfathered in to complete their work.

Despite all the controversy, Kirkland & Ellis brought me back into the fold as a litigation partner. I was grateful for that, as well as to George Mason Law School for inviting me aboard to teach and write *First Among Equals,* my long-postponed book on the Supreme Court. The law firm—and GMU—were especially kind, even courageous.

During his final day in office in January 2001, Clinton pardoned Susan McDougal, just as Jim McDougal predicted. Clinton described the convicted felon who helped bring Madison Guaranty to financial ruin as "horribly mistreated by the independent counsel." He left Webb Hubbell and Jim Guy Tucker languishing, but pardoned three other convicted Whitewater defendants.

In doing so, Clinton flagrantly bypassed the normal Justice Department procedures governing pardons. Even his go-along Deputy Attorney General, Eric Holder, rebuked this high-handed display of raw power. As did FBI Director Freeh, who later wrote that Clinton "tainted the old and honorable tradition of presidential mercy by his inability to rein in his own instincts, by his penchant for excess." In all, Clinton issued 177 pardons as he left office, including that of notorious fugitive financier Marc Rich.

Clinton's autobiography claimed that Susan and other Whitewater defendants were indicted because of Starr; his account left out all the damning evidence against them, and the fact that grand juries, not I, indicted them.

Notwithstanding his final-day confession of having lied under oath, Clinton left office immensely popular. His southern charm had conquered all. The nation's "first black president" repaired to his new office in Harlem. Arkansas, other than serving as the site of his presidential library, was in the Clintons' rearview mirror. They would make their lives—and launch Hillary's two presidential campaigns—from America's northeastern corridor, not Bill Clinton's native South.

But in the fullness of time, the culture would change significantly. In the first quarter of the twenty-first century, societal indulgence about the mistreatment of women, especially in the workplace, would come to a long-overdue reckoning. Victims began speaking out. Firings and resignations of abusive powerful men became an everyday story.

The Kathleen Willeys and other women who claimed to have been assaulted by Clinton would at long last get a hearing, respectfully, in the public square. The verbal assaults on women by the Clintons and their surrogates, who hurled demeaning epithets such as "trailer park trash," would become unthinkable in 2017 and 2018.

But the now-fading Clinton years were starkly different, culturally and politically, in terms of respecting the rights of all persons, especially those subject to the exploitative hands of the powerful. Both as governor and as president, Clinton could malign his jettisoned paramours and victims with little if any consequence. In those days, oddly, no one seemed to care about the exploitative power arrangement. That was just Saturday Night Bill from Hot Springs, Arkansas.

Those days, thankfully, are gone. And so, it would appear, are the Clintons. Tragically, their legacy, despite their accomplishments, despite their talents, is, above all, contempt: contempt for the rule of law that binds us together as citizens, and contempt for human beings—especially women—as inherently worthy of dignity and respect.

That was Bill Clinton, the protagonist of *My Life*, a life brimming with talent, but fatally infected by self-indulgent exploitation of the vulnerable. It all could have been radically different, and the country would have been in a better place. And so, too, would the White House, with the Age of Clinton now having given way to the Age of Trump.

I'm frequently asked whether I have any regrets. In response, I have often said that other than Congress's originally enacting and then reauthorizing the independent counsel law in the first place, I deeply regret that I took on the Lewinsky phase of the investigation. But at the same time, as I still see it twenty years later, there was no practical alternative to my doing so. If an independent counsel had been on standby, a sort of "call up the reserves" regime, then yes, the assignment should have gone to the ready reservist. But the governmental machinery in place at the time didn't work that way. There was no reservist standing by, as with the National Guard.

The president's premeditated perjury in the Jones federal civil rights case cried out for investigation, and we were the only logical shop for getting that job done efficiently. But we didn't just sally forth and launch yet another front on the multifaceted OIC inquiry. Instead, we went promptly to the Attorney General, and she readily agreed to seek expansion of our portfolio from the appointing court. Under the statutory reauthorization that Congress had passed and President Clinton himself had signed into law, the president had to be investigated. Bill Clinton signed his own impeachment warrant.

Some have been kind enough to suggest I would have been on the Supreme Court had I not taken on the Whitewater investigation, and especially the much-criticized Lewinsky inquiry. Maybe, but we'll never know. While serving as solicitor general, I had already been passed over by President George H. W. Bush in favor of David Souter.

That rejection was a bitter pill for me, with the president under whom I had faithfully served selecting an unknown judge from New Hampshire and elevating him to the highest court in the land.

Many conservatives would later rue that appointment, as Justice Souter became a reliably liberal vote on a closely divided Court. It was a costly and unforced presidential error. Justice Souter was even heard to say, privately, "I have the Ken Starr seat." Chief Justice Roberts has similarly been heard to say, "But for Whitewater, Ken would have my job."

Whether that's true or not, my opportunity to serve on the nation's highest court had passed me by. I would not have had another chance eight years later, as President George W. Bush wisely selected two sitting judges, Roberts and Samuel Alito, who were at least ten years younger than I. I was pleased and proud of those appointments.

By that time, I was in my late fifties, likely too old—and much too controversial—to merit serious consideration for appointment to the High Court. Presidents want longevity in their Supreme Court nominees, as we saw in 2017 with President Trump's choice of forty-eight-year-old Neil Gorsuch and, in 2018, Brett Kavanaugh. And presidents want Senate confirmability, which is what the choices of President Bush 43 elegantly provided.

And so, my public service drew to a close. But I left behind a record of integrity, of trying to do my honest best. As the banner we displayed in our Little Rock trial office said: "We are honored by our friends and distinguished by our enemies."

As for Bill and Hillary Clinton, the citizens of the United States deserved better. Talented they were, to be sure, but deeply flawed, fundamentally dishonest, contemptuous of law and process. That was a personal tragedy, but even more, a tragedy for our nation.

Afterword

URING THE WEEK BEFORE CHRISTMAS 2017, OUR DAUGH-
ter Cynthia was in the last month of an at-risk pregnancy. She
had lost her first child due to severe pre-eclampsia and desperately
wanted her family around her.

So a large contingent of us from Texas—Alice, my daughter Carolyn and her husband, Cameron, and their four children—trooped to
New York to enjoy Christmas with Cynthia and her husband, Justin.

I love Christmas in New York—all the lights, the chilly weather,
the beautiful store windows. Cynthia made arrangements for the
entire family to have an early Christmas Eve dinner at the Barclay, a
traditional restaurant in the West Village. Following that, we would
attend worship services at Grace Church near Washington Square.
I was looking forward to "Lessons and Carols" in that resplendent
setting.

Dinner had taken longer than we'd hoped, and as we left, gathering jackets and kids, I went toward the front door, worried that we were going to be late for the beginning of the church service.

People arriving for the next seating were standing around in the foyer. As I put on my coat and hat, I spotted a familiar face—a woman with shoulder-length dark hair, wearing a coat with a fur-trimmed hood, standing with several other people waiting to be seated. She looked around and locked her eyes on mine.

"She bears a remarkable resemblance to Monica," I thought. In all the chaos of 1998, I had never actually met Monica Lewinsky. Then I realized it *was* Monica.

I felt awkward. What do I do? I decided to step forward and greet her.

"You?" she said, not accusatory but quizzical. Like, "What are you doing here, in my world?"

We didn't shake hands, but I lightly touched her arm.

"I hope you are doing well," I said.

Our short exchange was pleasant and poignant. "Though I wish I had made different choices back then," Monica said, "I wish that you and your office had made different choices, too." There was no anger in her voice. "Let me introduce you to my family." The introduction was very brief.

My own family came toward the door. Monica's family moved toward their table, and I hustled my brood to catch several taxis for the Christmas Eve service. Our two families didn't speak to each other.

Monica later wrote a story for the March 2018 issue of *Vanity Fair* describing this brief encounter, portraying me as "somewhere between avuncular and creepy."

Monica still blames me for the heartache she experienced twenty years ago. I get that. She was very young and vulnerable, in an extraordinary situation with a man she loved. In the article, she seemed to be trying to figure out how to place her experience in the context of the remarkable changes that have recently gone on in our culture.

She was not trying to claim membership in either the #MeToo or the #TimesUp movement. She has always acknowledged that she had entered into a consensual relationship. But all that she experienced— Clinton's disavowal, the ridicule from his surrogates, her depression, her parents' fear and anxiety, the pressure from our office's insisting that she tell the truth—would have been difficult even for someone more mature, as I had personally seen with Kathleen Willey.

Monica seems to believe that Starr is the reason that her life irrevocably changed—not Bill Clinton, a man twice her age who took advantage of a lovely young person to meet his own needs. So be it. But it is also true that if Monica had cooperated during that first week, or even the first month, the country would not have been dragged through an eight-month ordeal.

In early June 2018, Bill Clinton had a unique opportunity to address his egregious behavior twenty years earlier. On a book tour, he was asked if he owed Monica Lewinsky an apology. "No, I do not," he told NBC's Craig Melvin. "I have never talked to her. But I did say publicly on more than one occasion that I was sorry. That's very different. The apology was public." He went on to portray himself as a victim, citing the fact that he had incurred $16 million in legal fees "defending the Constitution."

Later that week, Clinton went on *The Late Show with Stephen Colbert* to do damage control. Even comedian Colbert was surprised at his cluelessness. "It seemed tone deaf to me because you seemed offended to be asked about this thing when, in all due respect, sir, your behavior was the most famous example of a powerful man sexually misbehaving in the workplace of my lifetime," Colbert said. The judiciary had held him accountable; now it seemed the culture had finally caught up with Clinton.

In her fierce but misguided loyalty, Monica allowed herself to become a tragic figure of late twentieth-century America. She carries with her forever the living reality of the Clintons' victim-strewn path to power, the most visible casualty of the Clintons' contempt.

ACKNOWLEDGMENTS

I wrote much of this book drawing on memory but would have been unable to recount many of the details without the invaluable insight—and astonishing recall—of Hickman Ewing. His daily journal was an unerring source of lively detail and sparking recollections that had remained hidden in the recesses of my mental nooks and crannies. Jackie Bennett, Bob Bittman, and Sol Wisenberg, my senior colleagues in both Little Rock and Washington, D.C., served brilliantly and boldly on matters great and small during our tenure together. They, too, very kindly provided fresh eyes and vivid memories of those stormy times.

My wife, Alice, and daughter Carolyn were invaluable in editing my initial draft. Carolyn lived through the most challenging time, during her freshman year at Stanford, with round-the-clock security. My children Randall and Cynthia were likewise encouraging throughout the writing process, even though it brought back poignant memories of difficult times for our then-young family. They shared their memories, often painful, of times past. As was Carolyn's educational journey, their college

(Randall) and junior high (Cynthia) years were terribly disrupted by their father's having answered the call of duty.

My Waco-based research assistants, Drew MacKenzie and Luke Walker—later joined by Jake Adams toward the project's conclusion—are undergraduate (or recently graduated) students at Baylor University. They were immensely able and cheerful companions who made the daily deep dives into electronic archives extremely helpful.

My extraordinary agents Glen Hartley and Lynn Chu of Writers' Representatives, LLC, believed in this project from the start. They had been my agents for my first book, published in 2002, *First Among Equals: The Supreme Court in American Life.*

Bria Sandford, my wise and insightful editor at Sentinel/Penguin Random House, has the great spiritual gift of encouragement. Immensely talented, Bria was unfailingly supportive, while continually urging me to tell the Whitewater-Lewinsky story in a more accessible way.

Glenna Whitley, my tenacious book coach and now friend, took my initial draft, interviewed me for hours on end, reviewed numerous books about that controversial period in American history, and helped sculpt a story-filled narrative.

My friend of long standing Terry Eastland, a distinguished journalist and former Justice Department colleague, helped in the earliest days of the project, in both conceptualizing what the book could be and supplying helpful insights about the role of the media.

On the pages that follow, I identify every member of the Whitewater-Lewinsky team who co-labored with me during my tenure (1994–99). Their service to the Office of the Independent Counsel—and to the nation—deserves admiration and gratitude. The list does not include the numerous capable FBI and IRS agents assigned to the investigation. Each one served with distinction and fortitude. Former FBI Director

Louis Freeh assigned some of the most able men and women in the Bureau to labor alongside our team in Little Rock and in Washington, D.C. My profound thanks to Director Freeh, a model of integrity and dedication.

I am also deeply grateful for the sacrificial service of the men and women of the U.S. Marshals Service, so many of whom were summoned from around the country to protect my family when death threats abounded.

Over the years, many fellow Americans whom I did not know have come up to me and said they had prayed fervently for my family and me throughout the course of the investigation. Others sent messages of encouragement through email or snail mail. Those gracious words, in person or by pen, from kindhearted strangers brought comfort to our hearts and tears to our eyes. For those unnamed and almost countless friends of freedom under law, I am deeply thankful.

Special Thanks and Acknowledgments for the Service of the Office of the Independent Counsel Personnel from August 9, 1994, to October 18, 1999

Roger M. Adelman, SENIOR COUNSEL

Daniel R. Adrien, SUMMER INTERN

Sabrina L. Alexander, ADMINISTRATIVE ASSISTANT

Geneva L. Allen, RECEPTIONIST

Margaret E. Alvarez, LEGAL SECRETARY

Bernard James Apperson, DEPUTY INDEPENDENT COUNSEL

Caitlin O. Aptowicz, PARALEGAL SPECIALIST

J. Keith Ausbrook, DEPUTY INDEPENDENT COUNSEL

Alex M. Azar II, ASSOCIATE INDEPENDENT COUNSEL

Lawrence Bagley, CRIMINAL INVESTIGATOR

Charles G. Bakaly III, COUNSELOR TO THE INDEPENDENT COUNSEL

David G. Barger, ASSOCIATE INDEPENDENT COUNSEL

Mark J. Barrett, ASSOCIATE INDEPENDENT COUNSEL

Jerry Bastin, CRIMINAL INVESTIGATOR

John D. Bates, DEPUTY INDEPENDENT COUNSEL

SPECIAL THANKS AND ACKNOWLEDGMENTS

Stephen G. Bates, ASSOCIATE INDEPENDENT COUNSEL

Jackie M. Bennett Jr., deputy independent counsel

Elliot S. Berke, SENIOR COUNSEL IN CHARGE
   OF CONGRESSIONAL AFFAIRS

Dr. Alan Berman, CONSULTANT

Ronice D. Bevan, STAFF ASSISTANT

Cherry Joy Beysselance, LEGAL CONSULTANT

Thomas H. Bienert Jr., associate independent counsel

Stephen J. Binhak, ASSOCIATE INDEPENDENT COUNSEL

Robert J. Bittman, DEPUTY INDEPENDENT COUNSEL

William Black, CONSULTANT

Dr. Brian Blackbourne, CONSULTANT

James K. Blankinship, ASSOCIATE INDEPENDENT COUNSEL

Randy Boldyga, CONTRACT COMPUTER SUPPORT

Thomas P. Bossert, PARALEGAL SPECIALIST/EVIDENCE TECHNICIAN

Harvest Boyd, CONTRACT COMPUTER SUPPORT

John Brandon, CRIMINAL INVESTIGATOR

Ruth C. Brankstone, PARALEGAL SPECIALIST

Thomas C. Breighner, RESEARCH ANALYST

Kimberly Nelson Brown, ASSOCIATE INDEPENDENT COUNSEL

Tracee A. Brown, ADMINISTRATIVE ASSISTANT

John R. Bryck, PARALEGAL SPECIALIST

Elaine Burns, CONTRACT COMPUTER SUPPORT

John Burns, CONTRACT COMPUTER SUPPORT

Tina A. Byers, ASSISTANT INDEPENDENT COUNSEL

Jeb Coleman Cade, LEGAL ASSISTANT

William Cade, CRIMINAL INVESTIGATOR

Levi W. Chaconas, CLERK

Joseph W. Cleary, PARALEGAL SPECIALIST

Steven M. Colloton, ASSOCIATE INDEPENDENT COUNSEL

Ashford Connor, CONTRACT COMPUTER SUPPORT

Coy A. Copeland, CRIMINAL INVESTIGATOR

Julie A. Corcoran, ASSOCIATE INDEPENDENT COUNSEL

Kathryn A. Cottrell, ADMINISTRATIVE ASSISTANT

Pamela J. Craig, CONFIDENTIAL ASSISTANT

James N. Crane, ASSOCIATE INDEPENDENT COUNSEL

Robert Crouch, FACILITIES AND RECORDS SPECIALIST

Samuel Dash, ETHICS CONSULTANT

Thomas W. Dawson, ASSOCIATE INDEPENDENT COUNSEL

Cheri M. Dea, ADMINISTRATIVE SPECIALIST

Joseph M. Ditkoff, ASSOCIATE INDEPENDENT COUNSEL

Shireen E. Dodini, LEGAL SECRETARY

Eric Dreiband, ASSOCIATE INDEPENDENT COUNSEL

Eric A. Dubelier, ASSOCIATE INDEPENDENT COUNSEL

William S. Duffey Jr., deputy independent counsel

Colleen R. Duffy, SUMMER LEGAL CLERK

Rajeev P. Duggal, PARALEGAL

David L. Dunleavy, PARALEGAL SPECIALIST

Cynthia D. Earman, ARCHIVIST

Michael Emmick, DEPUTY INDEPENDENT COUNSEL

W. Hickman Ewing Jr., deputy independent counsel

Alison Ferguson, CLERK

Rita A. Ferguson, STAFF ASSISTANT

Lynda M. Flippin, PRESS OFFICER/SPECIAL ASSISTANT
   TO THE INDEPENDENT COUNSEL

Jason R. Foringer, SUMMER INTERN/LAW CLERK

Valerie Francies, CONTRACT COMPUTER SUPPORT

Anne V. Freden, SUMMER INTERN

SPECIAL THANKS AND ACKNOWLEDGMENTS

Richard D. Friedman, LEGAL CONSULTANT

Jeri Frye, CONTRACT COMPUTER SUPPORT

Meghan Gallagher, CLERK

Terrence J. Galligan, ASSOCIATE INDEPENDENT COUNSEL

Karl N. Gellert, ASSOCIATE INDEPENDENT COUNSEL

Deborah E. Gershman, STAFF ASSISTANT

D. Leah Giannini, RECORDS AND ARCHIVES OFFICER

Leland Giannini, CRIMINAL INVESTIGATOR

Lisa Gonsior, SUMMER INTERN/PARALEGAL

Ameen I. Haddad, LAW CLERK

Eric Hagans, PARALEGAL SPECIALIST

Rusty Harden, ASSOCIATE INDEPENDENT COUNSEL

Erin Harrington, LEGAL ASSISTANT

Judy Harris, ADMINISTRATIVE OFFICER

Rodger A. Heaton, ASSOCIATE INDEPENDENT COUNSEL

Cathleen C. Herasimchuk, ASSOCIATE INDEPENDENT COUNSEL

Robert Hirschhorn, JURY CONSULTANT

Phil Horton, CONTRACT COMPUTER SUPPORT

Victor Houston, CRIMINAL INVESTIGATOR

Karin J. Immergut, ASSOCIATE INDEPENDENT COUNSEL

Misty D. Jackson, SECRETARY

LeRoy Jahn, ASSOCIATE INDEPENDENT COUNSEL

W. Ray Jahn, ASSOCIATE INDEPENDENT COUNSEL

Eric H. Jaso, ASSOCIATE INDEPENDENT COUNSEL

Lindsey M. Jensen, CONFIDENTIAL ASSISTANT

Patricia C. Johnson, LEGAL ASSISTANT

Darrell M. Joseph, ASSOCIATE INDEPENDENT COUNSEL

Brett M. Kavanaugh, ASSOCIATE INDEPENDENT COUNSEL

George T. Kelley, CONSULTANT

William Kelley, LEGAL CONSULTANT

Richard C. Killough, ASSISTANT INDEPENDENT COUNSEL

Hyunjong Kim, RECEPTIONIST

Matthew B. Kirsener, LAW CLERK

Lisa K. Krupinski, MANAGEMENT ANALYST

Stephen A. Kubiatowski, ASSOCIATE INDEPENDENT COUNSEL

Michael Landess, RESEARCH CONSULTANT

Steve Learned, ASSOCIATE INDEPENDENT COUNSEL

Dr. Henry Lee, CONSULTANT

Gregory L. Lefever, ADMINISTRATIVE OFFICER

Greg Leiby, CONTRACT COMPUTER SUPPORT

Andrew D. Leipold, LEGAL CONSULTANT

Bradley E. Lerman, ASSOCIATE INDEPENDENT COUNSEL

Craig Lerner, ASSOCIATE INDEPENDENT COUNSEL

Gus Lesnevich, CONSULTANT

Cathy Lindsey, CONTRACT COMPUTER SUPPORT

Dawn L. Lipp, LEGAL SECRETARY

William S. MacCartee, PARALEGAL SPECIALIST

Gregory E. Maggs, LEGAL CONSULTANT

Ronald J. Mann, LEGAL CONSULTANT

John R. Martin, LAW CLERK

Kevin J. Martin, ASSOCIATE INDEPENDENT COUNSEL

Lindsey B. Matson, SUPERVISORY PARALEGAL SPECIALIST

Timothy J. Mayopoulos, ASSOCIATE INDEPENDENT COUNSEL

John E. McCarrick, LAW CLERK

Monica Molloy, PARALEGAL SPECIALIST

Walter Montano, PARALEGAL SPECIALIST

James M. Morris, CONSULTANT

Julie L. Myers, ASSOCIATE INDEPENDENT COUNSEL

SPECIAL THANKS AND ACKNOWLEDGMENTS

Judy M. Nance, SUPERVISORY PARALEGAL SPECIALIST
Monique M. Neaves, LEGAL SECRETARY
J. Forrest Norman, PARALEGAL SPECIALIST
Patrick M. O'Brien, ASSOCIATE INDEPENDENT COUNSEL
Sandra A. Oldham, ADMINISTRATIVE OFFICER
A. Louise Oliver, LAW CLERK
Edward J. Page, DEPUTY INDEPENDENT COUNSEL
Stephen C. Parker, ASSOCIATE INDEPENDENT COUNSEL
Margaret E. Parks, SUMMER INTERN
Robert H. Patterson Jr., legal consultant
K. Lawson Pedigo, ASSOCIATE INDEPENDENT COUNSEL
Jonathan I. Pomerance, PARALEGAL SPECIALIST
Linda Potter, STAFF ASSISTANT
Carolyn Pritts, RECORDS AND ARCHIVES OFFICER
Nicholas Pullen, SUMMER INTERN
Lucia Rambusch, PARALEGAL SPECIALIST
Elizabeth Ray, PUBLIC INFORMATION ASSISTANT
Robert W. Ray, ASSOCIATE INDEPENDENT COUNSEL
Mei Li Reedy, CONTRACT COMPUTER SUPPORT
Thomas Repczinski, LAW CLERK
Roberta Richardson, STAFF ASSISTANT
Jim Rickards, CONTRACT COMPUTER SUPPORT
Miguel Rodriguez, ASSOCIATE INDEPENDENT COUNSEL
Philip J. Rooney, FINANCIAL OFFICER
Nicholas Q. Rosenkranz, SUMMER INTERN
Rod J. Rosenstein, ASSOCIATE INDEPENDENT COUNSEL
Paul S. Rosenzweig, SENIOR LITIGATION COUNSEL
Ronald D. Rotunda, LEGAL CONSULTANT

Patricia S. Rowland, STAFF ASSISTANT

Debra Rubin, LEGAL SECRETARY

Neille M. Russell, CONFIDENTIAL ASSISTANT

William Rutledge, CONSULTANT

Amy D. Scivally, RECEPTIONIST

Thomas Serafin, INTERN/CLERK

Kevin M. Sigafoes, PARALEGAL SPECIALIST

Richard P. Simmons, PARALEGAL SPECIALIST

Edward H. Smith II, SUMMER INTERN

Deborah Stalford, PARALEGAL SPECIALIST

Amy St. Eve, ASSOCIATE INDEPENDENT COUNSEL

Timothy S. Susanin, ASSOCIATE INDEPENDENT COUNSEL

Anita P. Swartz, LEGAL SECRETARY

Mark Sylvester, PARALEGAL SPECIALIST

Julie Talley, SECRETARY

Hector Tapia, CONTRACT COMPUTER SUPPORT

Dillion Teachout, CLERK

Catherine A. Thie, MANAGEMENT ASSISTANT

Nora Thorne, CONTRACT COMPUTER SUPPORT

William H. Thullen, FINANCIAL CONSULTANT

Jennifer M. Tjia, PARALEGAL SPECIALIST

Mark H. Touhey III, DEPUTY INDEPENDENT COUNSEL

Michael L. Travers, ASSOCIATE INDEPENDENT COUNSEL

Bruce Udolf, ASSOCIATE INDEPENDENT COUNSEL

Erin S. Vagley, ADMINISTRATIVE CLERK

Donald Vinson, JURY CONSULTANT

Linda B. Walls, PARALEGAL SPECIALIST

Paul Walsh, CRIMINAL INVESTIGATOR

SPECIAL THANKS AND ACKNOWLEDGMENTS

Marcia L. Walter, ASSOCIATE INDEPENDENT COUNSEL

Bryan M. Winkelman, LEGAL SECRETARY

Mary Anne Wirth, ASSOCIATE INDEPENDENT COUNSEL

Solomon L. Wisenberg, DEPUTY INDEPENDENT COUNSEL

Gabrielle R. Wolohojian, ASSOCIATE INDEPENDENT COUNSEL

SOURCES

In writing this memoir, I have relied on my recollections of my time as independent counsel from 1994 through 1999. I have refreshed my memory through news sources, including the *New York Times*, the *Washington Post*, the *Wall Street Journal*, and other newspapers and magazines of the period, including *Time* and *Newsweek*. To flesh out the narrative, I have looked to books published after these events, including *Truth at Any Cost: Ken Starr and the Unmaking of Bill Clinton* by Sue Schmidt and Michael Weisskopf; *The Death of American Virtue: Clinton vs. Starr* by Ken Gormley; *Her Way: The Hopes and Ambitions of Hillary Rodham Clinton* by Jeff Gerth and Don Van Natta Jr.; *The Clinton Enigma* by David Maraniss; *Arkansas Mischief: The Birth of a National Scandal* by Jim McDougal and Curtis Wilkie; *Prosecutor, Defender, Counselor* by Robert B. Fiske Jr.; *My FBI: Bringing Down the Mafia, Investigating Bill Clinton, and Fighting the War on Terror* by Louis J. Freeh; *Monica's Story* by Andrew Morton; and *The Woman Who Wouldn't Talk* by Susan McDougal. I am particularly grateful for the input of my colleagues Hickman Ewing Jr., Jackie Bennett, Bob Bittman, Sol Wisenberg, Paul Rosenzweig, Ray and LeRoy Jahn, Steve Binhak, and Ed Page.

ILLUSTRATION CREDITS

INDEX